Progressive Web Application Development by Example

Develop fast, reliable, and engaging user experiences for the web

Chris Love

BIRMINGHAM - MUMBAI

Progressive Web Application Development by Example

Copyright © 2018 Packt Publishing

All rights reserved. No part of this book may be reproduced, stored in a retrieval system, or transmitted in any form or by any means, without the prior written permission of the publisher, except in the case of brief quotations embedded in critical articles or reviews.

Every effort has been made in the preparation of this book to ensure the accuracy of the information presented. However, the information contained in this book is sold without warranty, either express or implied. Neither the author, nor Packt Publishing or its dealers and distributors, will be held liable for any damages caused or alleged to have been caused directly or indirectly by this book.

Packt Publishing has endeavored to provide trademark information about all of the companies and products mentioned in this book by the appropriate use of capitals. However, Packt Publishing cannot guarantee the accuracy of this information.

Acquisition Editor: Shweta Pant
Content Development Editor: Onkar Wani
Technical Editor: Diksha Wakode
Copy Editor: Safis Editing
Project Coordinator: Devanshi Doshi
Proofreader: Safis Editing
Indexer: Tejal Daruwale Soni
Graphics: Jason Monteiro
Production Coordinator: Shantanu Zagade

First published: July 2018

Production reference: 1230718

Published by Packt Publishing Ltd.
Livery Place
35 Livery Street
Birmingham
B3 2PB, UK.

ISBN 978-1-78712-542-1

www.packtpub.com

*Thanks to my wife Beth for supporting and believing in me
as we journey through life together.*

mapt.io

Mapt is an online digital library that gives you full access to over 5,000 books and videos, as well as industry leading tools to help you plan your personal development and advance your career. For more information, please visit our website.

Why subscribe?

- Spend less time learning and more time coding with practical eBooks and Videos from over 4,000 industry professionals
- Improve your learning with Skill Plans built especially for you
- Get a free eBook or video every month
- Mapt is fully searchable
- Copy and paste, print, and bookmark content

PacktPub.com

Did you know that Packt offers eBook versions of every book published, with PDF and ePub files available? You can upgrade to the eBook version at www.PacktPub.com and as a print book customer, you are entitled to a discount on the eBook copy. Get in touch with us at service@packtpub.com for more details.

At www.PacktPub.com, you can also read a collection of free technical articles, sign up for a range of free newsletters, and receive exclusive discounts and offers on Packt books and eBooks.

Contributors

About the author

Chris Love is a frontend developer with 25 years of professional experience. He has won the Microsoft MVP award for 12 years and has authored multiple books. He has helped over 1,000 businesses of all sizes and from various industries.

Chris regularly speaks at user groups, code camps, and developer conferences, and also writes articles and videos to help fellow developers.

When he's not working on frontend development, you can find him spending time with his step-kids, doing karate, and taking part in Spartan races.

> *I would like to thank members of the Microsoft Edge and Google Chrome teams for being so accessible to me when I needed to ask questions. Most of us don't consider the passion the people making browsers have for the web. They work tirelessly to bring us a platform that enables us to build great experiences for real people and to make their lives better.*

About the reviewer

Amar Gharat has been working with various web technologies for the last 12 years, which includes developing creative and unique web applications using LAMP, open source, and cutting-edge technology, as well as delivering work on time with dedicated teamwork. He decided to contribute to this book as a reviewer while working on PWA projects. He has explored new technologies, such as Vuejs and Nuxtjs, to build PWA for our website and found them very interesting to work with. Another book he has reviewed is *Progressive Web Apps with React*.

> *I would like to thank Packt Publishing for giving me an opportunity as a reviewer to share my knowledge with others.*

Packt is searching for authors like you

If you're interested in becoming an author for Packt, please visit `authors.packtpub.com` and apply today. We have worked with thousands of developers and tech professionals, just like you, to help them share their insight with the global tech community. You can make a general application, apply for a specific hot topic that we are recruiting an author for, or submit your own idea.

Table of Contents

Preface 1

Chapter 1: Introduction to Progressive Web Apps 7
    Why we needed a new way to build websites 10
    Real-world PWA examples 11
    What are PWAs? 13
        Peak app 15
        PWA features 16
    PWA advantages 18
    PWA technical requirements 20
        The application shell 21
    2048 22
        The source code 23
        The application's code structure 23
        Adding node modules to the project 25
        Adding a manifest 28
        Adding a service worker 28
    Summary 31

Chapter 2: Creating a Home Screen Experience with a Web Manifest ... 33
    Why add to homescreen is important 34
    Making your PWA iOS web app capable 36
        The application title is set with another META tag 39
    The web manifest specification 41
        Referencing the web manifest file 41
        Web manifest properties 42
        Controlling the launch style 45
        Apple Safari web manifest support 47
    Validating web manifest files 48
    The Chrome improved add to homescreen experience 50
    The add to homescreen experience 51
        The Chrome add to homescreen experience 52
    Your add to homescreen responsibilities 55
        Disabling the homescreen prompt 59
    Tracking homescreen installs 59
    Polyfiling the homescreen experience on iOS and other legacy browsers 60
        Should you polyfil response caching? 62
    Microsoft Edge and Internet Explorer 62

Benefits await without Polyfils	64
Testing the add to homescreen experience in Chrome	65
Summary	66
Chapter 3: Making Your Website Secure	**67**
SSL history	67
How does TLS work?	69
What is HTTPS?	71
HTTPS advantages	72
Identity	72
Confidentiality	72
Integrity	74
Browsers are going out of their way to indicate HTTPS to the customer	75
Search engine optimization	75
No longer cost-prohibitive	76
Modern APIs require HTTPS	78
HTTPS can be significantly faster than HTTP	78
HTTPS adoption	79
Different types of SSL certificate	80
Domain-validated certificates	81
Organization-validated certificates	82
Extended-validation SSL certificates	82
How to obtain and install an SSL certificate	84
Migrating a website to HTTPS	85
Auditing the site for any HTTP:// link references	86
Auditing content and data	87
Updating social media links	87
Configure server auto-redirect of HTTP to HTTPS	88
Add and verify all domain protocol combinations in webmaster tools	89
Defining a canonical HTTPS link	89
Updating Google analytics to default to HTTPS	89
Updating the sitemap and RSS feed to HTTPS	90
Updating your robots.txt file	91
Summary	91
Chapter 4: Service Workers – Notification, Synchronization, and Our Podcast App	**93**
The service worker thread	95
Service worker browser support	96
Microsoft Edge service worker support	96
Safari service worker support	97
Is the service worker ready?	97
Polyfilling older browsers	99
The podcast application	99
The Fetch API	103

Introducing Fetch	104
Using the Fetch API	105
The response object	108
Service worker fetch	110
Polyfilling fetch in legacy browsers	111
Creating a service worker shell	**113**
The service worker life cycle	**113**
Caching	**114**
Using push notifications	**115**
Implementing push notifications	116
Setting up push notifications	117
Managing the user's subscription	120
Handling push notifications	123
Unsubscribing from push notifications	127
Handling a push subscription change	129
Background sync	**130**
Summary	**133**
Chapter 5: The Service Worker Life Cycle	**135**
Registering a service worker	**138**
Service worker clients	**140**
The service worker registration object	141
Updating a service worker	**143**
Service worker scope	**144**
Service worker updates	**147**
Service worker events	**148**
Summary	**149**
Chapter 6: Mastering the Cache API - Managing Web Assets in a Podcast Application	**151**
Using the Fetch API	**152**
Request object	153
Handling cross-origin requests	154
Managing request credentials	156
Controlling how a response is cached	156
Headers object	157
Adding Headers	158
Accessing Header values	159
Protected Headers	160
Body mixin	161
Response object	164
Response properties	165
Verifying a successful response	165
Caching responses	**166**
Caches object	**167**
caches.open	168

caches.match	168
caches.has()	168
caches.delete()	169
caches.keys()	169
The Cache object	170
cache.match()	170
cache.matchAll	171
Cache add and addAll	172
cache.put	172
Deleting Cached items	173
cache.keys	174
Summary	174
Chapter 7: Service Worker Caching Patterns	177
How the service worker cache works	178
Service worker events	180
Caching patterns and strategies	181
Precaching	182
Installing as a dependency	182
Installing not as a dependency	183
On activate	185
Real-time caching	186
On user interaction	187
On network response	188
Stale while revalidating	189
On push notification	190
On background sync	191
Cache only	192
Network only	194
Cache falling back to network	194
Cache and network race	196
Network falling back to cache	197
Generic fallback	198
Service worker templating	201
Summary	203
Chapter 8: Applying Advanced Service Worker Cache Strategies	205
What is PWA tickets?	205
Reviewing the PWA ticket application	207
Using the JSON server for an API	212
Making a database and the API	214
Using faker	216
Generating QR codes	217
Rendering the website	218
The PWA ticket rendering architecture and logic	219
The PWA ticket JavaScript architecture	220

The PWA ticket service worker architecture	224
The ResponseManager	227
Using the request method to determine the caching strategy	232
Matching routes with caching strategies	233
Cache invalidation strategies	235
Unique hash names and long time-to-live values	235
Maximum items in a cache	237
Purging stale responses using time to live	238
Executing ResponseManager	239
The Invalidation Manager	239
maxItems strategy	241
The time-to-live invalidation strategy	241
Using a real-time asset manifest	242
How much should you cache?	244
Summary	245
Chapter 9: Optimizing for Performance	**247**
The importance of WPO	248
Reducing image payload size	250
The cost of CSS and JavaScript	250
Proper test devices and emulation	253
Testing poor conditions using developer tools	254
Performing performance and PWA testing with Lighthouse	257
Using WebPageTest to benchmark performance	260
Key performance indicators	264
Time to first byte	264
The PRPL pattern	267
Implementing push with browser hints and the service worker cache	268
Using the app shell model and service worker to render the initial route	270
Service worker pre-caching important routes	271
Lazy-loading non-critical and dynamic routes	271
The RAIL pattern	272
How JavaScript clogs the pipeline	275
Why 14 KB is the magic number	276
Inline critical CSS	277
Minifying scripts with uglify	280
Using feature detection to conditionally load JavaScript polyfils	284
Lazy loading images	286
Summary	288
Chapter 10: Service Worker Tools	**289**
Using PWABuilder to scaffold your PWA	290
Generating a valid web manifest file	290
Building a service worker	293
Downloading your site's PWA assets	294

Scaffolded PWA images	294
Running PWABuilder locally	295
Auditing web pages using Lighthouse	**296**
Running Lighthouse from the Chrome Developer Tools	298
Running Lighthouse as a command-line utility	301
Lighthouse and headless testing	303
Running Lighthouse in a Node script	305
Continuous build with Lighthouse	306
Auditing web pages with Sonar	**307**
Using the Sonar CLI	307
Sonar components	310
Configurations	310
Connectors	310
Formatters	311
Parsers	311
Rules	311
Automating site audits with the Sonar node module	311
Making complex service workers with workbox	**312**
Installing workbox	313
Workbox structure	315
Service worker setup	316
Pre-caching with Workbox	317
Dynamic routes with Workbox	323
Caching strategies	325
Workbox cache invalidation	326
Adding background sync functionality	327
Using Google Analytics, even when the user is offline	328
Summary	**329**
Other Books You May Enjoy	**331**
Index	**335**

Preface

Progressive web apps (PWAs) mark a new era in delivering user experience. Now supported by every major browser and platform, PWAs eliminate many of the missing capabilities previously reserved for native apps. If you are a developer who works on application frontends, you need to understand what progressive web apps are, their advantages, and how to effectively architect modern web apps.

You will learn the basic PWA requirements, such as the web manifest file and how HTTPS works through advanced service worker life cycle and caching strategies. The book covers web performance optimization practices and tools to help you consistently create high-quality progressive web apps.

Who this book is for

If you're a web developer and frontend designer who wants to create the best user experiences, then this book is for you. If you're an application developer with knowledge of HTML, CSS, and JavaScript, then this book will help you capitalize on your skills to develop progressive web applications, which is the future of app development.

What this book covers

Chapter 1, *Introduction to Progressive Web Apps*, explains what progressive web apps are and the advantages they offer.

Chapter 2, *Creating a Home Screen Experience With a Web Manifest*, introduces the web manifest file and explains how it is used by browsers to design the home screen and launch experience after a PWA is installed.

Chapter 3, *Making Your Web Site Secure*, explains why HTTPS is a modern web requirement and how it works.

Chapter 4, *Service Workers - Notification, Synchronization, and Our Podcast App*, introduces service workers, the Fetch API, and implementing push notifications.

Chapter 5, *The Service Worker Life Cycle*, demonstrates how service workers are installed and updated, and how to manage the process.

Chapter 6, *Master the Cache API - Manage Web Assets in a Podcast Application*, takes a deep dive into how the service worker cache API works.

Chapter 7, *Service Worker Caching Patterns*, reviews common caching patterns you can use in your applications.

Chapter 8, *Applying Advanced Service Worker Cache Strategies*, applies caching strategies with invalidation techniques.

Chapter 9, *Optimizing for Performance*, explains what web performance optimization is and introduces some tools you can use to measure page load times to improve progressive web apps.

Chapter 10, *Service Worker Tools*, reviews four helpful tools to make developing and managing progressive web apps easier and more consistent.

To get the most out of this book

- Anyone who develops or is responsible for the technical aspects of application frontends or user experience will benefit from this book.
- A moderate background in modern web development is assumed.
- Knowledge of common JavaScript syntax is important because service workers are JavaScript files.
- Because many modern tools rely on Node.js, a basic understanding is recommended.
- Source code is managed on GitHub, which requires some knowledge of using Git source control.

Download the example code files

You can download the example code files for this book from your account at `www.packtpub.com`. If you purchased this book elsewhere, you can visit `www.packtpub.com/support` and register to have the files emailed directly to you.

You can download the code files by following these steps:

1. Log in or register at www.packtpub.com.
2. Select the **SUPPORT** tab.
3. Click on **Code Downloads & Errata**.
4. Enter the name of the book in the **Search** box and follow the onscreen instructions.

Once the file is downloaded, please make sure that you unzip or extract the folder using the latest version of:

- WinRAR/7-Zip for Windows
- Zipeg/iZip/UnRarX for Mac
- 7-Zip/PeaZip for Linux

The code bundle for the book is also hosted on GitHub at https://github.com/PacktPublishing/Progressive-Web-Application-Development-by-Example. In case there's an update to the code, it will be updated on the existing GitHub repository.

We also have other code bundles from our rich catalog of books and videos available at https://github.com/PacktPublishing/. Check them out!

Conventions used

There are a number of text conventions used throughout this book.

CodeInText: Indicates code words in text, database table names, folder names, filenames, file extensions, pathnames, dummy URLs, user input, and Twitter handles. Here is an example: "Mount the downloaded WebStorm-10*.dmg disk image file as another disk in your system."

A block of code is set as follows:

```
function renderResults(results) {
    var template = document.getElementById("search-results-
    template"),
        searchResults = document.querySelector('.search-results');
```

Any command-line input or output is written as follows:

```
npm install -g pwabuilder
```

Bold: Indicates a new term, an important word, or words that you see onscreen. For example, words in menus or dialog boxes appear in the text like this. Here is an example: "Select **System info** from the **Administration** panel."

Warnings or important notes appear like this.

Tips and tricks appear like this.

Get in touch

Feedback from our readers is always welcome.

General feedback: Email `feedback@packtpub.com` and mention the book title in the subject of your message. If you have questions about any aspect of this book, please email us at `questions@packtpub.com`.

Errata: Although we have taken every care to ensure the accuracy of our content, mistakes do happen. If you have found a mistake in this book, we would be grateful if you would report this to us. Please visit `www.packtpub.com/submit-errata`, selecting your book, clicking on the Errata Submission Form link, and entering the details.

Piracy: If you come across any illegal copies of our works in any form on the Internet, we would be grateful if you would provide us with the location address or website name. Please contact us at `copyright@packtpub.com` with a link to the material.

If you are interested in becoming an author: If there is a topic that you have expertise in and you are interested in either writing or contributing to a book, please visit `authors.packtpub.com`.

Reviews

Please leave a review. Once you have read and used this book, why not leave a review on the site that you purchased it from? Potential readers can then see and use your unbiased opinion to make purchase decisions, we at Packt can understand what you think about our products, and our authors can see your feedback on their book. Thank you!

For more information about Packt, please visit `packtpub.com`.

Introduction to Progressive Web Apps

Over 80% of 328 million active Twitter users are mobile. Twitter knew they needed their mobile experience to be faster, more reliable, and engaging. They chose to launch their default mobile experience as a **Progressive Web Application (PWA)** in April 2017, called Twitter Lite.

Their goals were simple, faster load times, more engagement, and lower data consumption. They were able to achieve all three when comparing general activities to the non progressive web app version:

- 65% increase in pages per session
- 75% increase in Tweets sent
- 20% decrease in bounce rate

> "Twitter Lite is now the fastest, least expensive, and most reliable way to use Twitter. The web app rivals the performance of our native apps but requires less than 3% of the device storage space compared to Twitter for Android."
> — Nicolas Gallagher, the Engineering Lead for Twitter Lite

This is just one example of online companies reaping the rewards that PWA offers. This book should serve as a starting point to arm you with the basic knowledge and confidence to create your first PWA.

In this book, you are going to learn how to build a PWA which will be ready for production use. In case you haven't created a PWA yet, you will learn how to make a simple PWA in the first part of this chapter.

Introduction to Progressive Web Apps

This chapter will cover PWA fundamentals and the advantages they offer over classic websites and native applications. You will also see how to upgrade an existing 2048 game web application to a PWA. You will learn how to add a web manifest and service worker to the application, enabling PWA features using a localhost web server.

The purpose of this chapter is to get a general idea of how PWAs work, why you want to deliver PWAs, and to give you the skills to easily create PWAs with basic functionalities.

This chapter will cover the following points:

- The purpose of PWA
- PWA advantages
- The basic technical requirements of a PWA
- The three primary user experience PWA goals
- How to upgrade an existing website and run it locally

The web as we know it is entering its third decade of existence. Over this time, the web has gone through many changes and enhancements. While the web possesses some great superpowers, it also had its limitations that inhibited it from delivering an experience in parity with native counterparts.

PWAs are a way to apply native browser technology to create web solutions that consumers want to add to their homescreen. Meanwhile, new web APIs are progressing to fill additional gaps in functionality between web and native apps.

The great thing about a PWA is existing websites can easily be upgraded to claim the PWA status. This can unlock new features in browsers and platforms to level up any website.

About a decade ago, not only was the web disrupted, but so was desktop computing when Apple released the iPhone. This ushered in a new era of mobile first computing. That era's web technology was not prepared for this rapid shift from desktops to handheld devices.

Changing to a mobile first world requires more than just responsive design techniques; it requires a new set of native APIs, capabilities, and coding techniques. The HTML, CSS, and JavaScript specifications and browsers have evolved over the past decade, catching up to the consumer expectations of client applications.

Today, we have a very rich set of native APIs and browsers, enabling everything from geo-location to voice input and camera manipulation. There are client platforms designed to provide a rich, mobile first canvas for developers to paint engaging user experiences.

In addition to great native APIs, browsers have added new features in service workers, web manifestations, and have begun requiring HTTPS to enable modern APIs. These three technical features are the core requirements to become a PWA. However, there is much more to the art of making a good PWA. This art requires a different approach to web development.

In this book, we are going to explore the requirements of a good PWA, and how to create new and upgrade existing websites as PWAs. Along the way, we will learn how to leverage new features such as IndexedDB, multi-media, and the Fetch API to add value to our applications.

As this book progresses, you will learn how to use service workers for caching, push notifications, and background synchronization. The next chapter delves into the web manifest file. `Chapter 3`, *Making Your Website Secure*, covers the subtleties of upgrading to HTTPS.

This book breaks down technical and experiential requirements so that you can create a good, PWA and demonstrates this with three sample applications:

- The first application is a simple game, 2048. 2048 was very popular about three years ago and I still find it very addictive. Even though it's a simple game, it will demonstrate how the web can compete on an even level with common native applications.
- Next, we will create a photo gallery website and see how to use service worker caching to create an application that loads instantly and runs with or without a network. The application will be comparable to many popular podcast players like iTunes and Stitcher.
- The final application is a consumer event ticket application. This application will demonstrate advanced service worker techniques like cache invalidation. I will also cover tools you can use to validate your applications and help you scaffold them for quality and consistency.

All source code is available on GitHub, with links provided in this book. You're welcome to clone and fork these repositories. Make local copies and modify them as you wish. I would love to see how you enhance the demo applications.

Why we needed a new way to build websites

When Apple released the iPhone in 2007, they initially intended that applications to be built using HTML. They provided an initial platform to create web applications. However, Mac developers cried put for a better native application solution and Apple answered. Apple did so with the caveat of taking 30% of the application's revenue and controlling the applications that were distributed through a closed App Store.

The closed App Store violates the openness of the web by introducing a third-party gatekeeper. This creates a layer of delay as Apple reviews your application. The review process can result in your application being censored or denied entry. The one advantage App Store offers is a sense of security and trustworthiness for consumers.

To make the App Store model interesting for Apple, they decided to take a big cut for tax-native applications. In return, Apple handles all payment and distribution infrastructure for applications. However, the web has not had a problem collecting money from consumers, nor a distribution issue.

Credit card merchant accounts typically take 2% to 3% of a transaction. Hosting has become a cheap commodity, often costing $10 or less a month for most websites.

The next perceived problem the web has suffered from is performance. Performance issues are amplified on mobile devices. Smartphones and tablets have underpowered CPUs compared to their desktop counterparts. And while more mobile devices use WiFi, cellular connections, even in the developed world, are still unreliable.

When the iPhone was first released, the web was still very static compared to what we experience today. Up to that point, the web was not a platform with animations and dynamic content.

Over the last decade, rich user experiences have become commonplace on the web with the rise of single page applications and many large frameworks. These changes have been driven in large part due to the user experiences consumers have come to expect from many native applications.

Many developers have tried to hack their way to mimicking native application experiences on mobile devices. This has led to some good progress as well as some bad experiences and coding practices.

Most bad experiences are due to a lack of awareness of the available APIs and how to use them. Poor coding techniques have also created more issues than perceived value.

A common mistake I have seen a lot is the application of server-side architecture in the browser. While outside the scope of this book, it is important to note that for a good modern web user experience, you may have to let go of preconceived notions of how to develop websites.

A prime example of misunderstanding how to use the web platform and the capability gap can be demonstrated by an interview in 2012 with Mark Zuckerberg, at a Tech Crunch event. You can check out the following link for the article: http://tcrn.ch/2hwN6HF

Facebook tried to make the web its primary platform, but due to many engineering mistakes and browser/hardware limitations, they failed. At that point, they switched to native apps as a primary focus and have since created a very large, walled off community of data and interactions.

As you will see later in this book, Facebook dominates the mobile native application space. This leaves very little room for anybody else to gain screen time.

This is where PWAs can empower businesses and organizations to engage with consumers at a deeper level. This book is designed to give you the tools and knowledge to create PWAs to reach consumers for less money and effort. The web possesses several superpowers that native applications can't touch. Now, with emerging native APIs, the web surpasses native applications.

Real-world PWA examples

Flipkart, the Amazon of the Indian sub-continent, embraced PWA as soon as the term was first mentioned. In many ways, they are the poster child of doing a PWA the right way.

Flipkart's consumer market consists of customers almost entirely on poor mobile connections. Their mobile devices have limited storage and may or may not have a reliable 3G connection. In fact, 63% reach the site via 2G. A client application experience that loads quickly and works even when the network is absent gives Flipkart a business advantage.

The Flipkart PWA (https://developers.google.com/web/showcase/2016/flipkart) was created by a small team of engineers in 42 days, a small investment on their part that has paid huge dividends by increasing conversions by 70%. These are just some of their published key performance indicators:

- Users time on the site with Flipkart lite vs previous mobile experience, 3.5 minutes vs 70 seconds
- 3x more time spent on site
- 40% higher re-engagement rate
- 70% greater conversion rate among those arriving via the Add to Homescreen feature
- 3x lower data usage

Over 50% of the Weather Channel's mobile usage comes from the web. Reaching consumers around the world is a priority. The web offers a reliable channel to reach everyone, which often means lower powered devices. Re-engagement and the delivery of timely information, such as storm warnings, was also very important.

The Weather Channel (https://developers.google.com/web/showcase/2016/weather-channel) created a PWA, implementing push notifications to deliver experiences matching their native application. This upgrade enabled their team to reach 178 countries and deliver weather forecasts while improving their load time:

- This PWA is now available in 62 languages and 178 countries
- 80% improvement in load time
- Based on this successful global test, the team will expand the PWA to its U.S site in 2017

Lancôme (https://developers.google.com/web/showcase/2017/lancome) rebuilt their mobile web presence as a PWA and increased conversions by 17%. As they tracked mobile web usage, passing desktop, Lancôme saw their conversions drop. After considering a native application, they decided investing in the web was the right way to go.

They determined customers were not likely to download a native application, nor use it often. They knew a web presence would have to be done right, as doing so could generate more rewards. They decided to rebuild their web presence from the ground up as a PWA.

Overall benefits:

- 84% decrease in time until the page is interactive
- 17% increase in conversions
- 15% decrease in bounce rate
- 51% increase in mobile sessions

iOS improvements:

- 53% increase in mobile sessions on iOS
- 10% decrease in bounce rates on iOS

Push notification benefits:

- 8% of consumers who tap on a push notification make a purchase
- 18% open rate from push notifications
- 12% increase in conversion rates on recovered carts via push notifications

If you are worried about browsers that do not support PWA technology yet, take note of the iOS statistics. Lancôme is not alone; almost every company embracing PWAs have reported similar improvements on iOS. Later, you will see how to polyfill caching and the Add to Homescreen experience in your applications to achieve similar results.

These are just a few samples of major brands that have adopted PWAs and reported benefits. There are many more smaller businesses also improving because they are building web experiences customers want to use. The great thing is you can start enhancing your existing web site today using examples from this chapter.

What are PWAs?

Two years ago, a Google Chrome engineer, *Alex Russell*, published the landmark blog post defining PWA. You can check the post on the following link: `http://bit.ly/2n1vQ2r`

With this blog post Alex declared that web could now stand toe to toe with native applications. But it goes beyond just native capabilities being added via service workers, and the Add to Homescreen heuristic also matters when it comes to building a website.

Another Google Chrome engineer, Chris Wilson said that Progressive Web Applications are a new level of thinking about the quality of your user experience.

What the Chrome team and other browsers want you to understand is that user experience is the most important part of your website or application. Browsers are providing you with the foundation to build great applications, but it is still up to you to make these experiences come to life.

I tend to think that there is a confidence issue web developers have compared to native application developers. There is still this perception that native rules everything. However, this is not really true. As we'll see later, there are far more accessible web pages than native applications., and there is much more room to grow your website's brand compared to a native application.

Native applications serve a purpose, and that purpose is starting to fade away. The former head of Opera, Bruce Lawson, a very popular browser on mobile devices, stated (http://bit.ly/2e5Cgry) that native apps are a bridging technology.

That's a very bold statement, comparing the web to native applications. But it's something to think about. There are often many bridging technologies that lead to the real consumable product.

For example, Netflix began by shipping DVDs in the mail. I'm sure you could still do that today, but the vast majority of Netflix members simply stream and download video content to watch. The DVDs were a mere bridging technology to get the company started and form a relationship with a very loyal customer base.

The expenses involved in distributing those DVDs became too much for them to make it their primary distribution channel. As technology improved, which led to an increase in broadband, Netflix was able to shed the bridging distribution technology and focus on the original goal of getting videos and movies the living rooms of members all over the world.

In much the same way, mobile was a brand-new platform for building application experiences. And just like desktop computing, it started with native applications, and the web eventually won them over. The web won the desktop just as mobile technology emerged, and it emerged in a big way.

PWA signify a retooling of the web to make it a mobile first platform. Your applications can run faster, work offline, and ask users for permission to be on their homescreen. Never before have we been able to deploy these experiences at this level on the web.

Peak app

Smartphone owners always lookout to download apps they think will be useful. If you are fortunate enough to have a consumer download your application, then odds are that they will delete it after one use if they find it troublesome or difficult to use.

According to a Nielsen study (http://www.nielsen.com/us/en/insights/news/2015/so-many-apps-so-much-more-time-for-entertainment.html) that average adult uses less than 30 apps per month. Over time the lack of using an app leads to the unused apps being purged.

Several studies estimate roughly 10% of apps are used enough times to be retained. This means even if your app is downloaded the odds are it will eventually be removed and probably never used.

Brands are spending between $8-12 in advertising to earn a single application download. This means the true customer acquisition cost is roughly $80-120. Good luck recuperating that expense.

The Apple and Google App Store's boast of 2 million or more applications. Some, dated, research shows nearly 60% of apps are never downloaded.

Apple recently made the barrier to success even higher by enforcing section 4.2.6 of their application guideline requirements. This section gives them the authority to reject and remove apps at their discretion. They have been purging apps in mass they don't consider meet these arbitrary guidelines.

Why have consumers stopped downloading applications? Space, both physical and temporal. Mobile phones and tablets only have so much disk space. Many applications now need 100 MB-1 GB of space. While a few 128 GB iPhones are sold, the typical iPhone size is 32 GB. After personal photos, videos, and music, there is little to no room for applications.

While we have become a society that can never seem to leave our mobile screens, there is still only so much time in a day. Market analysts pay close attention to what we do with our screen time. Kids watch videos and play silly games. Adults live in social media with Facebook and Snapchat owning their phones. Adults also play silly games, such as 2048.

Out of the top five applications one these App Stores, Facebook owns three. The average adult spends over 2 hours a day in the Facebook universe looking at photos and videos. Text messaging is being replaced with Facebook Messenger. Millennials are addicted to Instagram, sharing, liking, and commenting on photos and videos non-stop.

Facebook, Facebook Messenger, and Facebook-owned Instagram are the top three mobile applications. They are followed by YouTube, SnapChat, and Gmail. Two of those are owned by Google. After those applications, the distribution curve drops to nearly zero.

We, mobile consumers, have settled into usage habits and have found that the need for applications has passed.

Installing an application, even if it is free, consists of eight steps, each step losing 20% of the initial interested base. The reason Amazon implemented **one click** purchasing was to eliminate friction and increase sales.

The web is relatively frictionless. You click a link in an email or maybe search for something, clicking the best perceived result, and within a few seconds you have downloaded or installed the web page you need. Little to no friction and next to no device resources have been used.

In contrast to the distribution of app usage in a given month, the average consumer visits over 100 websites. That is roughly 20 times more variety than their application distribution. This means there is more opportunity to engage customers via the web than native applications.

The web satisfies two important consumer requirements of minimal resource investment. Very little time or disk space is needed. In fact, they do not need to uninstall your website when they clean out their device so that they can make more videos to share on Instagram.

This is where PWA have risen in importance. Companies want their icons on consumer's devices. This symbolizes a relationship and hopefully increases sales or other engagement statistics. When brand engagement is cheap for the customer, they are more likely to take the step to make you part of their daily life.

Browsers are providing the engagement platform, but you still need to meet their requirements. That is what you are going to learn in this book.

PWA features

Don't mistake PWAs as a specific technology. It is more of a marketing term describing the usage of modern platform features to provide a certain quality of experience. Without good user experience, the technology does not matter.

The Chrome team has identified four experience factors a PWA should offer:

- Fast
- Reliable
- Engaging
- Integrated

Research has shown that 53% of users will abandon a site if it takes longer than 3 seconds to load. Service worker caching makes page load time almost instant, but it cannot make animations faster. This requires knowledge of CSS animations and possibly JavaScript.

Applications that stutter or jump around the screen are said to be janky. If you have ever loaded a web page, for example, almost any news website, and had the content jump up or down just as you start reading, you know what I am talking about. This is a very poor user experience and can easily be avoided with proper coding practices.

Later in this book, you are going to learn about **RAIL (Response, Animation, Idle, Load)** and the **PRPL (Push, Render, Pre-cache, and Lazy- load)** patterns. These are coding best practices offered by the Chrome team because they understand how browsers work. They, and the other browsers, want the web to work for everyone.

Browser vendors are offering guidance to help developers create the class of web applications that will earn a place on customer's homescreens. This guidance starts with a mobile performance first approach.

Consumers need to have confidence in an application, and they need to know that the application is reliable. This means it should just work when called upon. To enable this, a web application should load if the device is online, offline, and anything in-between.

Service worker caching provides a proxy layer between the browser and the network. This makes the network a progressive enhancement. It also introduces a new class of programming web developers must master.

Later in this book, you are going to learn about different caching strategies and how to employ them in different scenarios to make websites just work.

Service workers open up a new layer of opportunity where web developers can add valuable features that improve performance, engagement, and data management. Service workers are designed to be extensible so future capabilities can be added. Right now, caching, push notifications, and background sync are supported, but there are many other features being debated in the W3C working groups.

Push notifications give you the ability to connect with a consumer any time you wish, increasing engagement. As shared earlier, both the Weather Channel and Lancôme increased engagement via push notifications.

Background sync is a channel you can now use to let your application run when the network is unavailable. When connectivity is restored, you can seamlessly synchronize with the server without disrupting the user. Their phone may even be in their pocket while your application catches up.

A web application needs to engage users enough that they will want to make it a permanent fixture on their devices. Once your web application has the minimum technical requirements—a web manifest, registered service worker with a fetch event handler, and served via HTTPS—the browser triggers native prompts for the user to add the web application to their homescreen. You will delve more deeply into this experience as this book progresses.

The web manifest, HTTPS, and service worker require different expertise to execute effectively. And in my opinion, they increase in complexity from the latter. That is why embracing PWA is often called a journey. It's something you can, and should, implement in steps.

PWA advantages

I teased you with the advantages the web has over native applications, but how do these advantages elevate the web's past native applications?

Let's borrow a demonstration from the Chrome team. An XY graph can show the differences between the web and native applications. The vertical axis represents **Capabilities**. The x-axis represents **Reach**. The reach being defined is how easy it is to discover and quickly access the application or website:

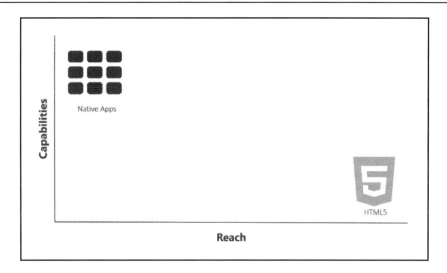

For many years, native applications enjoyed a capability advantage. They had tight native platform APIs and hooks that enabled native applications to do things that the web was not designed to do. For example, native push notifications allow brands to send messages to customers without the application being open.

However, apps are gated behind closed App Stores on Apple, Android, and even the Microsoft ecosystem. This makes finding applications very difficult. Many estimates show it takes between $8 and $12 a day to get a single app download.

The web, as I mentioned earlier, simply was not ready for this shift to mobile. There have been several APIs such as geo-location and some web notification capabilities. These APIs are not necessarily on the same level with their native counterparts.

Developers have lacked awareness of many modern APIs. Unfortunately, this lack of knowledge and confidence has caused websites to not take advantage of these capabilities.

Ten years ago, responsive design did not exist. However, today, not only do we have CSS media queries and a vast array of responsive CSS libraries, but we also have responsive images built-in to browsers. Now, websites can offer layouts and download appropriately sized images for all screen sizes without crazy hacks.

Compared to their native counterparts, websites have always been easily discoverable. You can advertise a domain in any media channel and people know how to load it. Search engines are much more sophisticated than App Stores and provide an easy interface to find just about anything. The big advantage search engines have over App Stores is the ability to deeply index web content.

Search engines index pages deep within a website and thousands upon thousands of web pages per site. App stores can only offer a single point of entry to download the app. The only *page* you have control of is a sales page. In that one page, you need to sell your app without the customer sampling your content and experience. Reach is and has always been the web's greatest superpower:

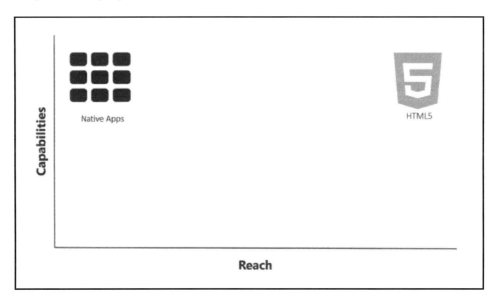

As the graph visualizes, the web is not only on equal footing with native applications—it exceeds native applications is most cases. Sure, there are still going to be edge cases where a native application is the best choice, but these are shrinking every time a browser adds a new feature.

PWA technical requirements

At a minimum, there are three core technical requirements to be a PWA. A website must have a web manifest file, be served using HTTPS, and must register a service worker with a fetch event handler. You will dive deeper into each one of these requirements in future chapters.

The web manifest drives the Add to Homescreen experience. HTTPS provides a layer of security and trust between your application and the browser. The service worker provides the extensible backbone for event-driven functionality to execute on a separate thread from the user interface.

A PWA should also use an application shell or common HTML and CSS. This is the most common application of Chrome, which is used on just about every page on the site. If you have any experience with single page applications, you should understand what an application shell is.

The application shell

A typical application shell typically contains a header, a main content area, and a footer. Of course, this can vary by application and site. The 2048 game differs because there is only one web page:

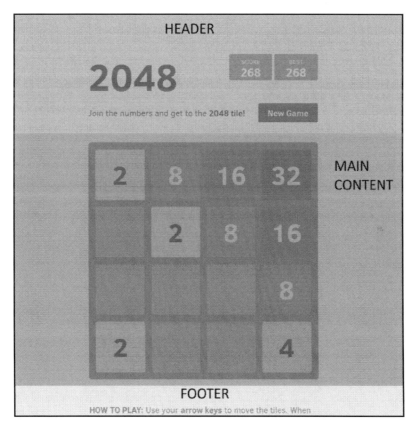

Application shells are common-place in single page applications because they dynamically render markup and data in the browser. This does not need to be the case with a PWA. The reason single page applications are so popular is their ability to create a more native-like transition experience because there is no request delay when a new page is requested.

[21]

Since a PWA can be cached locally, this does not mean you need a true application shell. If the application utilizes a cache first strategy, pages can load in a matter of milliseconds, often less than 100. This is perceived as instant by the human mind.

This does not mean you should not identify an application shell. Server and build rendering engines can use the application shell and an array of layouts to create server hosted markups. You will be exposed to this so that you can work as we build the photo gallery and podcast application.

2048

A few years ago, a popular application was a simple game called 2048. The goal is to combine blocks with numbers to ultimately total 2048. Blocks are numbered in multiples of 2. You can combine adjacent blocks with the same value to create a new block with their combined value.

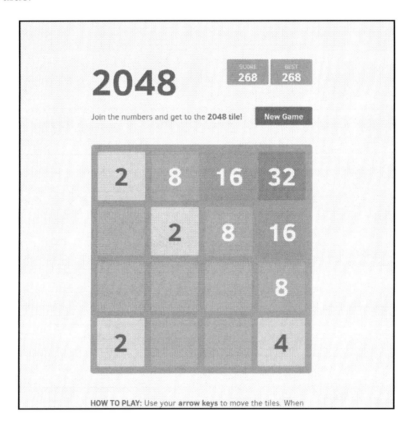

I wasted more time playing this game than I care to admit. It is easy to play and highly addictive. A well-crafted brew of endorphins and gameplay.

Fortunately, there were numerous open source knock-offs available on GitHub. Several were web applications. I would wager that native versions distributed through app stores were websites wrapped in a native shell, a hybrid application.

I chose a popular repository to fork for the book. The 2048 web application is simple and a perfect candidate to demonstrate how to make an exemplary PWA example:

The source code

The original application source code is available on GitHub (`https://github.com/gabrielecirulli/2048`). You can clone the repository and open it in a browser to play the game. Just be forewarned that it is addictive and could distract you from learning how to create PWAs.

I forked the repository in my GitHub profile (`https://github.com/docluv/2048`). My version adds the manifest, icons, service workers, and applies some code upgrades to make the application perform better and take advantage of newer APIs and browser features. The original code was written very well, but this was for browser capabilities of 3 years ago.

Feel free to star, clone, and fork my GitHub repository to customize it to your liking. A working version of the final application created in this book is available online (`https://2048.love2dev.com/`).

The application's code structure

Let's review how the game's source code is structured. I like this project because the code is simple and demonstrates how much can be accomplished with a small amount of code in the browser.

There are three asset folders: `js`, `meta`, and `style`. They contain JavaScript files, images, and style sheets that are needed to render and execute the game.

Introduction to Progressive Web Apps

You will also notice a `node_modules` folder. I added a local web server using `grunt connect`, which is a node module. The original game works just fine if you load the `index.html` file directly in the browser. However, due to security constraints, a service worker does not function without a web server. I will cover this in more detail shortly.

At the root-level, there are only handful of web application files:

- `index.html`
- `manifest.json`
- `sw.js`
- `favicon.ico`

The nice thing about the 2048 code is that it only requires a single HTML file. The `manifest.json` and `sw.js` files add the PWA functionality we are after. The `favicon.ico` file is the icon loaded by the browser for the address bar:

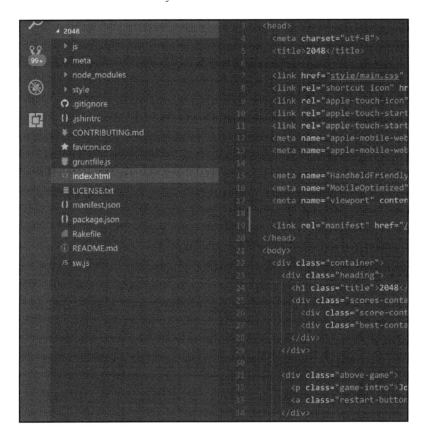

Adding node modules to the project

The original repository is a stand-alone game, meaning it does not require a web server to execute, just a browser. You can right-click the `index.html` file and choose to open it in your favorite browser. You can still do this after registering a service worker and may not notice any differences. But if you open the browser console (*F12* Developer Tools), you will most likely see an error.

This error can be attributed to service worker requirements. Service workers, like most new APIs supported by browsers, require HTTPS protocol. This requirement raises the default security level and gives the browsers a minimum level of trust in your site ownership.

The service worker specification relaxes this requirement for localhost addresses. Localhost is a common way to reference your local machine, which is typically a development environment. Because it is unlikely you are going to hack yourself, browsers tend to let you do what you want—except when you open files directly from the file system.

When localhost is used to load an asset, the browser is making a traditional network request, which requires a web server to respond. This means you, the user of the local machine, has gone through the effort of launching a local web server. This is not something the average consumer knows how to do.

A file, opened from the file system, is different. Anyone can send you an `index.html` file that loads scary code, designed to steal your identity or worse show endless loops of cat videos! By not honoring the direct file system, access browsers are protecting you from registering a malicious service worker script. Trusting a localhost web server makes development easier by avoiding the messy process of registering a localhost SSL certificate.

There are a variety of local web servers you can run. In recent years, my preference is node connect, which I execute as a Grunt task (`https://love2dev.com/blog/make-a-local-web-server-with-grunt-connect/`). Because connect is a node module, you can launch it directly from the command line or a custom script. There are modules for your favorite task runner, such as Gulp and so on. Besides, node is cross-platform, so everyone can use connect.

If you are familiar with installing node modules, you can skip ahead. If node and connect are new to you, this section will serve as a simple primer to get you up and running to run all the samples applications in this book on your local machine.

The first step to loading a node module is to install them from `https://www.npmjs.com/` or one of the emerging package manager sites. You can manage this from the command line if you like, or you can define the modules needed in a `package.json` file.

You can read more about the `package.json` format here (https://docs.npmjs.com/files/package.json). For our purposes, `grunt` and the `grunt-contrib-connect` module are `devDependencies`. You could also define a dependencies section if this were a node application.

Grunt is a task runner that gained popularity several years ago and is still my preferred task runner. Task runners, and there seems to be a new one every week, help you organize repeatable tasks into repeatable recipes. I use Grunt and custom node scripts to build and deploy my PWAs. Think about your task runner as a command-line control panel to manage your application:

```
{
    "name": "2048",
    "version": "1.0.0",
    "description": "2048 Progressive Web App",
    "author": "Chris Love",
    "private": true,
    "devDependencies": {
        "grunt": "*",
        "grunt-contrib-connect": "*"
    }
}
```

Both Grunt and the Grunt connect module are node packages and must be downloaded in order to execute. The `package.json` file gives npm a configuration so it can manage your packages. This way, you can quickly set up your project on any machine without having to maintain your node dependencies as part of the source code.

If you have cloned the sample repository, you will note that the node modules were excluded from the source code. That's because they are not part of the application itself. They are a dependency and npm helps you recreate the desired environment.

To install the packages, you need to open a command line and change to your source code's folder. Next, you must execute the following command:

```
>npm install
```

This kicks off the npm installation process, which downloads your modules and their dependency chain. When completed, you have everything you need to run or build your application.

Next, you will need to create a `gruntfile.js`. This is where you tell Grunt what tasks you want to run and how you want them to run. If you want to know the details of using Grunt, visit their website (https://gruntjs.com/):

```
module.exports = function (grunt) {
    grunt.loadNpmTasks('grunt-contrib-connect');
    // Project configuration.
    grunt.initConfig({
        connect: {
            localhost: {
                options: {
                    port: 15000,
                    keepalive: true
                }
            }
        }
    });
};
```

Since we are only using the connect module, the 2048 gruntfile is very simple. You need to tell Grunt to load the connect module, then register the task to run in the `initConfig` function.

2048 is a very simple application, which keeps our customization to a minimum. I arbitrarily chose port 15000 to serve the application and chose to have `keepalive` open. There are many options you can define. More details are available on the `grunt-contrib-connect` **npm page** (https://www.npmjs.com/package/grunt-contrib-connect).

The only task left to do is start the connect web server. This is done from the command line. If you still have the command line open from when you performed the npm install, you can reuse it. If not, repeat the process of opening a command line and changing to the project's folder:

```
>grunt connect
Running "connect:localhost" (connect) task
Waiting forever...
Started connect web server on http://localhost:15000
```

Execute `grunt connect` and you should see the preceding example output. Note that the command continues to execute. This is because it is a server, listening to requests on port 15000. You cannot execute additional commands at this prompt.

You can now load the 2048 game in your browser by entering `http://localhost:15000` in the address bar.

Adding a manifest

Adding a web manifest file should be the first step in upgrading an existing website. You can create your site's manifest file in a matter of minutes. In the tooling chapter, I will review a few online resources that can help automate the process.

Registering a PWA's web manifest requires a special link element in the HTML `head` element. The following code shows how the 2048 manifest file is registered:

```
<head>
     ....
   <link rel="manifest" href="manifest.json">
</head>
```

If you are familiar with referencing a style sheet, this syntax should look familiar. The difference is the `rel` attribute value being manifest. The `href` value points to the manifest file. You are free to name it anything, but manifest is the most common name.

The next chapter will go into more manifest file details. You can reference the project's `manifest.json` file to see how the 2048 game is configured. It contains the application's name, default URL, primary colors, and an array of icon image references.

Adding a service worker

Next, you need to register a service worker. This is done in what I call the client-side code, which is the JavaScript you are accustomed to writing. Service workers execute in a separate thread from the UI. I think about it as a background process. You still need to register the service worker for the site.

For simple registrations, like this example, my preferred method is a script block at the bottom of my site's markup. First, detect if service workers are supported. If they are, then attempt to register the site's service work. If the browser does not support service workers, skip the registration code so no exceptions occur.

Registration is done by calling the `navigator.serviceWorker.register` function. It accepts a single argument, which is a path to the service worker file. I will review more rules around this in later chapters.

The register function returns a promise. You can add code to log successful registration as follows:

```
<script>
  if ('serviceWorker' in navigator) {
      navigator.serviceWorker.register('/sw.js').then(function
       (registration) {    // Registration was successful
          console.log('ServiceWorker registration successful with
          scope: ', registration.scope);
      }).catch(function (err) {    // registration failed :(
          console.log('ServiceWorker registration failed: ',
          err);
      });
  }
</script>
```

We will start diving into details about service workers in Chapter 5, *The Service Worker Life Cycle*. To help you understand the example code, let me introduce some service worker fundamentals. Service workers are completely asynchronous. They enter an idle or sleep state if they are not needed. They wake up or spin up completely in response to the operating system or browser firing and events.

All logic execution is a product of events. You must register event handlers to execute your service worker logic. The 2048 service worker registers event handlers for the install, activate, and fetch events.

The 2048 game service worker pre-caches the entire application in the install event. You will learn more about caching strategies in Chapter 6, *Master the Cache API – Manage Web Assets in a Podcast Application*. For now, we will cache the application so it is available all the time, without any network chatter:

```
self.addEventListener("install", function (event) {
    console.log("Installing the service worker!");
    caches.open("PRECACHE")
        .then(function (cache) {
            cache.addAll(cacheList);
        });
});
```

Introduction to Progressive Web Apps

The 2048 service worker caches assets in the install event. The application assets are defined in an array in the server worker code. The cache API provides an interface to a special storage designed specifically to persist response objects. I will defer the details to later chapters:

```
var cacheList = [
    "index.html",
    "style/main.css",
    "js/keyboard_input_manager.js",
    "js/html_actuator.js",
    "js/grid.js",
    "js/tile.js",
    "js/local_storage_manager.js",
    "js/game_manager.js",
    "js/application.js"
];
```

The service worker also has an activate and a fetch event handler. A fetch event handler must be registered before the add to homescreen feature can be triggered.

The fetch event fires when the browser requests an asset from the network. This could be an image, stylesheet, script, AJAX call, and so on. The `event` parameter contains the request object and can be used to check your cache to see if the asset is available:

```
self.addEventListener("fetch", function (event) {
    event.respondWith(
        caches.match(event.request)
        .then(function (response) {
            if (response) {
                return response;
            }
            return fetch(event.request);
        })
    );
});
```

Without a fetch event handler, your application cannot work offline. There is no requirement that the handler catch any requests, just that it is registered. It is a minimal check for offline capability.

In the example fetch event handler, all caches are interrogated to see if there is an existing match to the request. If so, the locally cached version is returned. If not, the request is passed to the network.

That's it; congratulations! Your website is now a PWA, at least on your local machine:

At this point, loading the 2048 localhost site in Chrome should cause an add to homescreen prompt being displayed. If not, reload the page once or twice and apply focus to the browser tab. If you are still not seeing the prompt, check the console for any error messages and debug them accordingly.

Summary

In this chapter, you have learned the basics of PWAs by updating a basic game website. We also reviewed what progressive websites are and why they were created.

In the next chapter, you will learn more details about the homescreen prompt experience and how to make a proper web manifest file.

2
Creating a Home Screen Experience with a Web Manifest

Progressive web apps make a website feel like a native app. For a business stakeholder, this gives them the opportunity to use a free app store to engage customers. For real users, it means that the sites they routinely visit can be installed without any friction. Either way, it is a marketing opportunity to increase engagement by delivering a better user experience and an natural way to place their brand's icon in the customer's most important location: their homescreen.

Each platform (operating system and browser) implements a homescreen and how the application is launched in their own way, but most involve some sort of bookmarking process and opening experience driven by the web manifest file.

Chrome for Android places installed PWAs in the application shelf and allows PWAs to be managed like a native app in the device settings. Microsoft leverages the Windows Store and is formulating a free store installation process for future releases. Apple is still figuring out how they will implement these experiences, but they are building on their legacy experiences.

This chapter goes over how to create a web manifest file to describe your application to the platform and how you can programmatically prompt the user to add a PWA to their homescreen. You'll see me refer to the process of add to homescreen throughout this chapter, but it is only a name that refers to more. The term add to homescreen has sort of grown to be the de facto way of describing how PWAs are installed on the user's device.

The reality is more diverse as there is no official common specification for this process. On Android, you add application icons to the homescreen, and since this is where PWAs first saw adoption, this is how the term originated. Today, each browser and platform handles this process differently. Even unique browsers on Android vary from what Chrome has been practicing. During the writing of this chapter, Microsoft Edge required you go through the Windows Store to install progressive web apps, but even that is in flux.

As this chapter progresses, you will see how this concept applies to different browsers and platforms, and learn how to describe your PWA to the platforms using a web manifest file.

The following topics will be covered in this chapter:

- The web manifest file
- How the add to homescreen process works
- How to use legacy features to *Polyfil* the add to homescreen experience

Why add to homescreen is important

Reengagement is a key advantage that native applications have enjoyed over websites. The presence of their icon on the user's homescreen and app shelves provides quick, visual access to the brand's experience. It's subtle, but that icon is a constant visual reminder of the customer's relationship to the brand.

Browsers have provided a built-in mechanism for us to bookmark websites using favorites for years now, but these lists have become cluttered messes we often forget about. We have also been able to add bookmarks to the desktop, start menu, and even the windows task bar, but the process is manual, and most consumers do not know that it exists.

More modern browsers have started logging pages that you frequently visit and providing bookmarks to these common destinations when you open a new tab. This is an example of making the user more productive without asking them to *bookmark* a URL.

These bookmarks do not offer the same native experience that the progressive web app's add to homescreen experience does. Chrome on Android is leading the way with the most advanced PWA installation benefits by making all installed PWAs a WebAPK.

WebAPKs are a technical way to say that Chrome on Android will silently upgrade progressive web apps to an almost native app by packaging them as an APK (Android executable) during the installation process. They are still limited because they do not have access to Android-specific APIs like native Android apps do.

However, if you submit your PWA to the Windows Store and the customer installs it from the Windows Store, your progressive web app is a native app. It will enjoy all the benefits and capabilities as native apps do on Windows, including file system access and the ability to integrate with features like Cortana.

The ability to earn a place on a customer's home screen is important. Both native and web applications have mechanisms, but both have friction that reduces success and increase costs. There are 6-8 steps which you must use to coax a potential customer to install your app on mobile platforms. In 2012, *Gabor Cselle* estimated that each of these steps eliminates 20% of the mobile user's interested in installing your app (`https://blog.gaborcselle.com/2012/10/every-step-costs-you-20-of-users.html`). This means for a 6-step installation process that only 26% of users remain, as illustrated in the following diagram. That number falls to less than 17% if there are 8 steps:

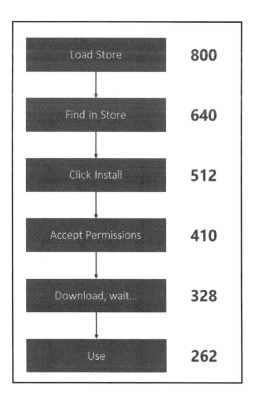

Of course, a user only starts the app installation process if they know how to/can find you in the app store. This means that your company must invest time and money driving traffic and brand awareness. Recent research reveals that this would cost between $8-14 on iOS and slightly less on Android.

Yet, for a few pennies paid per click, Facebook, **pay-per-click** (**PPC**), or banner ad campaigns can drive the same engagement to a website. Even better, if your page has a good, organic SEO profile, you can drive volumes of targeted traffic for free! However, earning a place on the customer's homescreen is not as easy. That's because it is not an obvious process.

Rewinding to the original iPhone launch, third-party apps were not available till 6 months later. At WWDC, Steve Jobs announced the third-party app solution HTML5 + AJAX (https://www.apple.com/newsroom/2007/06/11iPhone-to-Support-Third-Party-Web-2-0-Applications/):

> "Developers can create Web 2.0 applications which look and behave just like the applications built into iPhone, and which can seamlessly access iPhone's services, including making a phone call, sending an email, and displaying a location in Google Maps. Third-party applications created using Web 2.0 standards can extend iPhone's capabilities without compromising its reliability or security."

With that proclamation, Apple provided a simple, and sort of hacky, way to drive the homescreen experience on iOS. The non-standard techniques required adding iOS Safari specific META tags to each page and having appropriate sized homescreen images.

Making your PWA iOS web app capable

When Apple introduced iOS, the original app recommendation was to use HTML5, CSS3, and JavaScript to create rich client-side user experiences. Apple has not removed web app support and has enhanced some capabilities over time. The iOS web app experience is driven by custom metadata that's added to a web page's HEAD.

Chapter 2

Much of the Apple meta data has served as a model for the modern web manifest specification. Before the web manifest specification was created, Chrome on Android integrated support for the Apple meta data to drive a similar experience.

The web app experience on iOS is triggered when your website contains Apple-specific META tags, corresponding icons, and when the user has added your site to their homescreen.

The first piece you need is a png file as the default homescreen icon. The file should be named `apple-touch-icon.png` and it should be present in your site's root folder.

Individual pages can have a unique icon with a `link` reference in the `HEAD`:

```
<link rel="apple-touch-icon" href="/custom_icon.png">
```

It is even better to specify icons for different screen sizes and densities. The platform will determine which icon works best for the device. If no icon is specified, the root folder is searched for icons with the `apple-touch-icon` prefix:

```
<link rel="apple-touch-icon" href="touch-icon-iphone.png">
<link rel="apple-touch-icon" sizes="152x152" href="touch-icon-ipad.png">
<link rel="apple-touch-icon" sizes="180x180" href="touch-icon-iphone-retina.png">
<link rel="apple-touch-icon" sizes="167x167" href="touch-icon-ipad-retina.png">
```

When the required meta data is supplied, you must then coax the user to initiate the iOS add to homescreen process. This starts when they press Safari's share icon:

[37]

Creating a Home Screen Experience with a Web Manifest

This triggers the Safari **share** menu, which contains more than just options to share the URL: it contains icons to bookmarks and saves the site to the home screen, as shown in the following screenshot:

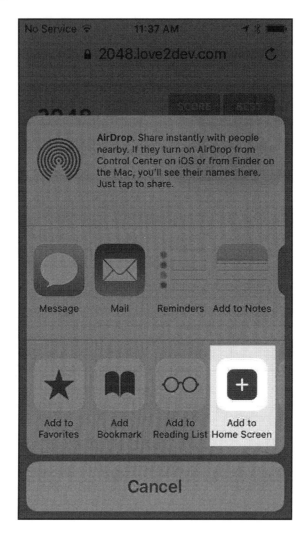

Similar to the home screen icon, the Launch screen image can be specified. Think of this as a splash screen. This is done with a LINK element and a reference to the startup image. If no image is specified, a screenshot of the last time the app was launched is used:

```
<link rel="apple-touch-startup-image" href="/ meta/apple-touch-startup-
image-640x920.png">
```

The application title is set with another META tag

This is similar to the name and short name manifest properties I'll discuss in detail in the the *web manifest* section. If no META value is supplied, the `title` element value is used:

```
<meta name="apple-mobile-web-app-title" content="2048 PWA">
```

Check the output in the following screenshot:

Next, you should control how your web app appears to the user. iOS allows you to either launch the app in the browser or as a standalone mode. Standalone mode removes the browser, but retains the iOS status bar across the top of the screen. Check the following code for this:

```
<meta name="apple-mobile-web-app-capable" content="yes">
<meta name="apple-mobile-web-app-status-bar-style" content="black">
```

When in standalone mode, there is no address bar, so you may need to adjust your UI to allow customers to copy URLs and go back to previous screens. The navigation concerns are the same that native application designers negotiate, and every application has different requirements.

The status bar can also be styled with the `apple-mobile-web-app-bar-style` value. This value is only used when your app is launched in standalone mode. You can change the default grey to either black or translucent black.

Unfortunately, you cannot theme the color to match your application theme or hide it altogether:

If you have done everything according to Apple's specifications, when a user launches the 2048 game, it should consume the entire screen, as demonstrated in the preceding screenshot.

Apple may have paved the way for a more intimate relationship with web brands on iOS, but their approach was never a common standard. This has changed in the era of progressive web apps as the W3C standardized, which is a meta data format to describe your web app to the platform.

The web manifest specification

The Web Manifest describes the progressive web applications with meta data and JSON formatting. Browsers parse the manifest file to create the add to homescreen icon and launch the experiences.

Now, instead of polluting each page's HEAD with extra meta data, the browser can load an external file containing standard properties and values formatted using JSON.

The web manifest specification (https://w3c.github.io/manifest/) provides some guidelines for browsers to establish an add to homescreen experience. How browsers implement the experience is left open ended, making an avenue for creativeness. I will cover this topic in more detail after reviewing the manifest file.

Referencing the web manifest file

The web manifest file must be referenced in the document's HEAD, as mentioned in the following code:

```
<head>
   ....
   <link rel="manifest" href="manifest.json">
</head>
```

Manifests should be served using the application/manifest+json MIME type. This is an important setting because it is often overlooked.

> You should research how to define or add MIME types in your web server of choice.

Many servers block requests to files based on their type by default. This often leads to manifest files returning 404 or 403 type status codes. I see similar issues raised when PDF documents need to be served. You may need to coordinate with your network administrators or devops team to make sure that your servers are properly configured.

> Do not cache the web manifest file using your service worker. You may not be able to update the file without updating your service worker. They should remain decoupled.

Web manifest properties

Owning your application's appearance is vital to ensuring the best user experience. Every application has unique use cases, eliminating the idea that one size fits all for progressive web applications. While most applications will want to copy a native application full screen experience, some will want to maintain a visible address bar. A standardized manifest file provides brand owners a communication channel with the browser to deliver the best branded experience.

The manifest should contain a series of properties, including `name`, `short_name`, `description`, `icons`, `orientation`, colors, and a default page. These are used for the homescreen and launch experience.

A minimal list of manifest properties is as follows:

- `name`
- `short_name`
- `description`
- `icons`
- `orientation`
- `theme_color`
- `background_color`
- `start_url`

There are additional official properties which you can specify within the manifest, but their use cases are limited. I would also point out that because the document uses JSON, a mutable data structure notation, it is extensible, and some browsers are experimenting with proprietary properties. Don't worry if you are using a non-standard property – you won't break other browsers because they just ignore those values.

There are two name properties; `name` and `short_name`. The `short_name` is used with the homescreen icon and other places where spaced is constrained. Where space allows, the `name` property is used.

This is what the first four properties look like in the 2048 app:

```
{
  "name": "2048",
  "short_name": "2048",
  "description": "[provide your description here]",
   "start_url": "/",
...
}
```

The `start_url` defines the initial URL that's loaded when the homescreen icon is selected. This eliminates the scenario where the user adds the PWA to the homescreen from a deep link, like a news article. In the past, the icon would be a bookmark to that article, not the home page.

The `start_url` can be any URL within the application's scope. It does not need to be the public home page; it can be a special PWA home page. You can also use QueryString values to drive additional tracking and dynamic behavior from the server.

Next, the `icons` property is an array of `icon` objects defining the URL to an icon, the MIME type, and dimensions:

```
"icons": [
    {
       "src": "meta/2048-logo-70x70.png",
       "sizes": "70x70",
       "type": "image/png"
    },
...
    {
       "src": "meta/2048-logo-600x310.png",
       "sizes": "600x310",
       "type": "image/png"
    }
 ],
```

While different image types are supported, I recommend using .png as Chrome is looking for at least one .png of 144 x 144 dimensions. You should include at least four icons, one being at least 144 x 144, but 192 x 192 is better. In Chapter 10, *Service Worker Tools*, I'll show you how to use https://www.pwabuilder.com/ to help you automate the process of creating a full set of images.

Creating a Home Screen Experience with a Web Manifest

My rule of thumb is to include a dozen or more icon variations to account for differences in potential platform requirements and opportunities. Windows Live Tiles can be 600 pixels wide and can be scaled down to less than 70 pixels wide.

It is also a good idea to use some art direction when creating icons. Some logos do not work well in smaller situations. If you add your icon to the homescreen and find it difficult to locate, chances are your customers will too.

A splash screen image is drawn from the icons array. Chrome chooses the image that is closest to 128dp for the device. The title is simply pulled from the name member. Specify the background color using the appropriately named `background_color` property.

The following image shows how the Flipkart.com site's colors and logo icon are used to create a brief splash as the web app is loaded:

Reference your PWAs icons as URLs using an array. Each item in the array is an object that describes the icon. Include the src URL, the sizes property, and MIME type. I recommend using .png files since Chrome currently requires this format.

Controlling the launch style

The manifest has properties which are used by the platform to know how to launch the application. The `display` property allows you to control how the Chrome browser is rendered. The default value is `browser`, which launches the PWA in a browser, with Chrome.

The `minimal-ui` option launches the PWA as an application, but with a minimal set of navigation UI.

`standalone` launches the PWA as a full screen application. The application takes up most of the screen, but some browser elements, like the status bar, may be rendered. Check the following code to understand the properties:

```
"display": "fullscreen",
"orientation": "landscape",
```

`fullscreen` mode launches the application in full screen and application mode without any browser elements. To the end user, it feels like they have opened a native app.

The values currently supported for the display are as follows:

- `fullscreen`: Launches the application in full screen.
- `standalone`: Similar to fullscreen, but may have a system UI visible.
- `minimal-ui`: Adds some minimal browser navigation UI components to the standalone view.
- `browser`: Opens the PWA as a regular web page in the browser.
- `orientation`: This property defines what angle the application renders. The primary choices are landscape and portrait. The values should be self-explanatory. No, you cannot render your app at a 45 degree tilt!
- The full set of orientation options are as follows:
    - `any`
    - `natural`
    - `landscape`

- portrait
- portrait-primary
- portrait-secondary
- landscape-primary
- landscape-secondary

The `theme_color` and `background_color` are used to represent the app and provide the default background color. The difference between these two colors is in how they are applied:

```
"background_color": "#fff",
"theme_color": "#f67c5f",
```

The background color refers the default background color of the `BODY` elements. This is typically set in the site's CSS. If not, it defaults back to the browser's default. Today, the de facto background color is white, but in the early days, it was grey.

The `theme_color` defines what color the operating system uses to visualize the application. This includes the task switching experience. Each platform offers different user experiences related to how apps are presented, so application of the theme color will vary.

If your application uses a language that is right to left, you can specify that using the `dir` property. The direction is then applied to the `name`, `short_name`, and `description` fields.

The `lang` property relates to `dir` because it designates what language the site uses. It is also applied to the text properties. The value should be a standard language tag (https://developer.mozilla.org/en-US/docs/Web/HTML/Global_attributes/lang) consisting of a 2 or 3 character code followed by an optional subtag, for example, `en-US` or `en-GB`.

If you happen to have a native app available that provides functionality not available in your PWA, you can indicate its availability using the `prefer_related_applications` field and setting it as either true or false. Use this in conjunction with the `related_applications` value to hint at how to install the native app:

```
"related_applications": [
  {
    "platform": "play",
    "url":
"https://play.google.com/store/apps/details?id=com.love2dev.2048",
    "id": "com.love2dev.2048"
  }, {
```

```
    "platform": "itunes",
    "url": "https://itunes.apple.com/app/2048-pwa/id123456789"
}]
```

Chrome recently added support for the manifest scope property, adding more control over how a PWA and the pages it links to are rendered. I will review how Chrome specifically uses this property within the concept of the WebAPK or *improved add to homescreen experience* section later.

The `scope` property defines the web application's context or range of URLs that are considered to be part of the progressive web application. Platforms can use this as they see fit, but the consensus is that if the user navigates within the scope, the browser will render PWA according to the manifest's `display` property. Any navigation outside of this scope results in the page being rendered with the full Chrome browser.

Apple Safari web manifest support

Since Apple released the iOS 11.3 and Safari 13 updates, basic support for the web manifest specification was included. There are some limitations to the current usage and support of the web manifest:

- The home screen icon is still referenced from the `apple-touch-icon`
- Transparent icons are not supported
- No 3D touch menu support
- No splash screen
- Can't lock orientation
- Display `fullscreen` and `minimal-ui` not supported properly

Apple still has work left so that they fully support using the web manifest, but it is a start. I believe that over the coming months we should see support being improved. One thing browser vendors struggle with is turning the ship to support modern ways of providing functionality.

Migrating from a 10-year-old way of providing user experience like touch icons and mobile web app capable features to a different mechanism is tough. If they do it too fast, they can and will break many sites, which is something all browser vendors fear. So, expect the transition to be gradual.

I would also like to point out that the PWA support, especially relating to service workers, is not yet supported in webviews used by many native apps. This also means that any hybrid applications will not have access to these features as a PWA, including the service worker.

Pseudo browsers like Chrome, Edge, and FireFox on iOS also do not support any progressive web app functionality on iOS. These browsers use the webview to render pages and not their own engines. So, for now, they are also limited.

The positive news is that Safari supports all major browsers on all major platforms, and nows support basic web manifest consumption.

Validating web manifest files

The web manifest is a simple JSON document, but it's easy to make typos or forget things. If your site is not properly registering the manifest file, you will need to troubleshoot the issue. Fortunately, there are a few resources to help you validate your file.

Google hosts a simple online validator (`https://manifest-validator.appspot.com`) where you can enter either a URL or just paste the manifest code into the page. It will parse your manifest and let you know if there is an issue:

> This page is meant to be used to test the validity of a Web Manifest. The parser follows the rules from the W3C specification.
>
> **Enter a Website URL**
>
> https://2048.love2dev.com   [VALIDATE]
>
> **Paste a Web Manifest**
>
> [   ]
>
> [VALIDATE]
>
> **Upload a Web Manifest File**
>
> [Choose File] No file chosen
>
> Success: Manifest is valid!
>
> Manifest URL: https://2048.love2dev.com/manifest.json
> JSON parsed successfully.

The nodejs Web Manifest Validator (`https://github.com/san650/web-app-manifest-validator`) is a module you can include in your automated testing workflow to validate a manifest file. It is a couple of years old, so you may need to fork the project and update it if you are using newer manifest features. Remember that the manifest specification is not final and can and will change over time.

These are not the only tools. There are a few other node modules available as well as Lighthouse and Sonar. I will cover those tools in `Chapter 10`, *Service Worker Tools*, along with PWA Builder, which can generate your manifest.

The Chrome improved add to homescreen experience

Some time in 2017, the Chrome team announced changes to the PWA installation experience called the improved add to homescreen experience. At the time, it was not as much about the automatic prompt, but that has been part of the change. It has more to do with how PWAs behave on Android and that it is more like a native application.

These changes were multifaceted and start with the web manifest scope property. This property is relatively new but allows the browser to know how to limit PWA functionality on an origin (domain name).

When you set the scope value to /, you are telling the platform that the progressive web application's capabilities apply to all paths within the origin. This may not always be the case, especially on larger sites and enterprise applications. Often, these sites are segmented into different applications.

If you changed the scope to say /hr/, then only URLs under the /hr/ folder would be part of the PWA's scope. This means that those URLs will be opened according to the web manifest file configuration. URLs not within the /hr/ folder will open normally in the browser.

When a PWA is installed using Chrome on Android, it automatically creates an unsigned WebAPK, which makes the PWA a native app. Within the WebAPK, an Android manifest is created, which includes intent filters.

Intent filters tell Android how URLs within the origin should be opened. For PWAs, this means that the app is launched according to the manifest configuration or directly in the browser if outside of its scope.

Here is what these intent filters look like in the WebAPK:

```
<intent-filter>
  <action android:name="android.intent.action.VIEW" />
  <category android:name="android.intent.category.DEFAULT" />
  <category android:name="android.intent.category.BROWSABLE" />
  <data
    android:scheme="https"
    android:host="2048.love2dev.com"
    android:pathPrefix="/" />
</intent-filter>
```

The `pathPrefix` value changes to match the web manifest scope value:

```
<intent-filter>
  <action android:name="android.intent.action.VIEW" />
  <category android:name="android.intent.category.DEFAULT" />
  <category android:name="android.intent.category.BROWSABLE" />
  <data
    android:scheme="https"
    android:host="love2dev.com"
    android:pathPrefix="/hr/" />
</intent-filter>
```

These changes have not stopped with Android as recent updates have also been applied to Chrome OS and are in the near future for desktop Chrome. Google is in the process of replacing the Chrome OS apps with progressive web apps, giving similar capabilities to the previous web apps that are available on the platform.

Chrome is also bringing more of the add to homescreen experience to desktops as well. However, this will vary by operating system as there are different user expectations on each platform.

The good news is that if you make good progressive web applications, you will just benefit from these changes.

The add to homescreen experience

The emergence of an automatic prompt to a visitor to add your progressive web app to their homescreen is exciting. In the past, Chrome would eventually display a prompt to install a progressive web app, but that has changed recently. The rules determining when the prompt triggers are still valid, but now only trigger the `beforeinstallprompt` event.

How the user prompt triggers is where each browser can choose a different path. Some of the requirements are defined in the web manifest specification, but the experience is left open ended for browsers to implement as they see fit.

Right now, Chrome has the most mature process. They established the following criteria to automatically trigger the add to homescreen experience:

- Has a web app manifest file with:
    - A `short_name` (used on the homescreen)
    - A name (used in the banner)

- A 144 x 144 .png icon (the icon declarations must include a mime type of image/png)
    - A `start_url` that loads
- Has a service worker registered on your site:
    - Has a fetch event handler
    - The Fetch event handler cannot be a noop function, it must do something
    - Is served over HTTPS (a requirement for using service worker)
    - Is visited at least twice, with at least five minutes between visits
- FireFox, Samsung, and Opera have similar requirements. FireFox will trigger the experience on Android, but not the desktop. You can allow the experience on desktop, but it is hidden behind a flag.

These browsers typically provide a simple visual queue in the browser's address bar. Here is how FireFox on Android displays the indicator:

Notice how it uses a house with a + to indicate that the site can be installed. To its right, you will also see an Android logo silhouette. The little Android head indicates that an app is available. In this case, it is detecting the PWA I installed from Chrome, which created a WebAPK.

The Chrome add to homescreen experience

The clear leader in the progressive web application experience is Chrome. They should be, since they created the concept. They have also had time to experiment with the concept to see what works, what doesn't, and what consumers and developers expect.

This has led them to continually improve the process to the point that Chrome on Android creates a WebAPK when the app is installed, elevating the app to a similar level as native apps. Recently, they extended this functionality to Windows and ChromeOS, with plans to implement it on macOS soon.

Here, you can see some recently installed progressive web apps in my Windows Start menu:

So, what exactly is a **WebAPK** and the **enhanced add to homescreen experience**?

I have already explained this: it is where the Chrome packages progressive web apps in an apk package is called a **WebAPK**. If you are not familiar with Android native application development, all of the assets are packaged in a single file called an apk.

As an oversimplification, this is just a zip file containing the application's assets. Windows does something similar with the appx format. What Chrome does when it creates a WebAPK is akin to using Cordova to generate a native application from a website.

The Chrome team instead decided to create a duplicate channel to maintain and give PWAs similar control, as native apps implementing this hybrid approach was most efficient. They first shipped this capability in Chrome 57. The big difference between a native Android application and an installed progressive web app is no access to platform APIs.

The application appears like any Play Store installed application on the device. The icon can be placed on the homescreen, is visible in the app shelf, and can be managed through the Android platform settings.

Here is how the 2048 PWA is surfaced in the Android application management interface:

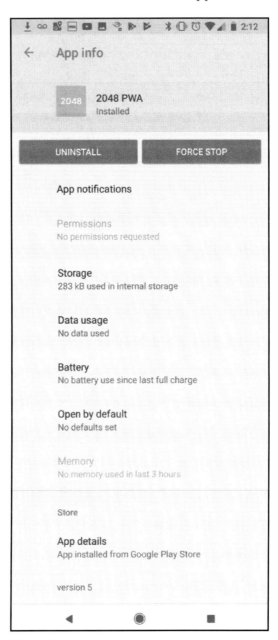

As Chrome implements this functionality on other platforms, you may or may not find the same level of control. For example, you still can't manage a Chrome installed PWA from the control panel on Windows.

The application uses the same storage settings as the web page. Clearing storage for the domain will also clear the storage for the installed PWA. This means that cookies and cached content will be removed.

Another benefit is when the web manifest file is updated to reference a new icon or change the name value. This will be updated on the homescreen icon.

Google is not hoarding this functionality to themselves. They have provided documentation and reference for other user agents (browsers) to implement similar functionality (`https://chromium.googlesource.com/chromium/src/+/master/chrome/android/webapk`). This means that we could see FireFox, Samsung Internet, UC Browser, and so on implement similar functionality soon.

Your add to homescreen responsibilities

At Google I/O 2018, it was announced that Chrome on Android will no longer include an automated add to homescreen prompt. Instead, it is your responsibility to create the user experience. Ultimately, the Chrome team decided to fall more in line with how other browser vendors are crafting their experiences.

The manifest specification takes time to define skeleton rules and minimal requirements for the add to homescreen experience. Rather than limiting all browsers to the same rules, the specification defines *instalability signals* that can be used as part of the add to homescreen prompt algorithm.

The prompt sequence should honor a modicum of privacy considerations and wait for the document to be fully loaded before issuing a prompt. The process should also allow the user to inspect the application name, icon, start URL, origin, and other properties. It is also recommended that the end user be allowed to modify some of the values. For example, changing the application name on their homescreen.

This is where the `beforeinstallprompt` event comes into play. This is your hook to a proper signal to prompt the user to install your progressive web app.

Creating a Home Screen Experience with a Web Manifest

This event triggers when heuristics are met to trigger an add to homescreen experience. But instead of a native or built-in prompt from Chrome, you are responsible to prompt the user at an appropriate time after this event triggers.

Why did they change this? I am not 100% certain, though personally I thought it was a good idea to help promote web app installs. But this is somewhat intrusive and does not fall in line with other best practices. For example, when we look at enabling push notifications later in this book, you should not automatically pester the visitor to enable notifications.

There should be a little courtship before asking for the next level of engagement. I hate to use this analogy, but it has become canonical at this point; you can't just walk up to every pretty girl and ask them to marry you. It is a much longer process, where mutual trust must be earned.

Asking a visitor to add your icon to their homescreen is not exactly the same as marriage, but is more like asking them to go steady or be exclusively dating.

To use the `beforeinstallprompt` event, add an event listener callback in your site's JavaScript:

```
var deferredPrompt;

window.addEventListener('beforeinstallprompt', function (e) {
// Prevent Chrome 67 and earlier from automatically showing the prompt
  e.preventDefault();
// Stash the event so it can be triggered later.
  deferredPrompt = e;

  showAddToHomeScreen();

});
```

There are a few moving parts I need to review. First is that the event object (`e`) has two unique properties, platforms, and `userChoice`. Platforms are arrays indicating if the user can install a native app or a progressive web app. The `userChoice` property resolves a promise indicating if the user chose to install the app or not.

The other piece used in this code is the `deferredPrompt` variable. This is declared outside the event handler, so it can be used at a later time, in this case within the `showAddToHomeScreen` logic.

The `showAddToHomeScreen` method is called as soon as the event fires in this example, but a better practice is to defer the action to an appropriate time. Think about a user in the middle of an important application task. A sudden prompt to install the app would be a confusing distraction. It would serve you and the user better if you deferred the prompt till the action completes.

The `showAddToHomeScreen` method displays a special overlay, asking the user to install the app:

```
function showAddToHomeScreen() {
    var a2hsBtn = document.querySelector(".ad2hs-prompt");
    a2hsBtn.style.display = "flex";
    a2hsBtn.addEventListener("click", addToHomeScreen);
}
```

I added a simple overlay to the 2048 application that slides up when made visible. Check out the following screenshot:

Once the prompt is accepted, the user is presented with the native add to homescreen prompt, as shown in the following screenshot:

Creating a Home Screen Experience with a Web Manifest

Finally, the `addToHomeScreen` method utilizes the `deferredPrompt` variable that we saved a reference to in the `beforeinstallprompt` event handler. It calls the prompt method, which displays the built-in dialog that's pictured in the preceding screenshot:

```
function addToHomeScreen() {

...

    if (deferredPrompt) {
      // Show the prompt
      deferredPrompt.prompt();

      // Wait for the user to respond to the prompt
      deferredPrompt.userChoice
        .then(function (choiceResult) {

          if (choiceResult.outcome === 'accepted') {
            console.log('User accepted the A2HS prompt');
          } else {
            console.log('User dismissed the A2HS prompt');
          }

          deferredPrompt = null;

        });
    }
}
```

The method then uses the `userChoice` method to perform tasks based on the choice. Here, I am just logging the choice to the console. You could persist a token indicating the state, or cascade additional logic to perform additional tasks.

I think this is a good opportunity to initiate a thank you or onboarding experience.

The 2048 application is a very simple add to homescreen experience. You can expand this functionality to educate the user or tell them the benefits of adding your app to their homescreen. Flipkart has a neat educational sequence that explains how to install the app and why they should. It is a good experience to model and one of the reasons why they have been successful in using progressive web apps.

Disabling the homescreen prompt

The `beforeinstallprompt` event can also be used to suppress Chrome's automatic prompt. This time, like breaking the default form submission, call the `preventDefault` function and return false:

```
window.addEventListener('beforeinstallprompt', function(e) {
  e.preventDefault();
  return false;
});
```

This will block the behavior in Chrome. Right now, I don't know how to suppress the prompt on other platforms as they do not support the `beforeinstallprompt` event yet.

Tracking homescreen installs

Once the homescreen install prompt displays, the user can choose to add the PWA to their homescreen, or ignore the prompt. Businesses should track and measure everything possible to make better decisions. Knowing how many homescreen installs there have been and what rate customers install their PWA provides insight into their marketing and technology investments.

Chrome supports the `beforeinstallprompt` event, which can be used to track this activity. You can add a handler to this event and log each user's choice:

```
window.addEventListener('beforeinstallprompt', function(event) {
  event.userChoice.then(function(result) {

  if(result.outcome == 'dismissed') {
    // They dismissed, send to analytics
  }else {
    // User accepted! Send to analytics
  }
  });
});
```

You can POST the user's choice to your analytics system. This could be a custom API to your internal analytics or even tied to your third-party service, like Google Analytics.

The `beforeinstallprompt` is part of the web manifest specification, but at the time of writing this book, it is only supported by Chrome. Hopefully, other browsers will add support soon.

Browsers that don't support `beforeinstallprompt` can also provide feedback. The web manifest's `start_url` can be set either to a special start URL, or a custom querystring value appended to the default URL. You will need to add logic to your log analyzer to track this behavior. Besides just knowing how many homescreen installs you have, you can also track how many times users have launched your PWA as opposed to those who have not installed your PWA.

Polyfiling the homescreen experience on iOS and other legacy browsers

A common question developers and business owners ask is how to enable progressive web application features on iOS and older browsers like Internet Explorer. While all features cannot be hacked in these browsers, much of it can.

When the iPhone was released, the initial application model was the web. They created an advanced experience for web apps that included the add to homescreen experience. Unfortunately, they did not make an automatic prompt experience. Who knows how advanced this might be today if developers did not cry out for the native app model.

What we can do is still leverage this capability and use Matteo Spinelli's add to homescreen library (http://cubiq.org/add-to-home-screen) in combination with Apple's guidelines. Doing so allows your web apps to launch from user's home screens, with or without Chrome. This is shown in the following screenshot:

It is important that you avoid duplicating homescreen prompts by not loading the **Add to Home Screen** library unless needed. The simplest way I have found to determine if the polyfil is needed is by using feature detecting service worker support. I chose this since browsers supporting service workers have some sort of add to homescreen experience. This may or may not remain true in the future, so be ready to change criteria if things change.

Without going into details, I like to dynamically load JavaScript references when a page is loaded. This process involves a series of feature detections to polyfil various requirements like Promises and the Fetch API:

```
if (!'serviceWorker' in navigator) {
    //add to homescreen polyfil
    scripts.unshift("js/libs/addtohomescreen.min.js");
}
```

> You can read more about dynamically loading scripts in *Jake Archibald's article* (https://www.html5rocks.com/en/tutorials/speed/script-loading).

You will also need to dynamically add the add to homescreen stylesheet. This time, add a feature detection script to your document's HEAD:

```
<script>
    if ('serviceWorker' in navigator) {

        // add addToHomeScreen CSS
        cssLink = document.createElement("link");

        cssLink.id = "addToHomeScreen";
        cssLink.rel = "stylesheet";
        cssLink.type = "text/css";
        cssLink.href = "css/libs/addtohomescreen.css";
        document.head.appendChild(cssLink);

    }
</script>
```

Users have been able to install web apps like this since the iPhone was released, but the process is manual and largely unknown by end users and developers alike. The lack of an automated prompt has been a key missing component of this feature. The experience it creates seems to be a model that the Chrome team and other platforms modeled to surface the progressive web application homescreen prompt.

Matteo's library only prompts the user and starts them down the manual process. but there are still a few extra steps that aren't intuitive that users must complete. The new native add to homescreen process has a pseudo automatic pipeline you can integrate. I think the add to homescreen library may serve as a good reference for designing your experience, so it is worth your time to look at it.

Should you polyfil response caching?

Request caching can also be polyfiled using IndexedDB. However, now that most browsers support service workers and caching, I don't think this approach has a wise use of resources. Outside of mobile use, Internet Explorer is the main browser without service worker support. At the time of writing this book, IE should really be used primarily in enterprises when their line of business applications have not been upgraded to modern standards.

This means a very small percentage of potential users that may open your PWA will do so in a browser without service worker support. When they do, it is pretty safe to say that they are most likely on a desktop of some sort with a reliable network connection.

Despite developing hundreds of applications using an early implementation of client-side asset caching, I have officially deprecated this approach from my recommendations.

Microsoft Edge and Internet Explorer

When Windows 8 shipped, Microsoft quietly shipped support for what they called a **Hosted Web App** (**HWA**). These are websites that reference a valid web manifest file and are served via HTTPS.

HWAs were an early precursor to progressive web apps. The obvious difference is no service worker requirement, which you would expect since the concept of a service worker had not be created yet.

To be a HWA, you would create a `.appx` file for your application containing the manifest file and a reference to the public URL. Then, you would submit the HWA appx to the Windows Store and consumers could install the HWA from the store.

The advantage of being a HWA is that these web apps have full access to all the Windows platform APIs, just like any native application. The reason that they have this privilege is that once installed, they form the store and are full blown applications.

The main difference is that the UI components and business logic are all just web pages. This gives you the benefit of also being able to update the application immediately, without going through the audit delays that plague all mobile app stores.

In many ways, this is a cross between a traditional native app and the WebAPK functionality supported by Chrome on Android.

Microsoft even created an online tool called Manifoldjs to help with the HWA creation and submission process. In recent years, Manifold has been remodeled and has a new name, PWA Builder (`https://pwabuilder.com`).

Today, PWA Builder takes any public website and provides the resources to convert it into a Progressive Web Application and submit it not only to the Windows Store, but also compile Cordova apps for the Apple and Google Play stores.

If you are wondering, there are many HWA and PWAs already in the Windows Store. Twitter and Pandora are a pair of high profile Windows progressive web apps. In fact, Twitter is in the process of deprecating all their native apps to PWA in the future.

I will go into more detail about PWA Builder in `Chapter 10`, *Service Worker Tools*. Trust me, you will not want to skip this chapter, as PWA Builder and the other tools we have mentioned have all become staples of my PWA workflow.

Today, Microsoft Edge supports service workers, which means that the concept of HWA has evolved into the consumption of progressive web apps. The same process applies to store submission and you still have full, native application capabilities.

Windows 8 and Internet Explorer also support native Live Tiles for web applications pinned to the start screen. When Edge and Windows 10 were released, Live Tile support did not make the cut. This does not mean you cannot add websites to the start menu, though.

In Microsoft Edge, the user can open the menu via the . . . icon in the top right corner. This exposes a menu of many options, one being **pin this page to Start**. Another option is to add the page to the taskbar:

As you may recall, Internet Explorer supported a rich pinned site feature in the Windows 7 era. Recently, support for the pinned sites has returned. Like iOS, you can customize this experience via `meta` tags:

```
<meta name="application-name" content="2048" />
<meta name="msapplication-square70x70logo" content="meta/2048-logo-70x70.png" />
<meta name="msapplication-square150x150logo" content="meta/2048-logo-152x152.png" />
<meta name="msapplication-wide310x150logo" content="meta/2048-logo-310x150.png" />
<meta name="msapplication-square310x310logo" content="meta/2048-logo-310x310.png" />
<meta name="msapplication-TileColor" content="#ECC400" />
```

Pinned sites still work from Internet Explorer, but as enterprises upgrade to Windows 10, the use of Internet Explorer as a primary browser is quickly fading. This does not mean you should skip the pinned site meta data. I still include it, for now.

I don't want to put these solutions in a negative space because they are both good first attempts to advance the web platform to give users a better user experience. Maybe you can see how these attempts have served as a reference for the modern web manifest specification.

Now that Microsoft Edge has shipped service workers, the team is busy working on what their **add to start menu** (my term, not theirs) will look like. They provided some early protypes at the 2018 Build conference, but at the time of writing this book, there is nothing definitive.

My best guess is that some time in the late summer or early fall we may see something more concrete from Redmond at their annual Edge Developer Summit.

Benefits await without Polyfils

Even if you don't polyfil the add to homescreen behavior, your web application will see user engagement gains on iOS and other non-PWA platforms. Many companies are publicly sharing their improvements in various progressive web application case studies.

Wego, an online air travel booking service, reported a 50% increase in conversions and 35% longer sessions on iOS. Mynet increased page views by 15%, and a 23% lower bounce rate on iOS. Lancôme increased iOS sessions by 53%. These are just a small sampling of positive progressive web application case studies.

These companies are reaping the rewards of PWAs on iOS because, by nature, properly architected websites perform better. Plus, creating a progressive web application forces you to put the customer first, not the developer. When you do this, you create a better user experience, which directly correlates to improved key performance indicators.

Following progressive web application guidelines forces you to deliver a user first experience that works across all platforms.

Testing the add to homescreen experience in Chrome

The developer experience would not be complete without the ability to test the add to homescreen experience. Chrome has added tooling which allows you to see how your web manifest file is interpreted and manually trigger the prompt.

Launch Chrome's developer tools by using *F12* and select the **Application** tab. There are many choices to help you debug various aspects of a progressive web application. Under **Application**, there is a **Manifest** choice. This will display the properties of your web manifest file, including each icon. This is a quick way for you to determine if your manifest is interpreted correctly, as you can see in the following screenshot:

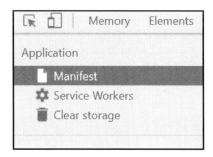

There is also a link to manually trigger the **Add to Home Screen** experience. Check out the following screenshot:

Clicking the link in the developer tools will trigger the **Add to homescreen** prompt. Take a look at the following screenshot:

The best way to test your experience is to deploy your progressive web app to the cloud, with HTTPS enabled. Open your site in a PWA supporting browser and do your best to adhere to the rules to trigger the add to homescreen prompt.

It is always a best practice to test your site across multiple devices. I recommend at least one iPhone, Android, and desktop with multiple browsers. Having these real user experiences available gives you confidence that your deployed PWA works as expected.

Summary

The line between native and progressive web applications is very blurred, thanks in part to the web manifest and add to home screen experience. No longer is the homescreen reserved to native applications; the web is welcomed by all platforms.

Today, most browsers provide a first-class app experience for progressive web applications, and while Apple has yet to adopt the progressive web application standards, they were the first to make the web into an app experience. It is up to developers and businesses to adopt and implement the rich add to homescreen capabilities.

Triggering the add to homescreen experience is the first step in levelling up your web presence.

Even if the user has not added your PWA to their homescreen, you can still take advantage of progressive web app features. However, before we dive into service workers, let's take a look at adding SSL to your website.

The next chapter covers security or use of HTTPS, which is one of the three primary technical requirements so that an app can be a Progressive Web App.

3
Making Your Website Secure

It's surprising that no website utilizes HTTPS today. Securing a website was difficult in the past, but most barriers to security have been erased in recent years. Some of those barriers included the price, technical requirements, and performance concerns.

To qualify as a progressive web application, a website must be served via HTTPS. Service workers are gated behind HTTPS because they run in the background and are designed to perform tasks that could compromise privacy if they are not protected.

With reduced and eliminated barriers, search engines and browsers have increased HTTPS's visibility to consumers because of improved search engine rankings, visual queues in the browser, and the gating APIs behind HTTPS:

This means that every website now has incentives to migrate from HTTP to HTTPS. But there are still some issues that you will need to deal with for a successful HTTPS strategy.

In this chapter, you will learn the following topics:

- What SSL/TLS and HTTPS are
- Common objections, reasons to migrate today HTTPS
- An HTTPS migration strategy

SSL history

The **Secure Socket Layer** (**SSL**) certificates represent the underpinnings of trust in most web and internet transactions. Trust is the key word when it comes to SSL and HTTPS. When a website uses SSL, the communication between the browser and the server is encrypted, but to obtain an SSL certificate, you must establish a level of trust with an issuing authority.

To enable SSL, you must install a certificate on your server. Certificates are issued by a **certificate authority (CA)**. Today, there are many certificate authorities, and it would be difficult to list them all. You should search for the best provider for your needs. I will discuss a few in this chapter. You will also learn about the different types of certificates and the additional features that CAs *package* them with. In the not too distant past, Network Solutions was the only authority from which available to purchase a certificate.

Not only were they the only game in town, you had to navigate lots of red tape. If they did not like your paperwork, they would reject you. It was almost impossible for individuals to buy a certificate as domain ownership needed to be tied to a registered business.

This limited availability led to high prices for annual certificates. The average blog, business, or organization never considered using SSL because of the cost. This limited SSL to sites that transferred sensitive information, such as credit card and bank account numbers, because of the original barriers.

The certificate cost was not limited to just the annual certificate cost—hosting a secure site was prohibitive. Because web technology had not evolved, SSL was limited to a single domain per IP address. This meant that sites needed to pay for a dedicated IP address and, often, a dedicated web server. $4.99-a-month shared-hosting plans were not an option if you wanted encryption.

The HTTPS story has changed since then. There are many free and low-cost certificate authorities, removing the annual cost barrier. HTTP protocol and web server technology has also advanced. Today, you can host multiple sites on the same IP address using different certificates and host headers (domains).

Server Name Indication (SNI) was added to the TLS specification in 2003 (`https://en.wikipedia.org/wiki/Server_Name_Indication`). This allows servers to host multiple domains on the same IP and port number using TLS. Originally, the server managed the host header name translation once the HTTP connection was established, or after the TLS handshake.

The 2003 TLS specification change has the client include the domain name as part of the TLS negotiation. Now, web servers can use their internal host header tables to determine the desired website.

How does TLS work?

TLS is an encryption protocol that works on top of TCP and sometimes UDP as well. Because it sits on top of the transport layer, it allows protocols higher in the chain to remain unchanged, such as HTTP, for example.

The protocol hides the actual data being sent across the wire. Attackers can only see what port, domain, and IP address are connected with it. They could also track how much data is being transferred.

Once the TCP connection is established, the TLS handshake is started by the client (through the browser or another user agent client application). The client starts the TLS conversation by asking a series of questions:

- Which version of SSL/TLS is it running?
- What cipher suites does it want to use?
- What compression methods does it want to use?

The client chooses the highest level of the TLS protocol supported by both the client and server. The compression method is also selected.

Once the initial TLS connection is established, the client requests the server's certificate. The certificate must be trusted by the client or an authority party that the client trusts. Examples of certificate authorities are Network Solutions, GeoTrust, Let's Encrypt, and Amazon.

After the certificate is verified, an encryption key is exchanged. The key depends on the cipher that is chosen. Once the key is exchanged, the client and server are able to perform symmetric encryption.

The client tells the server that all future communications are to be encrypted:

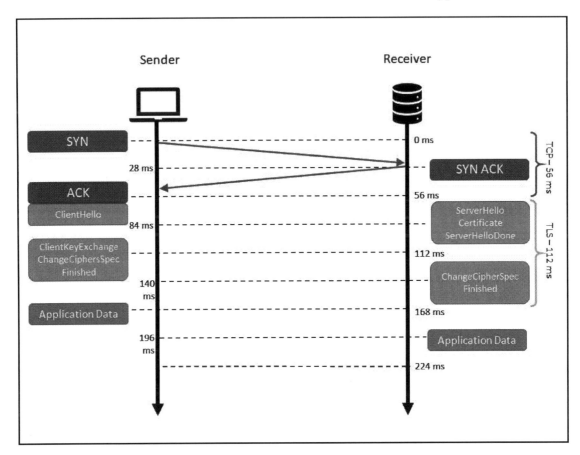

The client and server perform a final verification in which the client's MAC address is verified by the server. The server receives an initial authentication message from the client that is decrypted and sent back to the client for verification.

Encryption keys are generated uniquely for each connection, and are based on the authentication message. Assuming the handshake completes successfully, the client and the server can now communicate securely.

Secure TLS connections between the client and server have at least one of the following properties:

- As symmetric cryptography is used to encrypt the transmitted data, it is the reason why the connection is secure. The negotiation of a shared secret is both secure and reliable (the negotiated secret is unavailable to eavesdroppers and no attacker can modify the communications during the negotiation without being detected).
- Public-key cryptography is used to authenticate the identity of the communicating parties. The authentication procedure could be made optional, but typically it is required for the server.
- To prevent the undetected loss or alteration of the data during transmission, each transmitted message includes message integrity check using a message authentication code

What is HTTPS?

HTTPS is HTTP within SSL/TLS. TLS establishes a secure tunnel for bidirectional binary data communications between two hosts (the web server and browser). **HTTP (Hypertext Transport Text Protocol)** is the communications protocol that the client and server use to talk to each other:

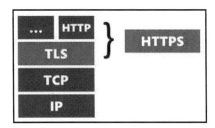

So, think of HTTP as water inside a pipe. The pipe is the TLS encryption and the water is the data. The primary difference between HTTPS and the water analogy is that HTTPS is bidirectional and plumbing isn't.

There are other communication protocols that support TLS, such as web sockets (WSS), email (SMTPS), and FTP (FTPS).

HTTPS advantages

The first, and often only, feature you will think of when someone asks about SSL or HTTPS is encryption. This is a good reason to use HTTPS, but it is not the only reason, and not even the most important reason.

HTTPS gives us three security properties:

- **Identity**: Certificate proves the server is the real server
- **Confidentiality**: Only the browser and server can read the data being passed between them
- **Integrity**: The sent data is what the other party receives

Identity

When you install an SSL certificate and enable HTTPS, you are telling the world that they can trust your site's identity. Once that secure channel of communication is opened between the client and server, both can have confidence that the conversation is to whom they expect.

Both the client and the server establish a communication channel by verifying each other's identity. The certificate is used to verify this identify. Each part of the conversation requires a token, known only to the client and server.

Confidentiality

Without HTTPS, your connection could be hijacked via a man in the middle attack. The address in the browser may tell you that it is the domain you expect to have loaded, but in reality, it could be bad guy in the middle.

Let's start by defining different scenarios:

Normally when you connect to a website using HTTP, the conversation is in plain text. In general, the conversation contains nothing sensitive. But a bad person could snoop on your traffic and use the information they find to do bad things, as shown in the following image:

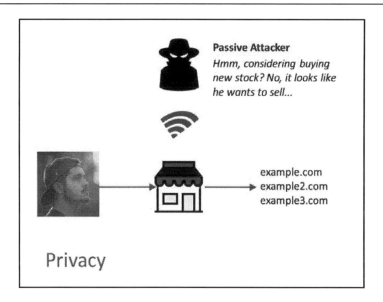

This is amplified when you use public Wi-Fi. These networks are great for connecting to the internet for free, but poor for personal security.

Once the eavesdropping bad guy identifies your session, they could intercept the conversation and route you to their server. Now any information you share with the desired site is sent to the bad guy's server instead, as shown in the following image:

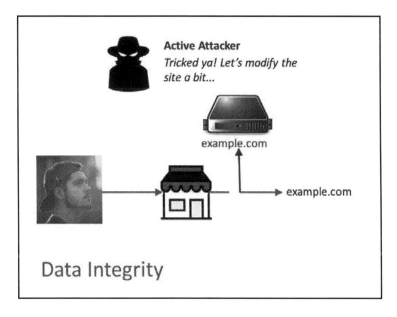

While somewhat sophisticated, it happens more times than you might think.

Let's change the scenario so that all those involved are using HTTPS. Now all the communication is encrypted. The only thing the bad guy can see is what domain(s) you visit, not even the URLs on those domains, as shown in the following image:

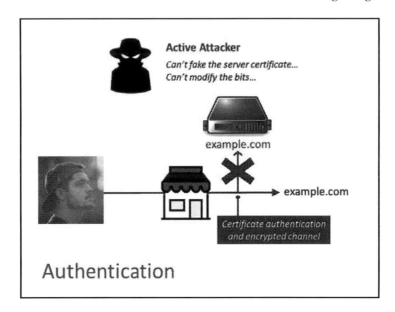

The connection between the client and server cannot be hijacked. If a bad actor tries to hijack the session, both the client and server know there is a problem and the conversation ends.

Integrity

Because the connection is encrypted and third-party actors cannot tamper with data, each end knows the data is valid. This is because the man-in-the-middle attack is thwarted.

It is not just bad guys you need to worry about. Third-party content, such as ads, could be injected into a response anywhere along the way with HTTP. For example, an ISP or your local coffee shop could modify the request and response to reroute you to a different server or change the content you view.

HTTPS gives both the customer and the server confidence that the conversation contains the real data. There is no guarantee that the data received by either the client or the server is correct when HTTP is used.

Browsers are going out of their way to indicate HTTPS to the customer

Have you noticed those padlocks in the browser address bar? Chances are you have, but that you don't really think about it until you feel something is a little fishy. Browsers have gradually been stepping up the user experience for the average consumer in recent years:

Soon, Chrome will start making it very apparent when a page contains either a password or credit card field. If those fields are present and not served via HTTPS, they will display a big red visual warning indicating to the customer that the page is not secure.

Recently, Chrome started showing a warning when a site is loaded using HTTP when in Incognito mode, as shown in the following image:

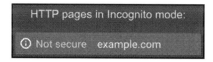

Chrome is not the only browser that is increasing visual prompting when a site is not served with HTTPS: Microsoft Edge, FireFox, and Opera have all announced plans to increase visual cues. This will, of course, lead to fewer and fewer scams succeeding, but will also cut into legitimate business conversions because they have neglected the application of HTTPS.

Search engine optimization

Google and other search engines have publicly stated that they consider HTTPS sites to be more authoritative than nonsecure sites with the same information. The reason is twofold. First, the average web surfer will trust an HTTPS site more than a non-HTTPS site. It might just be a simple blog, or it could be a giant bank—whatever the site is, the perception of security goes a long way.

Independent surveys have shown a correlation between higher rankings and HTTPS (see `https://backlinko.com/search-engine-ranking`). This makes sense because search ranking signals highly correlate with better user experience. HTTPS is a user experience factor because it conveys trust to the consumer.

So even if your site does not handle *sensitive* information, you should still implement HTTPS to boost your visitor's confidence in your brand and your search engine rankings.

The second reason search engines are pushing businesses and organizations to implement HTTPS is to verify ownership. You cannot install a legitimate TLS certificate without some sort of ownership verification. A certificate issuer will send an email to trigger a verification process based on the domain's WHOIS record. When you register your domain, you must supply real contact information, including an active email address.

Bad guys tend to register domains with fake or false contact information so they cannot be traced. By requiring HTTPS, search engines are showing that there is a modicum of trust in the site's ownership.

As the web moves toward HTTPS as the default, there will be fewer and fewer SPAM websites. Bad guys won't get SSL certificates, at least not easily.

No longer cost-prohibitive

Since the beginning of SSL, certificates have come with a cost. Typically, this was an annual cost. In the past (around 15 years ago), certificates typically cost between $100 and $500 a year. You can think about it like an annual business license. In fact, to complete a certificate request, you often needed a proof of business or organization. The issuing process was also time-prohibitive. It often took 3–14 days to get a certificate. The issuing authority had a staff that evaluated every certificate request and the accompanying paperwork. A very archaic process for a digital platform.

While enterprises do not blink at a $100-a-year fee for their web site, the average small business does. There are thousands of small businesses for every enterprise. As well as traditional small businesses, there are millions of businesses, blogs, forums, and other entities that make little to no revenue from their site. They can barely justify their hosting overhead. HTTPS is just not viable at those rates.

Another cost you might not think about is IP addresses. In the beginning, SSL required a dedicated IP address. Despite millions of possible IP addresses, there were not enough, not even close. The limited supply of IP addresses also raised the price of HTTPS. This could have added another $100 or more a year to the cost of hosting a site. Today, this has changed. Now a certificate maps to a domain. This eliminates this tax.

Today, HTTPS requirements and costs have all relaxed. There are many low-cost certificate providers. In fact, you can obtain a certificate for free from Amazon or Let's Encrypt (https://letsencrypt.org). The latest stats Let's Encrypt shares are over 50 million certificates issued.

Up to this point, I have referred to SSL, but that name is not exactly correct anymore. **Transport Layer Security** (**TLS**) is the proper term used today. The security protocol continues to evolve over time. SSL was originally created by Netscape, which is now owned by AOL.

To avoid potential legal issues, TLS was first drafted in 1999 in RFC 2246 (see https://tools.ietf.org/html/rfc2246). The primary intent behind the name change was to separate the encryption protocol from Netscape and make it more *open* and *free*.

SSL and TLS are interchangeable in general conversation as most people will understand what you mean.

Which protocol version you implement is limited by your server platform. Because TLS 1.2 is very well established at this point, it is difficult to find a server platform or browser that does not support version 1.2. But Qualys has some advice:

> "There are five protocols in the SSL/TLS family, but not all of them are secure. The best practice is to use TLS v1.0 as your main protocol (making sure the BEAST attack is mitigated in configuration) and TLS v1.1 and v1.2 if they are supported by your server platform. That way, the clients that support newer protocols will select them, and those that don't will fall back to TLS v1.0. You must not use SSL v2.0, because it is insecure."

Fortunately, when you create a TLS certificate, the protocol version is handled for you. Later in this chapter, I will go through the steps to create a certificate in AWS and Let's Encrypt, both free services.

Modern APIs require HTTPS

We are currently at a point in our technological development where new high-value APIs and features are being added quickly. These include service workers and HTTP/2, both requiring HTTPS. WebRTC and now Geo-Location also require HTTPS. Any API that deals with personal information either is or soon will be gated behind HTTPS (`https://www.chromium.org/Home/chromium-security/deprecating-powerful-features-on-insecure-origins`).

While these APIs could work without HTTPS, the security wraps these features in confidence. Think about it for a moment—the deeper a platform lets you integrate, the more they will require of your application.

Requiring HTTPS ensures a minimal amount of security and trust, and thus enough faith from potential platforms that you are not going to do evil things.

HTTPS can be significantly faster than HTTP

Some technologies designed to make websites faster only work with HTTPS. One example is a protocol enhancement known as HTTP/2. Take the HTTP versus HTTPS test to see this in action (see `https://www.httpvshttps.com/` for details).

When I first saw research showing HTTPS to be faster, I admit I was skeptical. I saw how much time the encryption adds in network waterfalls. Fortunately, the folks managing browsers and network stacks have done us a solid and smoothed out many of the issues that cause SSL to be slower than non-SSL, as illustrated in the following quote from Adam Langley at Google:

> "On our production frontend machines, SSL/TLS accounts for less than 1% of the CPU load, less than 10 KB of memory per connection and less than 2% of network overhead. Many people believe that SSL/TLS takes a lot of CPU time and we hope the preceding numbers will help to dispel that."

Because HTTP/2 multiplexes requests through a single connection, there is only one TLS handshake that must be completed. This reduces the time to retrieve assets and server load. Now the client and the server only need to perform a single handshake and encryption cycle.

The goal of HTTP/2 is to improve performance by undoing the shortcomings of the HTTP/1.1 specification. HTTP/2 eliminates connections by multiplexing responses, compressing headers, prioritizing responses, and allowing server-side push, as shown in the following image:

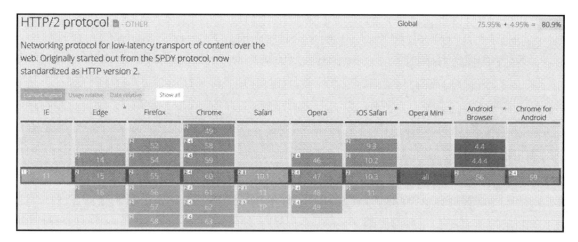

All browsers support HTTP/2 and most servers do as well. Windows 2016 was the last major operating system to ship HTTP/2 support. Since it is relatively new, there are not many production deployments online.

HTTP/2 does not change any of the HTTP semantics. Status codes, verbs, and other such phrases are things we have used for years, and thus will not break existing applications.

The de facto implementation that standard browsers are enforcing is HTTP/2 over TLS. While you could technically use HTTP/2 without TLS, browsers do not allow this approach.

The combination of the single connection and TLS handshake in concert with the other performance benefits that HTTP/2 offers mean that TLS is consistently faster than HTTP.

HTTPS adoption

According to the August 2017 Qualys survey (see `https://www.ssllabs.com/ssl-pulse/`), 60.2% of the sites they analyzed had proper SSL configuration. It is important to note that their survey is limited to 138, 672 of the most popular websites, a small sampling of the hundreds of millions of sites currently available online.

The HTTP Archive reports 64% of the top 500,000 websites use HTTPS (`https://httparchive.org/reports/state-of-the-web#pctHttps`) shown in the graph. The good news is both surveys show a positive trend toward more sites using SSL:

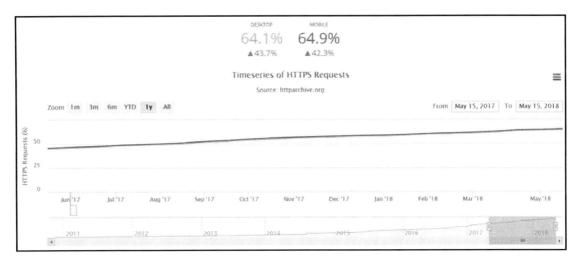

Unlike the past, every website should now use HTTPS instead of plain text HTTP. Securing your website via HTTPS is about more than security—it is about building trust. When you implement HTTPS, you not only add a layer of security: Your customers can see that dedication to security and feel more comfortable about doing business with your brand. Most consumers and non technologists get the purpose of HTTPS. They don't care about the technical implementation, they care about the trust. When you implement HTTPS, you are eliminating a layer of stress that your customer might have if you didn't use HTTPS. SSL adds value to your overall user experience, and that is why search engines and browsers are pushing everyone toward HTTPS everywhere. There are several reasons why you should use HTTPS with every website.

Different types of SSL certificate

SSL certificate can be organized into two types: **validation level** and **secured domains**.

Certificates can be issued for multiple domains and even wildcard domains. But because of the extended validation specification, these certificates can only be issued for a single domain, not multiple or wildcard domains. This is because of the sensitivity of the verification process.

There are a couple of different types of SSL certificates based on the method that you choose to confirm your identity. The three levels increase in complexity and vary in the type of information requested to validate the certificate.

Domain-validated certificates

The **domain-validated SSL certificate** (**DV certificate**) is the most basic, and validates the domain associated with the SSL certificate that is registered. To validate a DV SSL certificate, the owner (or someone with admin rights) approves the certificate request via email or DNS.

The email recipient proves their administrative privileges over the domain by acknowledging receipt and sending confirmation to the provider. Additionally, they may be required to configure certain DNS records for the associated domain. The process may take a few minutes to a few hours to order and validate a DV certificate.

This should be the most common type of certificate used because any site can quickly install them for little or no cost. If your site might be the target of phishing or other forms of fraud, you should probably invest in a certificate that requires more authentication:

Browsers will visually indicate a site that is served with proper HTTPS, typically with a green padlock. The domain-validated certificate is the minimal certificate required for this status.

The following screenshot shows how FireFox displays the certificate's information. Here is my current Love2Dev.com certificate, a domain-validated certificate:

```
This certificate has been verified for the following uses:
SSL Client Certificate
SSL Server Certificate

Issued To
Common Name (CN)         *.love2dev.com
Organization (O)          <Not Part Of Certificate>
Organizational Unit (OU)  <Not Part Of Certificate>
Serial Number             0D:F6:ED:58:9B:65:43:B9:4C:D7:B7:0C:1E:7B:02:C6

Issued By
Common Name (CN)          Amazon
Organization (O)          Amazon
Organizational Unit (OU)  Server CA 1B

Period of Validity
Begins On                 January 3, 2017
Expires On                February 4, 2018
```

You can see that it only lists the common name (domain) and leaves the **Organization** and **Organizational Unit** empty.

Organization-validated certificates

An **organization-validated SSL certificate** (**OV certificate**) validates the domain ownership, plus the organization information included in the certificate, such as the name, city, state, and country. The validation process is similar to that of the domain-validated certificate, but it requires additional documentation to certify the company's identity. The order can take up to a few days because of the company validation process.

Offers more company information and thus trust to the end user. Most consumers will never check the details of a certificate, but it can help convey more trust.

Extended-validation SSL certificates

Extended Validation SSL certificates (**EV certificates**) require more company data validation than DV and OV certificates. Domain ownership, organization information, and legal proof and documentation are all required. The order may take from a few days to a few weeks because of the extended validation process.

A *green address bar* in the browser containing the company name is the distinguishing attribute of extended-validation certificates, and is an immediate reward for the extended-validation certificate. It is not really a green bar, but your organization's name is listed in the address bar with a nice green font, indicating a trusted site, as shown in the following screenshot:

Comparing an extended-validated certificate to the preceding example, the **Organization** and **Organizational Unit** fields have properties, as shown in the following screenshot:

The OV and EV certificate types do not reflect an increase in the level of encryption; instead, these reflect a more stringent validation of the individual/company that owns the website domain. A good rule is that the more sensitive the data that your site manages, the higher the level of verification you should use.

If you do use an organizational- or extended-validated certificate, make sure you start the renewal process ahead of your expiration date. These certificates take days and weeks to issue because of the diligence required. If your certificate expires, you could go days without being properly secured.

How to obtain and install an SSL certificate

Every server platform has its own steps to generate a certificate request and install an issued certificate. But the common steps include the following:

1. Generate a **certificate signing request (CSR)**
2. Order an SSL certificate from a CA
3. Download the intermediate certificate from the CA
4. Install the intermediate certificate on the server

There are multiple certificate authorities to choose from today, such as GeoTrust, DigiCert, Symantec, and Network Solutions. You can compare the prices as well as the types of certificates that they offer to find the best solution for you. We will review the different types of certificates later in the chapter.

Traditionally, you generate an unsigned key from your web server software or administration panel. This is usually a file with an encrypted string. You submit this file to the CA as part of the order process.

Once the verification process is complete, the CA will issue the certificate, another file. Your web server then allows you to install the certificate for the site.

Today, the process has become less manual. Many are making it an automated feature that is included with web server control panels. Many are including automated LetsEncrypt.org certificates.

WordPress (https://wordpress.com/)is the biggest player to adopt an HTTPS-only policy. They upgraded all the sites that they host to HTTPS in 2017 using a built-in LetsEncrypt tool.

Amazon AWS offers free certificates for Cloud Front and their network load-balancer services. These are domain-validated certificates, and take about 30 seconds to process; just a shining example of how far the SSL world has come since the mid 90s.

Migrating a website to HTTPS

Regardless of whether you have a new or existing site, you should have a system to ensure that your site is implementing HTTPS correctly. Installing a certificate is just the start of the process. You must make sure that different aspects of your site are referencing HTTPS correctly.

This includes the links in your pages, handling links to your site, and your analytics and search engine profiles.

Even if your site uses HTTPS, the HTTP portion of any page that includes HTTP content can be read or modified by attackers. When an HTTPS page has HTTP content, it's called **mixed content**. You might think the page is secure, but it isn't because of the mixed content.

When a page has mixed content, browsers have visual queues to alert the user to the insecure state. You cannot rely on seeing https in the address bar—look for the green lock. The following screenshot shows an unsecured URL in the browser bar:

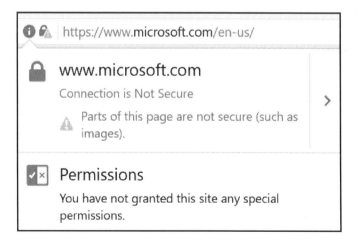

Making Your Website Secure

The image shows that Microsoft's home page is not secure, even though the site is loaded via HTTPS. It contains references to insecure assets. The following screenshot is an example of what might be causing the problem:

```
▼<noscript>
    "<img alt="" width="1" height="1" src="http://c.microsoft.com/trans_pixel.aspx" />"
  </noscript>
```

There is more to migrating your site than just cleaning up asset references. This section should be a guide or checklist for you to define an HTTPS migration strategy for your websites.

As a bonus, this list can serve as a portion of your full site-readiness checklist because it includes several best practices that are often overlooked.

Auditing the site for any HTTP:// link references

It does not matter if you have a single-page website or one that contains a million URLs, you need to audit each page for external `http://` link references. This include anchor tags as well as any link tags you may have in your document's head.

All third-party hosted assets, such as CSS, JavaScript libraries, images and fonts on public CDNs, as well as third-party services, such as **Google Analytics (GA)**, are prime targets for HTTP references. These are often overlooked because they are not "owned" by the business.

By now, any reputable third-party service offers HTTPS support. If it does not, you may need to require them to offer HTTPS or find a new provider it they refuse.

As with the preceding Microsoft example , you should also make sure that all references to assets in your site are either HTTPS or are simply absent of the protocol. This would update the site and be ready for any potential future protocols:

```
//:c.microsoft.com/trans_pixel.aspx
```

The best practice is to make all references protocol-less. Instead of changing all references to `https://`, change them to `//`. This approach is more forward-thinking because you are making any future communication protocols that may evolve easier to adapt.

When using a protocol-less reference, the user agent applies it to the primary protocol of the asset or external link. This way, the user should have a more seamless browsing experience.

Auditing content and data

Google advises that you should consistently reference external URLs using the HTTPS protocol to send a clear signal to the ranking engine that your site has HTTPS.

Content, such as a blog or general text, is often entered by non developers through a content-management interface. This means that the raw content or site data is persisted in some form of a database, and would not be part of a source-code audit.

You could spider your entire site and produce a report. This could be done with a simple node module or some other utility. Similarly, you should also run a script over your site's persisted data for external HTTP references.

The key is to audit your entire site to identify these potential problems. Every website will require some form of custom audit and update process. I suggest you automate as much as you can; that way, you can rapidly make updates and repeat the process as part of your build.

Once you update content, deploy (preferably to a test server) and audit the results. Chances are that you missed some references and will need to address them. Correct those issues and try again, until you pass the test.

Updating social media links

I wanted to highlight social media links as a common example of the previous step. All social media networks use HTTPS. Since most sites link to their social media profiles as part of the site's main layout, these should be the first links you update.

Because these links are typically contained in the site header, footer, or both, they propagate to every page. From a source code perspective, this app-shell file is a single file, and in audits like these, it is often overlooked.

When globally updating something, such as the protocol that is being used to reference a link, you need to audit your source code as well as your content. This includes every archetype file, such as the master and child layout files.

Configure server auto-redirect of HTTP to HTTPS

Legacy links and natural consumer tendency is to reference URLs via HTTP. Your web server should be configured to send a 301 redirect to the user agent telling them to permanently load the HTTPS address.

A 301 redirect is a permanent address change. You are telling the user agent that the address they are seeking is no longer valid, and to instead go to a new address. By redirecting HTTP to HTTPS, you are effectively telling the world not to ask for insecure content anymore.

This process varies by web server, so consult your platform's documentation for more guidance. Most servers can do this using a simple setting.

If you are using a content-delivery network, and you should for any consumer site, you should be able to configure this redirection in your CDN configuration.

A `301` redirect works by receiving a request from a user agent and including a 301 header in the server's response. For example, an HTTP request to `www.example.org` would look like the following:

```
GET / HTTP/2
Host: www.example.org
```

The server returns a `301` response, which includes the permanent location, as shown in the following code:

```
HTTP/2 301 Moved Permanently
Location: https://www.example.org/
```

You should also configure a proper 301 redirect any time you change your site's routing. When migrating from HTTP to HTTPS, you are changing every route in your site.

Add and verify all domain protocol combinations in webmaster tools

The addition and verification of all domain protocol combinations in webmaster tools is another commonly overlooked migration task. If you are serious about search engine ranking, you will have your site properly registered with both Google and Bing's webmaster tools.

Details of both webmaster platforms is out of the scope of this book.

The best practice is to register all four ways in which your site might be referenced. You should register both HTTP and HTTPS versions for your primary domain and the www. alias. If you do not have all four registered, you will not have a fully registered site, and may suffer some search engine ranking issues.

Defining a canonical HTTPS link

Another SEO practice you might overlook is defining the canonical link. Google and other search engines use this as a signal to know the original source of the content. In this case, any reference using an HTTP URL will be considered a duplicate of the HTTPS version. Take the following code:

```
<link rel="canonical" href="http://example.com/foo">
```

You should update this to the following:

```
<link rel="canonical" href="https://example.com/foo">
```

This will avoid the duplicate content penalty, which in this case would dilute the link juice. By defining a `canonical` link, you are telling the search engine where to direct the ranking authority.

Updating Google analytics to default to HTTPS

Another update you should make concerns your analytics service. Since GA is the most common consumer service, I will demonstrate how to update GA.

Making Your Website Secure

In the current GA dashboard, there is an **ADMIN** option at the bottom of the menu, as shown in the following screenshot:

This brings up the administration for your site. The center column **Property** has a **Property Settings** option. Select it:

In the **Property Settings** panel, change the **Default URL** to use the HTTPS protocol and save:

Updating the sitemap and RSS feed to HTTPS

Just as you did with your site's source code and content, you should also make sure your `sitemal.xml` and RSS feed sources are updated to use HTTPS. These files are used by search engines and, of course, anyone that subscribes to your RSS feed. They serve as a known directory of your website.

The links in your sitemap are considered to be a source of authority to the search engines. Links in your RSS feed propagate to feed readers, and thus are the way many engaged visitors will enter your site. It is important that you bring them through the door in the best way.

Updating your robots.txt file

Just in case your `robots.txt` file has full URLs, you should update those as well. Generally speaking, you include relative paths if you are allowing and disallowing access to spiders. One file you most likely have the full reference for is your `sitemap` file:

```
User-Agent: *
Disallow:


Sitemap: https://example.com/sitemap.xml
```

While not as common, some sites maintain a `disavow` file for search engine spiders. They do this to avoid penalties from negative links. This file should also be updated to use `https://`, which reinforces the site's protocol profile with the search engines.

Summary

As you can see, HTTPS is important to implement, but does require some diligence on your part to properly configure your site. As TLS, certificates, and HTTP advances, the barriers that previously held sites back from implementing HTTPS have been removed.

Progressive web applications require HTTPS because it is a higher level of user experience. They also require a registered service worker, which also requires HTTPS. HTTPS unlocks the modern web's capabilities; without it, your website is relegated to a smaller set of capabilities.

Because TLS ensures the conversation between the client and server is not altered by a man in the middle, and because eavesdropping is mitigated, all sites should adopt HTTPS. You are adding a level of trust for your customers, and opening the gates to the latest features the web has to offer.

4
Service Workers – Notification, Synchronization, and Our Podcast App

In Chapter 1, *Introduction to Progressive Web Apps*, you read about how the web has fallen short in the mobile era and why progressive web applications can level your website to equal or even better capabilities than native options. Service workers are the most important part of a progressive web application because they are the application's backbone.

The web manifest and the home screen icon enhance the ability to develop a relationship with the customer and control the launch experience. Service workers enable a programmatic user experience enhancement when a page is loaded and even when it isn't.

Service workers sit between the browser and the network and act as a proxy server. They provide more than just a caching layer; they are an extensible backbone:

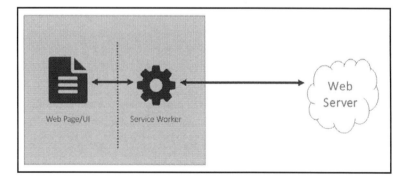

For the coder, **service workers** are JavaScript files, making them familiar to most web developers. These scripts are more like Node.js modules than a web page script. They execute on a separate thread from the UI service workers, so they do not have access to the DOM.

The service worker programming model is more functional than what you might use for the user interface. The node comparison makes sense in that the service worker programming is headless and used to perform calculations, with many tasks being traditionally reserved for the web server.

Service workers also differ from UI scripts because they are completely asynchronous. This means some APIs, such as XHR and localStorage, are not supported. Instead, you should use the Fetch API and **IndexedDB (IDB)** to connect with APIs and persist data. When a browser supports service workers, they must also support promises, providing a natural asynchronous interface.

A note about `XMLHttpRequest`, when initiated from the client the request passes through the service worker. You cannot initiate an XHR request from a service worker.

Service workers are designed to be an extensible platform, allowing for additional APIs to be added over time. Cache is the only extension API that the specification details. Native push notifications and background sync are examples of additional APIs that are enabled by service workers. In the future, you can expect many more APIs to be added.

Caching enables offline and instant asset loading. I think the best term to describe this feature is a proxy server in the browser. Advanced service workers act almost like a complete web server stack. A well-crafted service worker can assume rendering responsibilities currently allocated to ASP.NET, Node Express, and Ruby, and many more.

The last chapter covered adding HTTPS to your site. If you were not sold on the concept yet, you will be now. Service workers also require SSL. The main reason service workers require SSL is to enable APIs and other features requiring a higher level of trust.

The power service workers that have been enabled could be used for evil purposes. In addition to requiring SSL, they are also limited in scope to a single domain. They do not have the ability to manipulate anything outside the scope of the domain that hosts the script.

This is a good thing because a third-party script cannot register a service worker and do bad things to your site.

On the surface, this may seem simple, but there is an art to mastering service workers. The following chapters are designed to give you the foundation needed to create service workers that enhance any website.

In this chapter you will learn:

- The service worker threading model
- Service worker browser support
- How the example podcast application works
- An introduction to the fetch API
- How to create a basic service worker
- The service worker life cycle
- Service worker caching basics
- How to use push notifications
- An introduction to background sync programming

The service worker thread

Service workers run within their own context or thread outside the UI. Because the service worker thread is separate from the UI, it does not have access to the DOM.

The service worker scope is event driven, meaning the platform (browser or operating system, depending on your point of view) initiates the service worker. When the service worker initiates, it does so with the intent of responding to an event, such as a web page opening, a push notification, or another event.

The process stays alive long enough to service the need. This time is determined by the browser and varies by platform. There is no fixed time defined in the service worker specification.

Running in a separate context from the normal JavaScript offers many advantages to service workers. The first is that a service worker script does not block the UI from rendering. You can use this feature to offload non-UI work to the service worker. An example we will see in a later chapter shows how to use client-side templating to render markup in the service worker and not the UI thread.

This gives you a way to separate tasks into more appropriate threads. Now, you can perform calculations such as math or rendering markup in response to an API call and return it to the UI thread to update the DOM.

The service worker can communicate with the UI thread through the messaging API. You can pass text messages back and forth between threads. You can also modify responses from the server before they reach the UI thread.

Features like push notifications are possible because service workers execute in their own context. A service worker can spin up in response to an event triggered by the operating system and not because a page is loaded.

In the past, web-based push notifications have been possible by using web workers. These are great tools, but only execute when the browser is open. Service workers differ because the operating system can spin them up due to an external stimulus. The only real requirement is that the client device should be powered on.

Service worker browser support

Service worker is a relatively new technology, leading to a common question: is it safe to use service workers? What we are really asking is, how many browsers support service workers?

The good news is all major browsers have shipped basic service worker support. Chrome has been the leader as they have been largely responsible for initiating the concept and managing the specification. The technology has received enthusiastic support from other browser vendors including Microsoft, FireFox, Samsung, and Opera.

As of the Spring of 2018 all modern browsers had shipped updates to general consumers with at least service worker caching support. Of course, older browsers won't support service workers. But their usage is winding down as consumers upgrade phones and laptops.

Microsoft Edge service worker support

At the september 2017 Edge Web Summit, Microsoft announced they were shipping service worker support behind a flag. The goal is to flesh out any bugs in the implementation before general consumer support ships.

In the Spring of 2018 support for service workers was shipped to general consumers with when Windows RS4 was released.

Safari service worker support

If you are not familiar with how Apple announces web API support, they don't. New features quietly ship and are left for developers to discover, at least in most cases.

In a surprise release Apple updated Safari in March 2018 to support service workers:

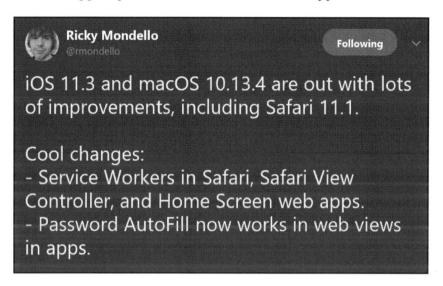

There are some limitations to Safari service worker support. For now, they do not support native push notifications or background sync. I don't consider these missing features a reason to avoid integrating them in your applications. Remember progressive web apps are about taking advantage of features as they are available. You can still create viable work around to these features.

Is the service worker ready?

Jake Archibald maintains a GitHub site that tracks each mainstream browser's support of service worker-related features (https://jakearchibald.github.io/isserviceworkerready/), called is *service worker Ready*..

The site features rows, focusing on each primary service worker feature and their requirements with each browser's icon. The grayscale browser icons indicate that support has not shipped. Icons with a yellow background have shipped partial support. A green background indicates full support of the feature:

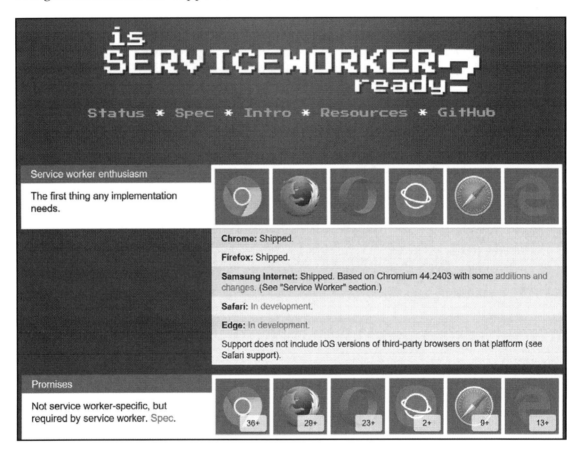

As you can see the major browser players all support service workers.

Now that all modern browsers support service workers you may think there is no reason to work about browsers without service worker support. But there are still an important percentage of browser sessions using Internet Explorer and legacy Android browsers. This means you may want to consider fallback options.

Polyfilling older browsers

Polyfills are libraries or fallbacks you can reference as needed to add support for modern features to browsers lacking support. Not all modern features can't be polyfilled, but many can. Some are not direct polyfills, but leveraging other APIs to create the desired experience.

The good news is that you can polyfill a service worker caching to a point. This can be done using `IndexedDB`. You will need an extra layer of JavaScript to manage the site's assets and API calls. We will touch on this technique in the advanced caching chapter.

In addition to using `IndexedDB` to cache assets, you can also use `appCache` as an offline and asset caching fallback.

Push notifications cannot be polyfilled, but you can utilize alternative notification mediums. SMS texting and web worker notifications can provide ways for the business to engage with customers.

The podcast application

This chapter introduces you to different service worker concepts and features like the service worker life cycle, caching, and push notifications. To do this, we are going to build a simple podcast application. This application will demonstrate how to tackle the service worker life cycle and response caching:

The minimal podcast application requirements include:

- Fast loading
- Search podcasts
- Favorite podcasts
- Play audio files
- Persist episodes for offline listening

The application requires some server-side help, which for our purposes will be a set of snapshot data I took from public sources. The data is part of the project repository (https://github.com/docluv/PWAPodcast), so you can recreate the application.

You will learn how to register a service worker, the basics of the service worker life cycle, how service worker caching works, and how to use `IndexedDB` to persist data. You will also see how to utilize service worker cache and `IndexedDB` to persist MP3 media files.

The podcast application source code is organized by folders that correlate to each chapter's progress. The root folder contains common files to define the Grunt tasks to run local web servers, just like the 2048 application.

Inside each chapter's folder there are folders for assets, such as CSS, JavaScript, and images. Each route also has a folder with a single `index.html` file. This allows the application to use extensionless URLs. The data files are stored under the API folder.

The application consists of the following pages:

```
/ (home)
/podcasts/
/podcast/{slug}
/episode/{slug}
/search?q={term}
/later/
```

Each page is a static page, pre-rendered as part of the site build process. The logic behind this is beyond the scope of this book.

The application's data comes from the iTunes API. It did require some data manipulation to make it usable in the application. I have included the raw data files in the GitHub repository if you would like to use or study them.

The Apple data model needs to be transformed for the application. Instead of standing up a web server to host a formal API, the data is stored in a series of JSON files. The application will reference those files as needed.

The service worker is in the application's root folder. This file is the centerpiece of this chapter and we will spend most of our time changing it in each chapter. It will demonstrate the service worker life cycle and basic caching concepts.

Chapter 4

You can try the finished version at `https://podcast.love2dev.com`:

Home page of PWA Podstr

The home page contains a list of podcasts that the user is subscribed to. This is populated by an API call to retrieve the list. It is then rendered in the browser using `Mustache`. All API data is a set of JSON files, so there is no messy code needed to connect and stand up a database:

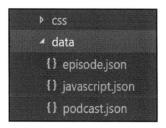

The podcast page displays details about the podcast and a list of recent episodes. The podcast data is also retrieved via an API call:

The episode page lists the title and description of an episode. It includes an AUDIO element that plays the mp3 file. Again, the page is rendered after retrieving the data from the server:

The Fetch API

Way back in 1996, Internet Explorer introduced the *iframe* element as a way to load web content asynchronously in a web page. Over the next two years, the concept evolved into the first implementation of what we now know as the XMLHttpReqest object.

Back then, it was known as XMLHTTP and was first shipped in Internet Explorer 5.0. Soon after, Mozilla, Safari, and Opera all shipped implementations of what we now call XMLHttpRequest.

Up to this point, web pages were static and required an entire reload when a user navigated from one page to another inside the same site.

In 2004, Google started making wide use of what we now call **AJAX** in Gmail and Google Maps. They showed us how to leverage in-browser requests to the server and how to manipulate the DOM in response to the server's payload. This is typically done by calling an API that returns JSON data.

As with any technology, as it is used, **implementers** get frustrated dealing with issues revealed through usage. In response to new use cases and issues, the technology updates, typically by releasing a new version.

Sometimes, those updates are so major a new technology, product, or implementation replaces the first version.

`XMLHttpRequest` provides a mechanism to make asynchronous calls to the server, but does so based on how the web and browsers worked over a decade ago.

Today, the web has expanded in many ways. One feature we now have ubiquitous support for is JavaScript Promises. We also have deeper insight into what types of content can be made using asynchronous calls to a server that we did not think about when AJAX was first being specified.

Introducing Fetch

After identifying common limitations of the `XMLHttpRequest` object, the Fetch API was standardized to provide a new, better thought out way to implement asynchronous HTTP requests.

The Fetch API is a brand new way to make AJAX calls. It was created to solve many of the problems we developers hack and work around to handle `XMLHttpRequest` limitations. The primary difference is that Fetch is asynchronous when using Promises.

It first started seeing browser implementations in the Spring of 2016 and now enjoys broad support by all modern browsers. If you have not started using Fetch to make asynchronous HTTP requests, you should start migrating as soon as possible.

Three key features that make Fetch stand apart from the `XMLHttpRequest` object is simpler syntax, native promise support, and the ability to manipulate requests and responses:

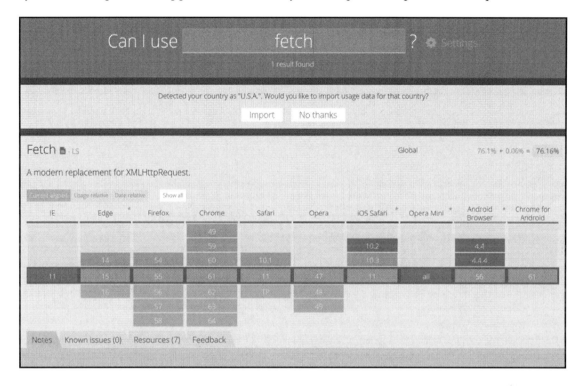

Using the Fetch API

Because AJAX has become a popular way to drive DOM manipulations, let's see how this is done using Fetch. This will be a slightly contrived example where a Podcast's logo is fetched and set to the corresponding `IMG` element:

```
var logo = document.querySelector('.podcast-logo');

fetch(".../600x600bb.jpg").then(function(response) {
  return response.blob();
}).then(function(logoBlob) {
  var objectURL = URL.createObjectURL(logoBlob);
  logo.src = objectURL;
});
```

If you are familiar with composing an XMLHttpRequest, this example should look very clean and simple. The first thing you will notice is that the only parameter needed is a URL. This is the simplest form of fetch.

This code does the same thing, but uses the XMLHttpRequest object:

```
var xhr = new XMLHttpRequest();

xhr.open("GET", ".../600x600bb.jpg", true);
xhr.overrideMimeType('text/plain; charset=x-user-defined');
xhr.send(null);

xhr.onreadystatechange = function() {
    if (xhr.readyState == 4){
      if ((xhr.status == 200) || (xhr.status == 0)){
          var logo = document.querySelector('.podcast-logo');
          logo.src = "data:image/gif;base64," +
          encode64(xhr.responseText);
      }else{
          alert("Something misconfiguration : " +
          "\nError Code : " + xhr.status +
          "\nError Message : " + xhr.responseText);
      }
    }
};
```

This is not quite as clean and not asynchronous. This example is rather simple. In most cases, AJAX requests require more complexity.

The fetch method returns a promise, which resolves a response object. This represents that response, not the image we wanted. Access to the image is done by calling the blob mixin, which also returns a promise.

The blob is the image, which can then be used by the URL.createObjectUrl function to convert the bytes to a usable image format that can be applied to the image's src property.

While contrived, this example demonstrates multiple aspects of the Fetch API you should familiarize yourself with. The API provides a simple surface to make requests, but allows you to make very complex request handler logic.

Along with the fetch method, the API also specifies request, response, and header objects. There is also a collection of body mixins, designed to manipulate different response types.

Instead of passing just the URL to the fetch method, you can also pass a composed request object. A request object contains the values to make network requests.

The request constructor has two parameters, the URL and an optional options object. You can also supply an existing request object, which may sound odd, but as you learn how to use service workers, you will realize this will be a common starting point.

The options parameter can contain the following properties:

- `method`: The HTTP request method: `GET`, `POST`, `PUT`, `DELETE`, and so on.
- `headers`: Custom request headers, which can be either a headers object or an object literal.
- `body`: Any body that you want to add to your request: a `Blob`, `BufferSource`, `FormData`, `URLSearchParams`, `USVString`, or `ReadableStream` object.
- `mode`: The request mode, for example, `cors`, `no-cors`, `same-origin`, or `navigate`. The default is `cors`.
- `credentials`: The requested credentials you want to use for the request: omit, same-origin, or include.
- `cache`: Similar to the properties used in the Cache-Control header. This tells the browser how to interact with the local cache.

Other, less common properties are cache, redirect, referrer, and integrity.

We can use the preceding example and expand it to use a custom request object:

```
var logoHeaders = new Headers();
logoHeaders.append('Content-Type', 'image/jpeg');

var logoInit = { method: 'GET',
                 headers: logoHeaders,
                 mode: 'cors',
                 cache: 'default'
        };

var logoRequest = new Request(".../600x600bb.jpg", logoInit);

fetch(logoRequest).then(function(response) {
  return response.blob();
}).then(function(logoBlob) {
  logo.src = URL.createObjectURL(logoBlob);
});
```

You should note that the fetch method will only reject when there is a network error. When an exception is thrown, the network cannot be reached, for example, when the device is offline. It will not fail for a non-2XX status code.

This means you must validate the response as being good, not found, a redirect, or a server error. You can build a robust logic tree to handle different status codes. If all you need to do is respond to a good request, you can use the `response.ok` property.

If the response has a 200-299 status, good, then the ok property is true. Otherwise, it is false.

You should handle exceptions differently than responses with status code. For example, if a response has a status code of 403, then you could redirect to a login form. A 404 status should redirect to a not found page.

If there is a network error, then you could trigger an appropriate visual response like an error message or triggering your application's offline mode experience.

The response object

The fetch method resolves a response object. This is similar to the request object, with a few differences. It represents a server response for a request.

The response object has the following properties:

- `headers`: The headers object
- `ok`: Indicates if the status in in the 200-299 range
- `redirected`: Indicates if the response is from a redirect
- `status`: The HTTP status code, for example, 200 for good
- `statusText`: The status message of the corresponding code
- `type`: The type of response, for example, cors or basic
- `url`: The response URL
- `bodyUsed`: A Boolean indicating whether the body has been used

There are several methods you should also know about:

- `clone`: Makes a clone of the response object
- `arrayBuffer`: Returns a promise that resolves to an `arrayBuffer`
- `blob`: Returns a promise that resolves to a blob
- `formData`: Returns a promise that resolves to a `formData` object
- `json`: Returns a promise that resolves the body text to a JSON object
- `text`: Returns a promise that resolves the body text

The preceding example showed how to use the blob method to create an image. A more common task web apps have is retrieving data from an API. Typically, the response is text, containing a JSON.

A common user task in a podcast application is to search for podcasts and episodes. Our podcast application has a search form built into the layout header. It has logic bound to it to call an API and return a set of results.

The Podstr application uses a single JSON file to serve as an example search result. This is done so we do not need to build a server-side search infrastructure. A production application would have a more formal setup.

The search results are formatted to contain two arrays, a list of matching podcasts, and another for matching episodes:

```
[
        podcasts: [
                {...}
        ],
        episodes: [
                {...}
        ]
}
```

The search results are displayed on the search page by rendering the results against a template. Retrieving the results is done via a fetch request that uses the JSON method:

```
var searchResults = document.querySelector('.search-results');

fetch("api/search?term={term}").then(function(response) {
    return response.json();
}).then(function(results) {
    renderResults(results);
});
```

The `renderResults` function runs the results object through a `Mustache` template and assigns the rendered markup to the `search-results` element:

```
function renderResults(results) {
    var template = document.getElementById("search-results-template"),
        searchResults = document.querySelector('.search-results');
```

```
                    searchResults.innerHTML =
                        Mustache.render(template.innerHTML, results);
       }
```

If you are not familiar with `Mustache`, it is a minimalist template engine. The render method takes an HTML template and merges a JSON object to produce markup. If you want to know more about using `Mustache`, visit the GitHub page (https://github.com/janl/mustache.js/).

The search page demonstrates how to make an API call to dynamically compose a page. This is common for web applications today. We don't go back and forth and let the server render new markup in response to an action, like submitting a form.

Instead, we migrated to a model that has evolved to what we commonly call a single page application. Pages are no longer static experiences, we can change them dynamically.

The ability to make an API call to the server without making a complete round trip. Fetch makes this possible and simpler than before. Template libraries like `Mustache` make it simple to render markup on the client.

If you are familiar with jQuery's ajax method, you will note some similarities to fetch. There are few key differences.

The promise returned from `fetch()` won't reject on HTTP error status, even if the response is an HTTP 404 or 500 error. Instead, it will resolve normally (with the `ok` status set to false), and it will only reject on network failure or if anything prevented the request from completing.

By default, fetch won't send or receive any cookies from the server, resulting in unauthenticated requests if the site relies on maintaining a user session (to send cookies, the credentials init option must be set).

Service worker fetch

Service workers rely on promises and asynchronous APIs. This eliminates platform features such as `XMLHttpRequest` from being used in a service worker. Service workers are dependent on the browser supporting promises and the fetch API.

A basic understanding of using fetch is a fundamental skill required for service worker programming. Service workers allow you to intercept all network requests before they are sent to the network. This is done by adding a fetch event handler:

```
self.addEventListener('fetch', function(event) {
  event.respondWith(
    caches.match(event.request)
      .then((response) =>{
        // Cache hit - return response
        if (response) {
          return response;
        }
        return fetch(event.request);
      }
    )
  );
});
```

The event handler receives a single `FetchEvent` object. There are two members of the `FetchEvent` object you need to know, which are `request` and `respondWith`.

The request property is the request object is being sent to the network. The `respondWith` method restricts the fetch event handler. It keeps the event handler *open* until the response is ready. The method also requires a response object to be returned.

The service worker fetch event allows you to intercept requests to the network. This power allows you to interrogate the request and return a cached response, compose a custom response, or return a network response. We will cover ways to use this power in the service worker caching chapters.

Polyfilling fetch in legacy browsers

Fetch and other modern APIs enjoy broad support by major browsers. However, there is still enough users using older browsers. Many enterprises still require employees to use obsolete versions of Internet Explorer. Many consumers that are happy with older phones and do not upgrade their devices or update software often.

This means we need to make our websites adaptable to these potential scenarios. Fortunately, many APIs can be polyfilled with JavaScript libraries. Fetch and promises are modern features that can easily be polyfilled.

Just like we feature detect service worker support, we can feature detect fetch and promise support. If those features are not supported, we can then load a polyfill. It is important that these polyfills are loaded in a dependent order where promises are followed by fetch, which is then followed by any site-specific code:

```
var scripts = ["js/libs/jquery.small.js",
    "js/libs/index.js",
    "js/libs/collapse.js",
    "js/libs/util.js",
    "js/app/app.js"
];

if (typeof fetch === "undefined" || fetch.toString().indexOf("[native code]") === -1) {
    scripts.unshift("js/polyfill/fetch.js");
}

if (typeof Promise === "undefined" || Promise.toString().indexOf("[native code]") === -1) {
    scripts.unshift("js/polyfill/es6-promise.min.js");
}
```

This is a technique of asynchronously loading scripts I borrowed from an HTML5 Rocks article (https://www.html5rocks.com/en/tutorials/speed/script-loading/#disqus_thread). Most of the time, the polyfills are not needed, but for those cases where a polyfill is needed, you need to control the order the scripts are loaded in.

The technique uses an array of script URLs and loops through them, appending each to the DOM while maintaining an order of dependence.

Because the polyfills are not needed all the time, they are only added as necessary. This is determined by checking for native support. In the example code, both promise and fetch are detected. If they are not supported, then they are added to the array of script URLs and are added before the other scripts.

Promises are also checked because fetch depends on promise support. The Podstr application only needs to potentially use the fetch and promise polyfill.

But there are many API polyfills that your application might need. The HTML5 Cross Browser polyfill (https://github.com/Modernizr/Modernizr/wiki/HTML5-Cross-browser-Polyfills) repository is a great place to find more. You can use the same feature detection technique to add them as necessary.

Creating a service worker shell

In Chapter 1, *Introduction to Progressive Web Apps*, we created a basic service worker that pre-cached the 2048 game assets. In this and the following chapters, we will dive deeper into the details of a service worker.

The service worker goes through several stages in its overall life cycle. A service worker is registered. Once the script is loaded, it triggers the 'install' event. At this point, the service worker is not in control of the client (browser tab).

When the service worker is cleared to control client contexts, the activate event is triggered. After this, the service worker is fully active and in control of any active clients, be they tabs or background processes.

Proper service workers take advantage of the event life cycle to manage data, like cached responses, to set the service worker context.

The podcast application starts with a simple service worker script containing handlers for the install, activate, and fetch events:

```
self.addEventListener('install', (event) => {
    //install event handler
});

self.addEventListener('activate', (event) => {
    //activate event handler
});

self.addEventListener('fetch', (event) => {
    //fetch event handler
});
```

As these chapters progress, we will fill in code to use each of these handlers. These updates will demonstrate the service worker life cycle, common caching techniques, and other important service worker concepts.

The service worker life cycle

Service workers obey a known life cycle that allows a new service worker to get itself ready without disrupting the current one. The life cycle is designed for the best user experience.

When a service worker is registered, it does not immediately seize control of the client. There are rules designed to minimize errors due to differences in code versions.

If a new service worker just took control of a client's context when it is expecting a previous version's logic, there could be issues. Even though the service worker operates on a separate thread, the UI code could have dependencies on the service worker logic or cached assets. If the new version breaks, the front-end your user experience could go sideways.

The life cycle is designed to ensure that an in-scope page or task is controlled by the same service worker (or no service worker) throughout its session:

The life cycle consists of the registration, installation, and activation steps. The installation and activation events can have handlers bound that perform specific tasks.

The life cycle also covers service worker updates and unregistration. These last two tasks may not be used as often, but developers should still be familiar with how they work.

Each stage can be used for different process phases to manage the service worker, cached assets, and possibly state data. The following chapter goes into details about the life cycle and how each phase can be used to make your application more performant and easier to manage.

You will learn how to register, update, and remove a service worker. You will also learn the service worker's scope and the definition of a service worker client. The chapter will also cover the install and activate events so that you can add code to manage the service worker's cache and active state.

Caching

One of the most important progressive web application features is the ability to work offline and load instantly. Service worker caching enables this super power. In the past, websites could function offline and even gain some performance benefits via `appCache`.

Service worker caching supersedes `appCache` and provides a better programmatic interface. `AppCache` is notorious for being difficult to manage and maintain.

When your page references an `appCache` manifest file and has a registered service worker, the service worker manages cache and the `appCache` is bypassed. This makes service worker caching a progressive enhancement from `appCache` and makes it safe to use both.

By enabling caching, service workers make the network a progressive enhancement. Because the service worker cache API is very low level, it requires the developer to apply custom logic to manage how network resources are cached and retrieved.

This leaves lots of room for creativity to apply different caching strategies in your application. `Chapter 6`, *Master the Cache API- Manage Web Assets in a Podcast Application*, dives into the core service worker caching concepts you need to master.

Using push notifications

Businesses have been using push to engage customers, even if their app is not open, for about a decade now. And why not? Research shows some impressive numbers related to brand engagement and revenue directly correlated with the tiny interruptions.

For example, Google has shared the following:

- 72% increase in time spent for users visiting via a push notification
- 26% increase in average spend per visit by members arriving via a push notification
- +50% repeat visits within 3 months

These values all point to the reason why brand and product managers love push notifications. Unfortunately, up to recent times, the web has been left out of this party. Many businesses have opted to go through the hassle of a native app solely to send push notifications.

The Push API gives web applications the ability to receive messages pushed to them from a server, whether or not the web app is in the foreground, or even currently loaded, on a user agent.

Implementing push in your application requires a server-based service, typically a cloud based service such as Google Cloud Messenger or AWS Pinpoint. There are numerous providers available.

Don't worry about your push provider. Web push notifications are based on an IETF standard, Generic Event Delivery Using HTTP Push (`https://tools.ietf.org/html/draft-ietf-webpush-protocol-12`). Make sure your provider is compliant and you should have no problems.

At the time of writing this book, Chrome, FireFox, Samsung Internet, and Opera currently ship push notification support. Microsoft Edge is in the process of shipping support. Apple has not released a potential timeline for Safari support.

It is important to note that each browser or user agent acts independently from other browsers. If a customer loads your web page from more than one browser, each will register a service worker. If each one also creates a push notification subscription, the user could receive multiple notifications.

This makes managing subscription logic in your application's service logic important. This is outside the scope of this book. As part of production logic, it is a good idea to query your server before attempting to register a user for push notifications. There are several options to handle this potential situation and you will need to determine what is best for your application.

If your brand also has a native app that offers push notifications, they will also be a separate subscription. This means you should track if the customer already receives notifications on the device as best as you can to avoid duplicating messages.

Implementing push notifications

In this section, you will learn some fundamentals of implementing push notifications:

- How to subscribe and unsubscribe a user for push messaging
- How to handle incoming push messages
- How to display a notification
- How to respond to notification clicks

The code is part of the Podstr application. I won't cover how to set up a push provider because they vary too much and are prone to changes to their administration interfaces. This creates a fluid environment that would only serve to create confusion with readers and potential providers. Plus, singling out a single provider could create an unwanted bias. Most providers have current documentation and JavaScript SDKs to help you create the server-side environment.

If you would like to stand up your own push service, Matt Gaunt, of the Google Chrome team, has published an example server you can clone (https://github.com/web-push-libs/web-push). This might serve as a decent test service, but I would not consider it a production quality service.

For our purposes, the Chrome developer tools provide enough to trigger the client-side logic and experience. You can find a link to the right of a registered service workers detail to emulate a push event:

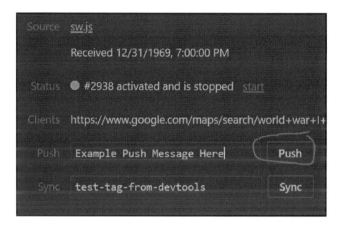

This link triggers an emulated push message with a simple payload: **Test push message from DevTools**. The Podstr application will use this event to trigger a message we can display to the user about new podcast episodes.

Setting up push notifications

To enable push notifications, there are several steps you need to follow. The first step is detecting if the browser supports push or not. If so, then you can proceed:

```
navigator.serviceWorker.register('/sw.js').then(function (registration) {
    if ("PushManager" in window) {
      //push is supported
    }
});
```

Since push is something you would configure after you register the service worker, you can check for support once the service worker is registered. Just like checking for service worker support, you can check if the window object contains a reference to the PushManager.

The PushManager has three methods to manage a user's subscription status. The getSubscription method returns a promise that resolves a PushSubscription object. If the user is subscribed, the subscription is an object, otherwise it is null.

It is up to you how you surface the state of push notifications in your application. My personal advice is to hide any visible queues if the browser does not support push notifications because it will confuse the consumer.

Most sites will simply prompt for permission to send push notifications. The ability to send notifications is gated behind user approval. The browser displays a yes or no dialog when you try to initiate the push notification subscription process.

It is also a good practice to allow users to opt out of push notifications. This can be done in application settings or on a configuration page. The Podstr application has a settings page that includes options to manage push notifications:

The code to manage push notification subscriptions is covered later in this section. You can provide an interface for the user either as a passive option, like on the configuration page, or actively via a notification.

As Android evolves, Chrome and possible other Android browsers will automatically convert progressive web apps that are added to the homescreen to WebAPKs. These are native applications that enjoy almost equal status with store apps. One feature they should have is the ability to manage push notifications in the app through the platform settings applications, but you should never rely on this as the only way to turn notifications off.

Chapter 4

For example, Twitter has adopted progressive web applications and can send notifications. I turned this on, but found it was pushing notifications for a single account (Scott Hanselman) to my phone. While I like Scott, I was expecting a bit more variety.

It took me a while to discover how to manage Twitter notifications. I found out how to block notifications for the site in Chrome faster:

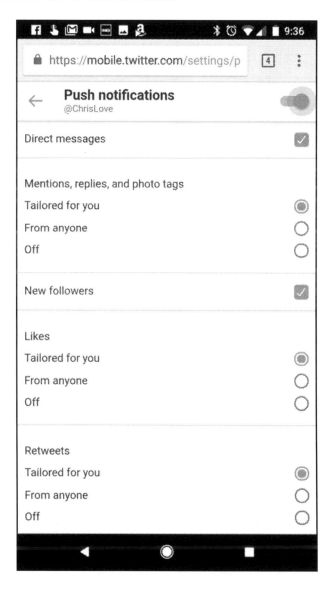

[119]

Twitter has many notification options which require a robust backend to manage. The Podstr application uses either an on or off choice. If this were a production application, I would build out more logic over time, like Twitter has done.

Managing the user's subscription

In the example code, if the subscription object does not exist, the `subscribeUser` function is invoked. The service worker registration object is passed as the only parameter:

```
registration.pushManager.getSubscription()
.then(function (subscription) {
        if(subscription === null){
                subscribeUser(registration);
        }
    });
```

The `pushManager` subscribe method has a single parameter, an object with two properties, `userVisibleOnly` and `applicationServerKey`.

The subscribe function returns a promise that resolves after the user has granted permission to send notifications and the browser sends a request to the push service.

As part of the subscribe function work flow, the User Agent is required to prompt the user for permission. If this is denied, the promise rejects with a `NotAllowedError`. You should always include a catch handler to the subscribe call.

According to the Push Notification specification (https://w3c.github.io/push-api/#webapp):

> *User agents MUST NOT provide Push API access to web apps without the express permission of the user. User agents MUST acquire consent for permission through a user interface for each call to the `subscribe()` method, unless a previous permission grant has been persisted, or a prearranged trust relationship applies. Permissions that are preserved beyond the current browsing session MUST be revocable.*

The `userVisibleOnly` property is a Boolean that indicates if the push notifications will always be visible to the user. Currently, you must set this property to true before browsers will let you subscribe a user:

> "If developers request the ability to use silent push (the ability to receive pushes without triggering a user-visible UI change) we currently reject the request, but in the future we plan to introduce a permission to enable this use case"
>
> – https://goo.gl/ygv404

```
User is unsubscribed.
Service Worker and Push is supported
⊗ Chrome currently only supports the Push API for subscriptions that will result in use
  pushManager.subscribe({userVisibleOnly: true}) instead. See https://goo.gl/yqv404 for
Failed to subscribe the user:  DOMException: Registration failed - permission denied
```

So, for now, you will need to display a message to the end user, even if there is no user feedback needed. For example, a caching strategy to update a site's cached assets can be triggered by a push notification. In those scenarios, you would display a notification to alert the user to the update.

The `applicationServerKey` property is also known as a WEBPUS-VAPID (voluntary application server identification for web push (`https://tools.ietf.org/html/draft-ietf-webpush-vapid-04`)). This value comes from your push service provider. It will be a rather long string of random characters and numbers.

The value should be base 64 URL safe encoded. The `urlB64ToUnit8Array` function converts it to a UInt8Array, which is expected by the subscribe function. The `urlB64ToUnit8Array` is a utility function you can find in the Podstr source code.

The User Agent should only accept notifications containing the subscribed `applicationServerKey`. Per the specification, this is a recommendation and browsers honor that advice:

```
    function subscribeUser(registration) {
        const applicationServerKey =
    urlB64ToUint8Array(applicationServerPublicKey);
        registration.pushManager.subscribe({
          userVisibleOnly: true,
          applicationServerKey: applicationServerKey
            })
            .then(function (subscription) {
                updateSubscriptionOnServer(subscription);
```

```
            console.log('User is subscribed.');
        })
        .catch(function (err) {
     console.log('Failed to subscribe the user: ', err);
        });
}
```

Once a subscription has been made, it cannot be altered. You must unsubscribe from the initial subscription and create a new subscription with the new options. For example, if you should change your push service, the client will need a new `applicationServerKey`:

Like all things in service workers, the subscribe function returns a promise. If there is not an exception, it resolves a `PushSubscription` object. This object contains various values about the subscription that could be useful to build a more robust user experience or management logic.

Properties (all read only):

- `endpoint`: The subscription endpoint
- `expirationTime`: Null unless the subscription has an expiration time
- `options`: An echo of the options used to create the subscription
- `subscriptionId`: The subscription ID

Methods:

- `getKey`: An `ArrayBuffer` representing the client's public key
- `toJSON`: A JSON representation of the subscription properties
- `unscubscribe`: Initiates a subscriber unsubscription process

The `updateSubscriptionOnServer` function, called upon a successful subscription, would normally be used to update the server. However, for our purposes, it is used to echo out the subscription object properties:

```
{
   "endpoint":
"https://fcm.googleapis.com/fcm/send/cRWeyfFxsE0:APA91bE8jAnZtPTHSG5pV9hNWt
TdS_ZFZT7FTDEpDEYwf8f_FvwuiLc6YDtxNigxKzyHhj9yzbhlJ4zm3M3wt0w1JPYQ41yhF38ye
XKhYVp_TFauMr_RnINOKiobCTCYIgj_X0PWlGQF",
   "expirationTime": null,
   "keys": {
      "p256dh": "BO0FEUNPej_U984Q-dVAvtv1lyIdSvOn01AV15ALu8F-
GPA7lTtZ8QfyiQ7Z12BFjPQLvpvypMrL4I6QqHy2wNg=",
      "auth": "lDiFiN9EFPcXm7LVzOYUlg=="
   }
}
```

Handling push notifications

After the consumer has confirmed a push notification subscription, you can send messages to the user agent. When a message is sent to the device, it determines what service worker to apply the message and trigger a push event.

The service worker needs a push event handler that receives an event parameter. The event object contains the message data.

The sever can send any text in the message. It is up to the service worker to parse the message and trigger the appropriate work flow.

PodStr only manages a new podcast's episode notifications. But a retailer might want to promote sales or remind a customer to complete an order. There is really no limit to what prompt you might send to your customer.

The latter message might not be a simple string -- it could be a stringified JSON object. If you need to process JSON objects, you will need to test it to see if it is a valid object before falling back to a string. The more message types you might have, the more complex event handler logic you will need.

For demonstration purposes, the Podstr push event handler will compose an `options` object that contains details about the new episode. This includes the episode title and podcast logo:

```
{
     "title": "CodeWinds - Leading edge web developer news and training | javascript / React.js / Node.js / HTML5 / web development - Jeff Barczewski",
     "description": "episode description here",
"image": "http://codewinds.com/assets/codewinds/codewinds-podcast-1400.png"
}
```

Push messages are handled by extensions to the core `serviceWorkerRegistration` object, which are obtained during the registration process or the `getRegistration` method. The method we are interested in is the `showNotification` method.

This method has two parameters, a title and an options object. The title should be a string that describes the notification. The Podstr application will use the episode's title.

The options object allows you to configure the notification and can be a combination of several properties.

Notification Object:

- `actions`: An array of objects that will display action buttons for the user to choose from.
- `badge`: The URL of an image to represent the notification when there is not enough space to display the notification itself.
- `body`: A string to display in the message.
- `dir`: The direction of the notification; it can be auto, ltr, or rtl.
- `icon`: The URL of the notification icon.
- `image`: A string containing the URL of an image to display in the notification.
- `lang`: Must be a valid BCP 47 language tag which is used for the notification language.
- `renotify`: If a notification uses a tag for a repeat display, this can be set to true to suppress vibrations and audible notifications.

- `requireInteraction`: On larger screens, if this value is true, the notification stays visible until the user dismisses it. Otherwise, Chrome and I assume other browsers will minimize the notification after 20 seconds.
- `tag`: An ID that allows you to find and replace the notification if needed. This can be done by calling the `getNotifications` method.
- `vibrate`: An array of numbers specifying a vibration sequence. For example, `[300, 100, 400]` would vibrate 300 ms, pause 100 ms, then vibrate 400 ms.
- `data`: This is an open field that you can optionally populate anyway you see fit. It can be any data type, like a string, number, date, or object.

The `action` property gives you the ability to add one or more action buttons to the notification. You can handle this selection in the `notificationClick` event handler.

An action object has the following properties:

- `action`: A `DOMString` identifying a user action to be displayed on the notification
- `title`: A `DOMString` containing action text to be shown to the user
- `icon`: [optional] A String containing the URL of an icon to display with the action:

The Podstr service worker looks for a simple JSON object in the notification event's data field. It parses the object and builds a notification object.

Be careful trying to parse the text because it may not be a JSON object. The best way to handle this situation is to wrap the parse method and associated logic in a try catch statement. Not the best scenario, but the only way, for now, to handle valid and invalid JSON object parsing:

```
try {
    var episode = JSON.parse(event.data.text());

    const title = episode.title;
    const options = {
        body: episode.description,
        icon: 'img/pwa-podstr-logo-70x70.png',
        badge: 'img/pwa-podstr-logo-70x70.png',
        image: episode.image,
        vibrate: [200, 100, 200, 100, 200, 100, 200],
        actions: [{
            action: "listen",
            title: "Listen Now",
            icon: 'img/listen-now.png'
        },
        {
            action: "later",
            title: "Listen Later",
            icon: 'img/listen-later.png'
        }]
    };

    event.waitUntil(self.registration.showNotification(title,
    options));

}
catch (e) {
    console.log('invalid json');

    event.waitUntil(self.registration.showNotification("spartan
    obstacles", {
        body: 'Generic Notification Handler',
        icon: 'img/pwa-podstr-logo-70x70.png',
        badge: 'img/pwa-podstr-logo-70x70.png',
        vibrate: [200, 100, 200, 100, 200, 100, 200]
    }));
}
```

If the notification contains plain text, a generic notification is displayed.

The `showNotification` method causes the message on the user's device. The function returns a promise that resolves a `NotificationEvent`.

Wrapping the `showNotification` method in a `waitUntil` function keeps the event handler open until the promise resolves so that the service worker does not terminate.

A `NotificationEvent` object has two properties: notification and action. The notification is a copy of the notification object used to create the notification. If there are one or more action buttons in the notification, the action value is the action object's action property defined in the notification object.

In our example, this value would be either listen or later. You can use this value to trigger a different response flow. If the user selects listen, you can go directly to the episode page and start playing the episode. If they say later, you know to download the episode's mp3 file and persist it in the cache:

```
self.addEventListener('notificationclick', function (event) {
    if(event.action === "listen"){
        listenToEpisode(event.notification);
    }else if(event.action === "later"){
        saveEpisodeForLater(event.notification);
    }
    event.notification.close();
});
```

The `notification.close` method programmatically closes a notification.

That is all it takes to display a push notification. Remember, all the code to process a push notification is handled in the service worker. For now, browsers require that you display a visible message when you process a notification. This does not mean the notification requires user interaction.

A push notification could trigger logic to be executed in the service worker like update the cache. If you require a response, you can configure action buttons and process the end user's choice.

Unsubscribing from push notifications

The only push notification task we need to implement is a way to unsubscribe the subscription. This can be done via the `pushManager`.

Before I dive into the details to unsubscribe a user from push notifications, I want to look at how we can provide a UI for the user to manage their subscription status.

Service Workers – Notification, Synchronization, and Our Podcast App

My preference is to include a management interface in the site's settings, configuration page, or section. For example, the Twitter PWA has a detailed notification configuration experience. It has a high-level page with links to four child pages, each offering more granular control over different notification aspects.

They are grouped as either filters or preferences. In the filters group, there is also a checkbox to enable a quality filter, which is a very high-level setting.

Push notifications are managed in their own group of pages. They have code to detect if push notifications are enabled for the site and, if so, give the user the option to enable push. Once they enable push, they can then tailor their notifications by type of activity.

The default choices can cause a crazy amount of notifications to be sent. So, if you are like me, take the time to trim the volume of notifications.

The Twitter Lite application can serve as a reference for a detailed push management interface. Fortunately, the Podstr application keeps its notifications simple. For our purposes, we will provide an interface to either turn notifications on or off:

Notifications can be toggled on or off, which triggers client-side logic to manage a subscription. The application must manage both `subscribeUser` and `unsubscribeUser` based on the user toggling a choice.

This is why there are separate subscribe and unsubscribe methods. Before I dive into the code to handle the toggling UI, let's review the `unsubscribeUser` method.

Just like the `subscribeUser` method, the `unsubscribeUser` method uses the service worker's `pushManager.getSubscription` method to obtain reference to the current subscription, if any.

If there is a current subscription, the subscription object's unsubscribe method is called. Unsubscribe returns a promise that resolves a Boolean indicating if the subscription was unsubscribed or not:

```
function unsubscribeUser(registration) {
    return registration.pushManager.getSubscription()
        .then(function (subscription) {
            if (subscription) {
                return subscription.unsubscribe()
                    .then(function(success){
                        console.log("user is unsubscribed ", success);
                    });
            }
        })
        .catch(function (error) {
            console.log('Error unsubscribing', error);
        });
}
```

If the service worker is unregistered, then any associated push notification subscriptions are deactivated.

When a notification subscription changes outside the control of the application, the `pushsubscriptionchange` event fires in the service worker. You can add an event handler to this event to handle the change as needed.

A subscription state can change by either the consumer or automatically by the service. The service might remove a subscription if it has become stale. In this case, you could create an automated resubscription process to renew the subscription.

If you are resubscribing a notification subscription, it must be done with the same options as the page used in the initial, frontend JavaScript. You can access the previous options by accessing the `oldSubscription` object in the event object.

Handling a push subscription change

The `pushsubscriptionchange` event is particularly handy if the subscription is automatically removed due to the subscription becoming stale. This can happen because many push services limit the lifetime of a subscription for security and due to inactivity.

Just like authentication tokens, push subscriptions can be seamlessly renewed without involving the user. This is what you can do in the service worker for a push subscription.

The `pushsubscriptionchange` event includes an `oldSubscription` object that contains the details of the original subscription. They can be used to create a new subscription:

```
self.addEventListener('pushsubscriptionchange', e => {
  e.waitUntil(registration.pushManager.subscribe(e.oldSubscription.options)
      .then(subscription => {
        // TODO: Send new subscription to application server
      }));
});
```

This saves you the hassle of persisting the values between sessions. Now, you can easily resubscribe the user in the service worker without disturbing the end user.

Background sync

The service worker cache enables a site to render offline. But that only helps when you have the page and assets available in the cache. What can you do if you need to post data or get uncached pages while offline?

This is where background sync can help. It enables you to register a request that will be fulfilled when the device is back online.

Background sync executes asynchronous tasks in the background, when a device is online. It works by building a queue of requests to fulfill as soon as the device is capable of connecting to the internet.

The way background sync works is you place a network request with a tag, registered with the `SyncManager`. The platform is responsible for checking if the device is online or offline.

If it cannot make the request, the sync places the request in a queue for that tag. The background sync periodically checks the ability to make a request, but not so much that it would drain your battery or consume excessive CPU cycles.

The background sync model possibly requires a new way to organize your application's code. To properly use sync programming, you should separate all requests into isolated methods from any event triggers.

For example, instead of making a fetch call directly in a button click event handler, you would call a method that fetches the asset from the event handler. This allows you to better isolate the call within a background sync registration.

The Podstr application allows the customer to select podcast episodes to listen to offline. This requires the user to select the episode, and the application will download the audio file and store it for offline consumption.

Of course, the application must be online to download the episode. You may also want to limit downloading a large file like an audio file for when the device is on WiFi and not cellular.

First, let's see how to register a request using background sync:

```
if ("sync" in reg) {
    reg.sync.register('get-episode');
}
```

Because background sync is very new, it is not supported by many browsers yet. That should be changing in the near future. For example, Edge has support behind the service worker flag.

To be safe, you should employ feature detection before using it. This can be done by checking if the service worker registration object supports "sync". If so, then you can register the request; otherwise, you can make the request as a normal request.

Sync requests are registered in your UI code, not the service worker. The service worker has a sync event handler, which is responsible for handling the network request.

Background sync works like a cloud-based messaging platform. Instead of placing a request directly, you post a message to a queue or buffer that can be accessed by both the placing and the responding parties.

In our example, Podstr stores requests for offline episodes in IDB. This is chosen because it is an asynchronous data store, available to both the client code and service worker. I won't go into the details of how this works in this chapter, as I am saving that for Chapter 6, *Master the Cache API- Manage Web Assets in a Podcast Application*, when we dive deeper into caching.

To make background sync work, you first need to place a message in the IDB queue. When the service worker receives a sync event to process episodes to listen later (`get-episode`), it checks the IDB queue for episodes and fetches each file.

You register the request by calling the sync's `register` method. This method accepts a simple tag name. This is passed along to the service worker's sync event handler.

The service worker registers a single sync event handler. Each time a background sync event triggers, the handler receives a `SyncEvent` object. It contains a `tag` property that identifies the event by the `tag` value which is supplied when you registered the synchronization:

```
self.addEventListener('sync', function (event) {
    if (event.tag == 'get-episode') {
        event.waitUntil(getEpisode());
    }
});
```

In this example, you can see that it is checking the value of the tag before calling the `getEpisode` function. The `getEpisode` function triggers the tasks required to retrieve the episodes in the listen later queue and downloads them for offline persistence.

You should notice the method is wrapped in a `waitUntil`. This is to keep the event handler live while the background task is being performed. Downloading a podcast episode could take a few minutes, and you do not want the service worker process terminating.

In this example, the podcast episodes will download in response to the background sync event being fired. This means the request(s) may not immediately initiate, but they will get downloaded.

The bonus is that these downloads will happen even if a Podstr page is not loaded in the browser. Plus, the download happens in a background thread, freeing up the UI from this cumbersome task. Now, the consumer is free to navigate around the application without waiting on the audio files to download.

Summary

Service workers are exciting and offer a great new context for developers to build rich, engaging user experiences while employing background activities. This chapter introduced you to different service worker concepts and the Podstr application.

You have now seen how to leverage both push notifications and background sync to build engagements, even when the customer is not viewing your application.

In the following chapters, you will see how the service worker's life cycle and caching work. By the end of this section, you will have a modest podcast application, demonstrating how to use service worker caching, push notifications, and background synchronization to create a user experience that rivals popular native applications using web technology.

The Service Worker Life Cycle

5

The service worker life cycle is one of the most important concepts you must master in order to create proper service workers. This part of the service worker discipline is often overlooked and leads to many questions and frustrations expressed on sites such as Stack Overflow. But mastering the service worker life cycle allows you to seamlessly register and update service workers.

I think developers overlook the life cycle because it is not obvious until they hit an obstacle due to not understanding the service worker lifespan. The issue that confuses most developers is when a service worker becomes active.

Service workers obey a known life cycle that allows a new service worker to get itself ready without disrupting the current one. The life cycle is designed for the best user experience.

When a service worker is registered, it does not immediately seize control of the client. There are rules designed to minimize errors due to differences in code versions.

If a new service worker just took control of a client's context, there could be issues if the client or page is expecting the previous version. Even though the service worker operates on a separate thread, the UI code could have dependencies on service worker logic or cached assets. If the new version breaks the frontend, your user experience could go sideways.

The life cycle is designed to ensure that an in-scope page or task is controlled by the same service worker (or no service worker) throughout its session:

The Service Worker Life Cycle

The life cycle consists of the registration, installation, and activation steps. The installation and activation events can have handlers bound to them so that they perform specific tasks.

The life cycle also covers service worker updates, maybe the most important life cycle step, and unregistration. These last two tasks may not be used as often, but developers should still be familiar with how they work.

Each stage can be used for different process phases to manage the service worker, cached assets, and possibly state data. This chapter goes into details about the life cycle and how each phase can be used to make your application more performant and easier to manage.

The following topics will be covered in this chapter:

- Registering a service worker
- Service worker clients
- Updating a service worker
- Service worker scope
- Service worker updates
- Service worker events

When a service worker is registered, the script is downloaded and then installed. At this point, it does not take over any active clients, including the page that registers the service worker. This is by design, to ensure that the client experience is not at risk of breaking due to changes in service worker code.

When a service worker becomes active, it claims or controls any clients within the worker's scope. Since there could be a previous worker controlling the clients, a new version does not automatically take over. This could lead to all sorts of trouble if there are logical differences between the two versions.

To avoid potential error states, the service worker specification errs on the side of caution. You can call the `skipWaiting` function in the install event handler to cause the new version to become active. When calling `skipWaiting`, you may still need to claim active clients:

```
self.addEventListener('install', event => {
   self.skipWaiting();
   event.waitUntil(
     // caching etc
   );
});
```

If you use `skipWaiting`, it is best to call the method before you proceed to any pre-cache activities, because they may take a while. This is why the pre-cache logic is wrapped in a `waitUntil` method.

The `waitUntil` method holds the event handler open until the tasks have finished processing. Think about holding an elevator door open until everyone gets on or off the car. If you have extending processing, the service worker will not shut down.

If the service worker is idle for a long period of time, the active service worker is terminated to reduce CPU load and other resources it might otherwise consume. This is a good thing because continuous service workers would drain your devices battery if it ran continuously.

Beware, if you force a new service worker to become active, you need to make sure that it will not break your application. Users don't like it when the user experience breaks and error messages are displayed.

A best practice is to execute some sort of testing to verify the integrity of your application. You may also want to warn the user that the application has been updated, possibly encouraging a manual refresh.

Never automatically refresh the page without warning the visitor as this could be confusing. The messaging API can be used to communicate with the user to coordinate the update.

If there are any errors during the service worker installation, the registration will fail and its life cycle will end. After installation, the service worker can become active. Once active, it can respond to function events such as `fetch`.

A common error during the installation handler is the cache. The `addAll` method may receive a 404 Not Found response. When this happens, the `addAll` method throws an exception. Since the install event cannot determine the error severity or context, it rolls back. The service worker never installs. This is represented by the red error block in the following flow chart.

You can catch exceptions and handle them gracefully. You can still make individual requests and cache those results. This requires a little more code, but gives you some insulation against a single request, causing the service worker install to fail. You can also make sure that good responses are cached, even when one fails.

The following flow chart demonstrates the core life cycle, but does not visualize how a service worker becomes active:

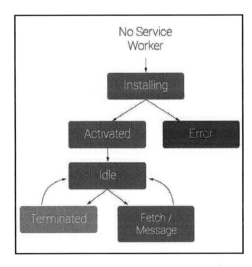

Registering a service worker

Service workers must be registered from a web page. This is done in a normal UI script. Before you call the `register` method, you should feature detect service worker support. If supported, the `navigator` object has a `serviceWorker` property:

```
if ('serviceWorker' in navigator) {
 }
```

If the browser supports service workers, you can then safely register your service worker. The `serviceWorker` object has a `register` method, so you need to supply a URL reference to the service worker script:

```
if ('serviceWorker' in navigator) {
 navigator.serviceWorker.register('/sw.js')
 .then(function(registration) {
 // Registration was successful
 });
}
```

The `serviceWorker.register("sw path"[, options])` function accepts two parameters. The first is the path to the service worker. This path is relative to the site origin or root folder.

The second parameter is optional, and is an object containing registration options. For now, the only option available is `scope`. An object was used to afford future modifications to the `register` function.

The `scope` option is a string reference to the path that is relative to the site's root the service worker is allowed to control. In the following example, a service worker is being registered for the human resources department. The same code would be used from the site's root domain or the `hr` subfolder because all paths are relative to the site's root:

```
navigator.serviceWorker.register('/hr/sw.js', {scope: '/hr/'})
  .then(function (registration) {
  // Registration was successful
  console.log('ServiceWorker registration successful with scope: ',
registration.scope);
  });
```

You could register a service worker for any path within the site from anywhere. The scope is still limited to where the service worker physically resides. This means you could also register the marketing and finance service workers from the HR application. However, HR would not have the ability to manipulate anything in those applications and vice versa.

A script can be stored at any level at or above its designated scope. For example, if all of your application's service workers were located in the site's root folder, they would each need a different `scope` value:

```
navigator.serviceWorker.register('/sw-hr.js', {scope: '/hr/'})
  .then(function (registration) {
  // Registration was successful
  console.log('ServiceWorker registration successful with scope: ',
registration.scope);
  });
```

The preceding example demonstrates how the HR department's service worker is stored in the domain's root folder. Setting the scope to `/hr/` limits its scope to the `hr` folder and below.

Misunderstanding scope is one of the most common mistakes new service worker developers make. The first step is to accept that service workers are different from the client-side JavaScript we have been authoring for the past two decades.

You should make an effort to separate your service worker scripts from your traditional client script files. Place the service worker file of your register in your application's root folder. You can still import scripts from other folders, giving you the freedom to reuse code across application scopes.

Scope is a valuable feature that guards against bad things happening due to external service providers or sites your customer may visit. You can think about it as a way to silo your logical business units. It is also a way to protect your applications from potential security threats if one application on your domain becomes compromised.

By default, a service worker is scoped to the folder the script resides in. The service worker is not allowed to control pages hosted at a higher folder level or in a sibling folder.

Service worker clients

I have mentioned the service worker clients several times in this chapter. The obvious definition is a browser tab with a site's page open. While this will be the case in most situations, it is not the only client type.

Because service workers execute in a separate context from a browser tab's UI thread, they can service multiple clients. This includes multiple tabs, push notifications, and background sync events. The latter two are clients without a traditional user interface.

The service worker specification says (`https://w3c.github.io/ServiceWorker/#service-worker-client-concept`):

> "A service worker client is an environment."

It goes on to define a series of potential client types. The concept of a service worker client is designed not to account for the obvious browser tab, but any process that might trigger a service worker event. For now, this includes push notifications and background sync events. The future is open as more features are being standardized to use the service worker infrastructure

The following screenshot shows the Chrome developer tools listing three different tabs that are open from the same site:

```
http://localhost:57661/

        Source   sw.js
                 Received 10/14/2017, 1:52:29 PM
        Status   ● #1078 activated and is running   stop
       Clients   http://localhost:57661/category/bedroom/   focus
                 http://localhost:57661/categories/   focus
                 http://localhost:57661/   focus
```

Each tab is a unique client. You can click the **focus** link to the right of any of the clients to immediately display the corresponding browser tab.

The following code allows you to check all of the service worker registrations for the current scope:

```
navigator.serviceWorker.getRegistrations()
  .then(function(registrations){
    registrations.forEach(function(registration) {
        console.log("registration: ", registration.scope);
      }, this);
});
```

You may be asking, why is there a `getRegistrations` method when you can only have a single service worker registered for a scope? The `getRegistrations` function returns a list of all registered service workers within the domain.

The `getRegistration` method works in a similar fashion but only returns the registered service worker for the current scope:

```
navigator.serviceWorker.getRegistration().then(function (registration) {
    if (registration) {
        console.log("registration: ", registration.scope);
    }
});
```

The `getRegistration` method has an optional parameter where you can specify a URL and it returns the service worker registration for the worker that controls the URL's scope. For example, if you supplied `/marketing/`, the `registration.scope` would return `{domain}/marketing/`, assuming that you have a service worker registered for that scope.

The service worker registration object

Registering a service worker creates an entry in a service worker registry that's maintained by the user agent. When you register or call the `getRegistration` or `getRegistrations` methods, they return a reference to the matching registration object(s).

The Service Worker Life Cycle

The registration object contains the following members:

Properties

- `scope`: The service worker's scope
- `installing`: If the service worker is installing, it returns a `ServiceWorker` object, otherwise it returns undefined
- `waiting`: If the service worker is waiting, it returns a `ServiceWorker` object, otherwise it returns undefined
- `active`: If the service worker is active or activating, it returns a `ServiceWorker` object, otherwise it returns undefined
- `navigationPreLoad`: Returns a reference to the service worker's `preLoadManager`
- `periodicSync`: Returns a reference to the service worker's `PeriodicSyncManager` for background synchronization
- `pushManager`: Returns a reference to the service worker's `pushManager`
- `sync`: Returns a reference to the service worker's `syncManager`

Methods

- `update`: Programmatically checks for a service worker update, bypassing caches
- `unregister`: Programmatically removes the service worker
- `getNotifications`: Returns a promise that resolves an array of notifications for the service worker
- `showNotifications`: Displays a notification identified by the title

Event

- `onupdatefound`: Triggered any time there is a new service worker

The following is an example of how the `updatefound` event might be handled. When it triggers, there should be a `serviceworker` object present in the registration's installing property. Here, the `serviceworker` object (`newWorker`) has had its state property interrogated:

```
reg.addEventListener('updatefound', () => {   // A wild service worker
//   has appeared in reg.installing!
const newWorker = reg.installing;
console.log("newWorker.state: ", newWorker.state);
// "installing" - the install event has fired, but not yet complete
// "installed"  - install complete
// "activating" - the activate event has fired, but not yet complete
```

```
//   "activated"  - fully active
//   "redundant"  - discarded. Either failed install, or it's been
//      replaced by a newer version

newWorker.addEventListener('statechange', () => {
// newWorker.state has changed
console.log("service worker state change");
});

});
```

This event could be used to perform a series of logic to prepare the client for updating, including notifying the user to reload the browser to take advantage of the newer version.

The `update` and `unregister` methods will be covered in Chapter 6, *Mastering the Cache API – Managing Web Assets in a Podcast Application*. Let's take a moment to see how push notifications work.

Updating a service worker

The following diagrams show the sequence a service worker goes through during a replacement cycle. The first diagram shows how a new service worker is registered and lives *next to* an existing service worker. The new service worker is not active, but hangs around, waiting for all active clients to close:

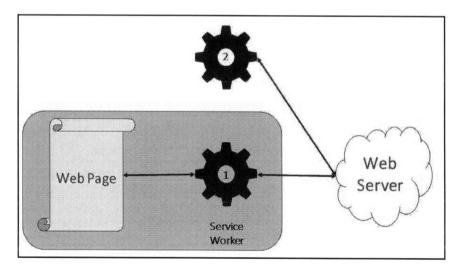

Once the clients are closed, the initial service worker dies and the new service worker begins its new active role:

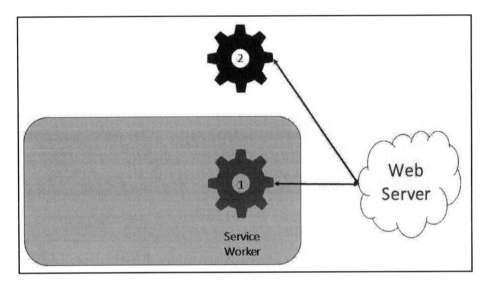

After the new service worker becomes active, it is the only service worker that's alive:

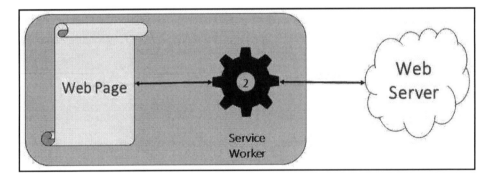

Service worker scope

As mentioned earlier, service workers are limited to a single domain. The domain is your site's address, such as `https://podcast.love2dev.com/`. This is a security feature. Limiting a service worker is known as the **service worker's scope**. This prevents external scripts from doing bad things to your site.

Imagine if your customer also visits your competition's web site, which installs a service worker. Without limits on service worker scope, they could conceivably manipulate your content or spy on you and your customer's private data.

In fact, a third-party script cannot register a service worker from a page on your site. This should keep external scripts and service providers from using service workers in conjunction with your domain.

A service worker is limited to the origin domain, and it is also limited to the folder in which it is physically located. This means you can register a service worker in any subfolder within the site's domain. The child script would control any request originating from its folder and below.

If another service worker were to register at a lower folder, then it would take control from that folder down and so on. Another way to think about a service worker's scope of control is downward, but not upward. A script residing in a subfolder does not execute in response to events triggered at the site's root.

Be careful about where your service worker file is located. The common practice is to store JavaScript files under a `/js` folder. This is fine for traditional UI JavaScript, but often leads to confusion when the service worker file is stored under the `js` folder. The best practice is to locate the service worker in your site's root folder or root folder of the scope it controls.

The scope determines which pages are controlled by the service worker. Once a page is controlled by a service worker, all HTTP requests originating from the page, regardless of the request URL, will trigger the service worker's fetch event.

Most of the time, this means that your service worker is located in the top folder of your domain's website. But there are many scenarios where this would not be the case. Large sites and corporate intranet sites are often collections of different, isolated applications.

In architectures where there are different application islands, each application can have its own service worker. For example, an enterprise might have sibling sites for HR, finance, and marketing. Each one can have a separate service worker. The different service workers are isolated from each other and cannot access the other applications' scope.

Each of these service workers could be registered anywhere within the site's root domain. This means you can register a child application's service worker from another scope. Each service worker is still limited in scope to the folder in which it resides and below.

The following screenshot shows that four service workers can be registered for a single site, each controlling their own scope:

Service worker updates

Updating the service worker file can be a tricky concept as well. There are several factors that determine when your service worker is updated. The update cycle does not start until the browser determines that there is a new service worker file available.

Once a service worker is registered, the browser treats the file like any other file when determining if there is a new version available. It makes a request to the server, which triggers a well-known cycle.

First, there is the local browser cache (not the service worker cache) for the file. If there is a local version available that has not become stale, it is retrieved. Next, the request is sent across the network to the server. If the server responds with a 304, it means that the browser has the most current version. If the file has not changed, then the service worker update cycle does not start. If there is a newer version, the service worker is updated.

The one exception to the basic update flow is a built-in guard against large Cache-Control header values. The browser will always retrieve the service worker from the server if it has not been updated within the past 24 hours.

Cache-Control headers tell the browser how long to persist a copy of a file in browser storage. For most assets, you want a long time to cache, for example, a year, because they don't change often. This could lead to a bad situation where your application is not updated.

For static assets such as style sheets and images, a common practice is to name them using a file hash generated value and assign a very long lifetime to them. This means any updates use a new file name and trigger a new request. You can certainly employ this strategy with service workers.

If you use the same service worker file name, then you should set a short lifetime. This can vary from a few minutes to a few hours. Anything over 24 hours will be ignored by the browser.

If the browser has not checked for a new service worker version within the past 24 hours, it will force a server-side check. This was added to the spec as a safety precaution just in case you deploy a service worker that causes major problems and you cannot force an update programmatically.

This scenario could play out if you have a long cache time specified for the pages in your site that register the service worker and have done the same for the service worker script. This means that the worst-case scenario you would experience would a full day from the time the bad service worker was installed.

Not the best solution to a bad problem, but at least there is an ultimate fail-safe to bail you out. If you find yourself in this situation, you can still deploy the update immediately and users that have not installed the buggy version will be spared.

Service worker events

There are two types of service worker events: core and functional. Core messages are fundamental to what makes a service worker a service worker. Functional events can be thought of as extensions to the central service worker backbone:

Core Events:

- Install
- Activate
- Message

Functional Events:

- `fetch`
- `sync`
- `push`

Each of these events can be used to trigger processing. The install and activate events are part of the life cycle. In `Chapter 7`, *Service Worker Caching Patterns*, we will dive into different caching patterns. The install and activate events are very useful to manage pre-caching assets and cleaning up your cache model.

When a new service worker is registered, the install event immediately triggers. The activate event triggers when the service worker becomes active. This means that any existing service worker is replaced with the new service worker.

The message event triggers when a message is sent from the client using the `postMessage` method.

Functional events are triggered in response to external actions. We have already looked at push and background sync. In `Chapter 6`, *Mastering the Cache API – Managing Web Assets in a Podcast Application*, we will review how the Fetch API works and start down the path of caching strategies.

Summary

The service worker life cycle looks simple until you start working with service workers. Understanding how the life cycle executes is helpful so that you can understand what the state of your service worker is.

The service worker life cycle is designed to help us avoid situations where you upgrade and could potentially break the application. A new service worker can be registered, but wait for any existing clients to close. When safe, you could use the `skipWaiting` method to allow a new service worker to immediately take control.

More complex applications may also have multiple service workers with different scopes. This allows larger applications to silo control across the different sub applications.

Now that you have a foundation in how to use the service worker and the service worker life cycle, in the next chapter, you will see how to use the Fetch and Cache APIs to make the Podstr app work offline and save episodes to listen to anywhere, anytime.

6
Mastering the Cache API - Managing Web Assets in a Podcast Application

The most important service worker superpower is the ability to use a local response cache, making the network optional. Service workers can do this because they can intercept network requests and check if a response has previously been cached before passing the request to the network. They can also be programmed to cache any network response for future use. This allows the website to possibly load instantly and regardless of the network state, which is another way of saying your web apps can work offline.

This super power relies on two newer platform features, Fetch and the Cache APIs. Before adding caching to the Podstr application, we need to learn the details of the APIs.

You first saw fetch in `Chapter 4`, *Service Workers – Notification, Synchronization, and Our Podcast App*, but it was only a simple introduction. Before we dive into using the Cache API, we are going to take a deep dive into the Fetch API and its support objects. After learning the details of these APIs, we can start stacking our skills to build caching strategies and make our web applications robust, offline progressive web applications.

The following topics will be covered in this chapter:

- How the Fetch API works
- The `Request`, `Response`, `header` objects and other Fetch API features
- How the Cache API works

Using the Fetch API

We have already seen the Fetch API being used in `Chapter 4`, *Service Workers – Notification, Synchronization, and Our Podcast App*, so let's do a quick review. Fetch is a modern replacement for `XMLHttpRequest`. It is asynchronous, relying on promises, and provides a more streamline interface to manage dynamic requests. You can customize requests by creating custom `Request` and `header` objects. Service workers rely on Fetch to make network requests.

The `fetch()` method takes two parameters, the URL that you are requesting (or a `request` object) and an `options` object. This method returns a `promise` object.

There are also some differences from how you may be accustomed to making AJAX requests. Fetch does not usually throw an exception on HTTPS status codes, only if there is a network problem making the request, which typically indicates a platform or hardware issue. Any response from the server, even if it is an error status code such as 404: Page Not Found or 500: Server Error is still considered a successful request.

This is because the browser cannot judge the success of the request in the eyes of the application. You are responsible for validating the response, which you see being done in the first code example, demonstrating a basic fetch request with a check for a successful response. If the response status is anything but 200 (good response), an error message is logged.

Another difference is how cookies are managed. Fetch does not send cookies to or from the server. This means if you rely on cookie-based authentication tokens, you will need to use the credentials property in fetch's initial options.

The `fetch` method accepts two parameters, a `request` object or URL and an optional `init` object. The first parameter is either a valid URL or a `request` object. If the URL is provided, fetch creates a default request to call the network. The `request` object is covered in the next section.

If the init parameter is not supplied or a property is not set, the default values are used. The `init` object can contain the following properties:

- `method`: HTTP verb; GET, POST, PUT, DELETE, and so on.
- `headers`: Custom HTTP headers are added to your request. They can be part of either a `header` object or an object `literal`.
- `body`: Any data passed to the server. It can be a `Blob`, `Buffer`, `FormData`, `QueryString`, or `String` object.

- mode: `cors`, `no-cors`, or `same-origin`.
- credentials: `omit`, `same-origin`, or `include` (required). It indicates how authentication cookies are handled.
- cache: `default`, `no-store`, `reload`, `no-cache`, `force-cache`, or `only-if-cached`.
- redirect: `follow` or `manual`.
- referrer: `no-referrer`, client (default), or a URL.
- referrerPolicy: `no-referrer`, `no-referrer-when-downgrade`, `origin`, `origin-when-cross-origin`, or `unsafe-url`.
- keepalive: Can improve performance by keeping the connection after the response is delivered.

When you supply just a URL or a URL and an init object, the `fetch` method creates a request from those parameters. When you supply your own `request` object, it contains those values. One of the cool things about the Fetch API is its ability to create a custom `request` object. This means you can intercept a request in your service worker and transform it into a different request.

Request object

The `Request` constructor has the same two parameters as the `fetch` method has, a URL and option initialization object. The following code modifies the fetch example to use a custom `request` object:

```
var myRequest = new Request("./api/podcast/" + id + ".json");

fetch(myRequest).then(function(response) {
      if (response.status !== 200) {
         console.log('Status Code: ' + response.status);
         return;
      }
    return response.json();
}).then(function(response) {
    console.log(data);
});
```

You can do much more than just create a `request` object from a URL. You can craft a request using various options. While most requests are simple GET requests, there are many times where you need to craft something custom. The `request` object gives you the flexibility to make these requests.

The following example shows how to manage a potential redirect situation where you have changed your primary image folder:

```
self.addEventListener("fetch", function (event) {

  event.respondWith(

    var re = /img/S+/g;

    if(re.test(request.url)){

        request = new Request(request.url.replace("img", "images"),
            {
                method: request.method,
                headers: request.headers,
                mode: request.mode,
                credentials: request.credentials
            });

    }

    return fetch(request)
        .then(function (response) {
            //process response
        })
    );

});
```

Of course, there are many other potential scenarios where you might need to modify a request before sending it to the network. Remember, if you make a custom request and cache the response, you will need to modify the request before checking the cache.

Handling cross-origin requests

You may also need to address a URL on a separate domain. Because of potential security holes, access to these URLs is often protected. You can access these URLs using **Cross-Origin Resource Sharing** (**CORS**), an additional layer, which relies on headers to control access.

It is up to the server to tell the browser if it is alright for the browser to access the resource. CORS is a protocol that enables these cross-origin requests. There are actually two requests required to complete a cross-origin request. The first is a pre-flight request (https://developer.mozilla.org/en-US/docs/Web/HTTP/CORS#Preflighted_requests) where the server tells the browser that the request is approved. After that, the original request is made.

Fetch will not make the pre-flight request unless the mode property is set to cors. The remaining part of the CORS request is handled in the response object. I will cover that in a later section.

There are four different request modes: cors, no-cors, same-origin, and navigate. You won't use navigate because it is only used to navigate between pages. Thus, it is created by the browser.

The default mode is same-origin, which limits requests to the same-origin. If a request to an external domain is made, an error is thrown:

```
var myRequest = new Request("./api/podcast/" + id + ".json",
                    {mode: "cors"});

fetch(myRequest).then(function(response) {
    if (response.status !== 200) {
      console.log('Status Code: ' + response.status);
      return;
    }
    return response.json();
}).then(function(response) {
    console.log(data);
});
```

A no-cors request limits the type of request methods to GET, HEAD, and POST. When using no-cors, the service worker is limited in how it can modify the request and what response properties it can access.

You can still request resources from a separate origin using no-cors, but the types of response types are limited. For example, you can fetch an image, but you are limited as to what you can do with the response. These are called **opaque requests**.

Managing request credentials

By default, fetch does not append cookies to requests. This is good for both security and performance. In most scenarios, accessing an API does require cookie-based authentication. For these scenarios, you need to set the credentials property to either same-origin or include. The default value is omit.

By setting the credentials option to include or same-origin, the request will include the authentication cookies. The include value triggers the request object to include the credentials for any target origin, and the same-origin limits the credentials to the same-origin:

```
var myRequest = new Request("./api/podcast/" + id + ".json",
                    {
                        mode: "cors",
                        credentials: "include"
                    });

fetch(myRequest).then(function(response) {
    if (response.status !== 200) {
      console.log('Status Code: ' + response.status);
      return;
    }
    return response.json();
}).then(function(response) {
    console.log(data);
});
```

Controlling how a response is cached

Another important request option is the cache property. This property controls how the browser uses its own cache. Since service workers provide a cache, you can programmatically control the browser cache, but it might seem a bit redundant and cause some unwanted responses.

The default cache value changes nothing; the browser checks its own cache before making a network call and the response is the best one based on the default caching rules.

However, by setting the request cache option to another value, you can force the browser to bypass or change the way it uses the browser cache. The options are as follows:

- `default`
- `no-store`
- `reload`
- `no-cache`
- `force-cache`
- `only-if-cached`

Since the service worker cache provides a superior method to cache assets, I tend to use it, and may want to remove the browser's cache from the pipeline. In this scenario, you would want to change the cache property to `no-store`:

```
var myRequest = new Request("./api/podcast/" + id + ".json",
                 {
                     mode: "cors",
                     credentials: "include",
                     cache: "no-store"
                 });

fetch(myRequest).then(function(response) {
    if (response.status !== 200) {
       console.log('Looks like there was a problem. Status Code: ' +
          response.status);
       return;
    }
    return response.json();
}).then(function(response) {
    console.log(data);
});
```

Headers object

Customizing request headers is important when crafting unique requests and responses between the client and server. The request headers property is a `Headers` object. `Header` objects are used by both `request` and `response` objects.

`Headers` are a way for the client and server to communicate extra information about the request and response. Think about them as meta data about the data being sent back and forth.

For example, when a response includes gzip compressed data, the Content-Encoding header tells the browser so it can decompress the body. Before returning a compressed response, the server looks for a corresponding header, such as accept-encoding, telling it that the client can accept a compressed response.

The `Headers` object manages the headers list. Member methods provide the ability to manage headers associated with a request or response.

Adding Headers

Headers can be added either in the constructor or via the `append` method. The following example uses the `Headers` constructor:

```
var httpHeaders = {
'Content-Type' : 'image/jpeg',
'Accept-Charset' : 'utf-8',
'X-My-Custom-Header' : 'custom-value'
};
var myHeaders = new Headers(httpHeaders);
```

Headers can also be added using the `append` method:

```
var myHeaders = new Headers();
myHeaders.append('Content-Type', 'image/jpeg');
myHeaders.append('Accept-Charset', 'utf-8);
myHeaders.append('X-My-Custom-Header', 'custom-value');
```

A final way to add headers is by using the `set` method:

```
var myHeaders = new Headers();
myHeaders.set('Content-Type', 'image/jpeg');
myHeaders.set('Accept-Charset', 'utf-8);
myHeaders.set('X-My-Custom-Header', 'custom-value');
```

The difference between `append` and `set` is the latter one will overwrite any existing values. While the `append` method adds the header value to the list of headers, the `append` method should be used for headers that allow multiple values.

An example multiple-value header is Cache-Control. There are many combinations you may need to set to provide instructions to different clients and intermediaries.

For example, the best way to manage cache on HTML assets with my CDN is to mark them as private, with a 3,600 seconds time to live. You may also include a value for CDN caching, maybe 300 seconds. This means my CDN will naturally invalidate after 300 seconds, reducing my need to force updates.

Using the `append` method requires up to three calls:

```
myHeaders.append('Cache-Control', 'private');
myHeaders.append('Cache-Control', 'max-age=3600');
myHeaders.append('Cache-Control', 's-max-age=300');
```

The `set` method writes the final value, overwriting any previous value:

```
myHeaders.set('Cache-Control', 'private, max-age=3600, s-max-age=300');
```

Headers are a complex topic, so I recommend finding more resources if you need to dig deeper into specific headers and their values. Wikipedia is a good place to start (https://en.wikipedia.org/wiki/List_of_HTTP_header_fields) as its page provides a very thorough list with details and further links to specifications.

There is a limit to the amount of headers you can manage. There are headers that are restricted to the browser and others that are restricted to the server, which means you are not allowed to change them.

If you try to append or set an invalid header, an exception will be thrown.

Accessing Header values

The `get` method returns a specific headers value:

```
Var cacheHeader = myHeaders.get('Cache-Control');
    //returns 'private, max-age=3600, s-max-age=300'
```

The `entries` method returns an iterator you can use to loop through all the headers. Each entry is a simple array, with the first entry being the header key name and the second member being the value:

```
// Display the key/value pairs
for (var header of myHeaders.entries()) {
   console.log(header[0]+ ': '+ header[1]);
}
```

The `keys` method also provides an iterator, but only returns a list of header names:

```
// Display the keys
for(var key of myHeaders.keys()) {
   console.log(key);
}
```

Conversely, you can get a list of values from the `values` method. The problem with this method is that the values are not directly correlated to their keys:

```
// Display the values
for (var value of myHeaders.values()) {
   console.log(value);
}
```

You can check if a header exists by calling the `has` method:

```
myHeaders.has(name);
```

A header can be removed using the `delete` method:

```
myHeaders.delete(name);
```

Protected Headers

Headers have a guard property. This flag indicates if headers can be manipulated. If you try to manipulate a header whose guard is set to immutable, an exception is thrown.

These are the possible guard states:

- `none`: Default
- `request`: Guard for a Headers object obtained from a Request (`Request.headers`)
- `request-no-cors`: Guard for a Headers object obtained from a Request that's been created with mode `no-cors`
- `response`: Naturally, for Headers obtained from Response (`Response.headers`)
- `immutable`: Mostly used for ServiceWorkers; renders a `Headers` object

The actual rules controlling how different headers can be manipulated is very detailed. If you want to know more about these details, I recommend reading the Fetch specification (`https://fetch.spec.whatwg.org/`).

Body mixin

The `Request` and `Response` objects both have a `body` property. This is actually a mixin or a class that implements the body interface. The body contains a data stream with methods to retrieve the contents according to the type.

Each `body` method reads the stream and converts it into the desired format. The stream is completely read and a `promise` is returned, resolving to the formatted data.

You have already seen how to use the `json()` method to read JSON formatted data. There is also the `text`, `blob`, `formData`, and `arrayBuffer` methods. Each one resolves the body to the corresponding format.

To review how to use JSON formatted data, let's see how to retrieve search results in the Podstr application:

```
function fetchSearch(term) {

    fetch("api/search.json?term=" + term)
        .then(function (response) {

            if (response.status !== 200) {
                console.log('Status Code: ' + response.status);
                return;
            }

            return response.json();

        }).then(function (results) {
            renderResults(results);
        })
        .catch(function (err) {
            console.log('No CORS Fetch Error :-S', err);
        });
}
```

Notice how the `json()` mixin is available as a method of the response. That's because each of the body mixins implements the Body interface and are added to the Response object.

The mixin returns a promise, resolving the JSON object. Remember, you cannot directly use the return value of the body mixins because they return a promise. You need to process the formatted data in a promise handler, which is the `then` method.

JSON may be the most common format used by modern APIs, but there are times when you retrieve other formats – the simplest being plain text.

Fetching plain text looks almost identical to fetching JSON. Instead of using the json mixin, use the `text` mixin:

```
fetch("api/simple.txt")
    .then(function (response) {
        if (response.status !== 200) {
          console.log('Status Code: ' + response.status);
          return;
        }
        return response.text();
    })
    .then(function(result){
        renderResult(result);
    })
    .catch(function (err) {
        console.log('Fetch Error :-S', err);
    });
```

The following example shows how to fetch an audio file (`ogg` format) and buffer the data to an `AudioContext` object:

```
source = audioCtx.createBufferSource();

fetch('./viper.ogg')
    .then(function (response) {
        return response.arrayBuffer();
    })
    .then(function (buffer) {
        audioCtx.decodeAudioData(buffer, function (decodedData) {
            source.buffer = decodedData;
            source.connect(audioCtx.destination);
        });
    });
```

So far, we have seen how to use a response body, but you can also set the body in a request. A common scenario is posting form data.

This example shows how to POST the contact form as a JSON object. The method is set to `'post'` and custom headers are supplied. The custom headers tell the server you are sending a JSON formatted body with the `Content-Type` header. You are also telling the server (the `Accept` header) that you expect a JSON object back.

The form is serialized or converted to a JSON object in the `serializeForm` method (not shown):

```
fetch("/api/contact/, {
    method: 'post',
    headers: {
        'Accept': 'application/json, text/plain, */*',
        'Content-Type': 'application/json; charset=UTF-8'
    },
    body: JSON.stringify(serializeForm())
}).then(function (res) {

    if (res.status >= 200 && res.status < 400) {
        // Success!
    return res.json();

    } else {
   console.log('Status Code: ' + response.status);
      return;
    }
}).then(function (resp) {
    //process the response
});
```

You can also post the raw form using the `FormData` object (https://developer.mozilla.org/en-US/docs/Web/API/FormData). Make sure that the API you are posting to can handle the form data:

```
    var form = document.querySelector("[name=contact-form]");

fetch("/api/contact/, {
    method: 'post',
    body: new FormData(form)
}).then(function (res) {

    if (res.status >= 200 && res.status < 400) {
        // Success!
    return res.json();
    } else {
   console.log('Status Code: ' + response.status);
      return;
    }
}).then(function (resp) {
    //process the response
});
```

The last aspect of the body you need to know about is the `bodyUsed` property. This can be checked to see if you can still use the body or not. A body can only be read once.

The body is a stream, which is a forward only set of data. Attempting to read the body more than once results in an exception being thrown.

If you need to read or use a body more than once, you should clone the request or response. A common scenario is when a service worker fetches a URL and caches the response while returning the response to the client. You will see this in more detail in the next chapter:

```
fetch(request)
    .then(function (response) {

        var rsp = response.clone();

        //cache response for the next time around
        return caches.open(cacheName).then(function (cache) {
            cache.put(request, rsp);
            return response;
        });

    })
```

Response object

The `response` object is almost identical to the `request` object. It is created when a request receives an answer from the server. Response objects also have headers and a body, the same object types as `request` objects.

Responses are normally created by the platform when a response is received from the server. However, you can create a new response. This is more common when you want to transform a response.

A scenario I have dealt with is accessing data from an older API that returned flat data. The flat data needed to be transformed into a multi-dimensional JSON object. Instead of repeating that CPU intensive process, I transformed the data and cached the transformed response.

The Response constructor has two parameters, a Body object and an initialization object. We have already gone over Body objects in Chapter 4, *Service Workers – Notification, Synchronization, and Our Podcast App*. The Response initialization object is slightly different than the `request` object.

Response object properties that differ from the `request` object are as follows:

- `status`: The status code for the reponse, for example, `200`
- `statusText`: The status message associated with the status code, for example, `OK`
- `headers`: Any headers you want to add to your response, contained within a Headers object or object literal of `ByteString` key/value pairs (see HTTP headers for a reference)

There are only three properties, one being a Headers object. The other two properties indicate the HTTP status. There is a code, status, and a text value, statusText.

Response properties

Most of the Response object properties are similar to a `request` object, most notably the Body and its mixins.

The `isRedirected` property indicates if the response is the product of a redirected (HTTPS status code `301` or `302`) response.

The type property is `readonly`, and tells us if the response had a network error (error), opaque (cross-origin with a no-cors request, cors, and basically inidicates a successful response.

The `url` property is the final response URL, after any redirects.

Verifying a successful response

As I mentioned earlier, fetch does not throw an exception or return an error if the response status is not 200. Instead, as long as fetch receives a response, it does not fail. It is still up to you to interrogate the response status to determine how you want to process the response.

The `ok` property is true if the status code is 200-299, and false otherwise. It can be a quick way to verify a request's success. Just be careful, as sometimes you can receive a 0 status code for cached, cross-origin responses.

In practice, many requests can have a range of successful status codes. HTTP status codes are grouped by 100s. 200-299 indicates a successful response, while 300-399 indicates a redirect and is accompanied by a new address. `400` indicates that the URL is not accessible, `404` being the most well-known. Other reasons a resource is not accessible have to do with authorization or permission to access the resource. Finally, anything in the 500 range indicates that there is a server-side problem.

Having a strategy to handle different statuses is important for the success of your application. Checking the `response.ok` value may not give you the entire story. I found that Chrome returns a status equal to 0 for external origin resources stored in the cache. The response is still successful, but limiting your logic to check for `response.ok` would lead to excess network requests.

Now that you know the details of the Fetch API, it's time to start learning how the Cache API works. The Cache API depends on the Fetch API because it caches request-response pairs.

Caching responses

We have been able to store content, including data and site assets using web storage and IndexedDB for several years. Using either medium requires a library or custom logic to manage site assets, which is why the service worker specification includes a specialized Cache API.

The Cache interface provides a managed storage mechanism for Request/Response object pairs. These objects are also referred to as network addressable resources, but you can think about them as just files or API responses.

The Cache API has a natural advantage over `IndexedDB` and `localStorage` because it is designed to abstract, persisting these assets by the `Request` and `Response` objects. This means that you can reference the assets using more than just a single key value, like `localStorage` provides.

Besides providing a managed interface to store assets, it also allows you to organize those assets into groups or caches. As we progress through the remaining chapters, you will see how to use this power to segregate the assets to make updating and invalidating easier.

Caches, like other browser storage services, are managed by the browser by origin, or domain. This prevents third parties from accessing the content that's stored your site. Your overall storage quota is also tied to the origin and allocated across the various storage services.

The amount of space available varies by device and is proportional to the available disk space. Like income tax, the rule governing your quota allowance varies by the amount of available space.

Ali Alabbas shared the following slide at the Microsoft Edge Developer Summit, explaining the rules governing storage quotas:

Quotas
IndexedDB & Caches API

VOLUME SIZE	DOMAIN LIMIT	OVERALL LIMIT
≤ 8 GB	20% of overall	50 MB
> 8 - 32 GB	"	500 MB
> 32 - 128 GB	"	4% of volume size
> 128 GB	"	4% or 20 GB (whichever is smaller)

If space becomes limited, the browser will arbitrarily purge stored data from the different storage providers. Unless you manage this process, you have no guarantee that your assets have remained cached.

The Cache API is part of the service worker specification because it is the backbone to make your progressive web application work offline. Without the ability to save assets for immediate access, your site could not work offline.

Caches object

The `Caches` object represents a collection of named caches and members to interact with those caches. The interface provides methods to open, create, iterate, and remove individual caches. You can also match cached responses over all the named caches without interrogating each one.

caches.open

The `caches.open` method returns a reference to a cache matching the name that's supplied. This reference is a `Cache` object, which is detailed in later sections. If a cache matching the name does not exist, a new cache is provisioned. This returns a promise; resolving a cache object allows you to manage cached responses in that cache:

```
caches.open(cacheName).then(function (cache) {
//do something here
});
```

caches.match

The `caches.match` method is a convivence method that works similarly to the `cache.match` method. It returns a promise that resolves to the first cached response matching the `Request` object passed to the method.

The nice thing about the `caches.match` method is how it handles interrogating all named caches for a match. It returns the first match it finds.

This means that if matching responses are stored in different caches, you have no control over which response is found. To avoid a scenario where an invalid response is matched, you need to ensure that your logic invalidates outdated cached responses before caching an update:

```
return caches.match(request)
    .then(function (response) {
   return response;
    })
```

caches.has()

If you need to check if a named cache exists, the `has` method returns a promise, resolving true:

```
caches.has(cacheName).then(function(ret) {
  // true: your cache exists!
});
```

caches.delete()

The `delete` method searches for a cache matching the name supplied. If a matching cache is found, it is deleted. A promise is returned that resolves true if a matching cache was deleted or false if one was not deleted:

```
Cached.delete(cacheName).then((ret)=>{ console.log(cacheName + " deleted: " + res});
```

You don't always need to add code to handle the response. Typically, you would log the activity. If no cache was deleted, it is most likely due to the cache not existing, which in that case you probably have nothing to worry about.

You should also note that if you delete a cache, all of the cached items are deleted along with it.

caches.keys()

The `keys` method returns a promise with an array of names (strings) for each named cache. This list can be iterated over for processing.

The following example is placed within the service worker activate event handler. It removes caches that were crafted for a previous service worker version. This concept was covered in Chapter 5, *The Service Worker Life Cycle*:

```
caches.keys().then(function (cacheNames) {
  cacheNames.forEach(function (value) {
    if (value.indexOf(version) < 0) {
      caches.delete(value);
    }
  });
  return;
})
```

Notice the `delete` method does not have any processing after a cache is deleted. If you wanted to log any problems regarding deleting a cache, you could do that here.

The Cache object

The Cache interface is a collection of methods and properties to manage stored responses. You cannot create a cache object; you must open a reference to a cache using the `Caches.open` method, which will be covered later. This reference is an instance of the Cache object, giving you access to the responses it manages.

cache.match()

The `match` method has two parameters, a `request` object and an optional options object. It returns a promise if a matching response is found to be resolved in the promise's return. If no response was found, the promise still resolves, but as undefined.

If no match was found, you can then continue with the appropriate logic, like forwarding the request to the network or returning a fallback response.

The `request` object parameter can be either a valid `request` object or a URL. If only a URL is provided, the method does an implicit conversion internally. Supplying a `request` object gives you more control because different responses could be cached by request variations.

For example, the same URL might have a cached response for both `HEAD` and `GET` methods, each being unique. Differing `QueryStrings` is another common example where similar URLs have different responses cached.

The optional `options` parameter allows you to provide more details to the `match` method about the specific request you want to match. You can think of it as a way of filtering potential matches.

The `options` object has a set of potential properties you can provide a value to match or filter against.

The potential options that are available are as follows:

- `ignoreSearch`: Indicates if you want to use the `QueryString` or not. The options are true or false.
- `ignoreMethod`: Indicates if you want to filter by the `request` method, for example GET, POST, DELETE, and so on. By default, match does use the request method to match a response.

- `ignoreVary`: When set to true, headers are ignored when retrieving a match. The URL is used as the filter, which means cached responses for different header combinations could match.
- `cacheName`: This limits matching responses to a specific cache name. Multiple responses could be cached across different named caches, but this specifies which cache should be used.

For most queries, you won't use these options because they are highly specialized. `ignoreSearch` has the most potential to be used because `QueryString` parameters are very common. Servers typically return different responses based on how these values vary:

```
return namedCache.match(request).then(function (response) {
   return response;
   });
```

cache.matchAll

Similar to the `match` method, the `matchAll()` method takes request and options (optional) parameters. The method returns a promise that resolves an array of matching responses. Unlike the same method on the Caches object, it only returns matches in the specifically named cache.

The main difference between `matchAll` and match is that the `match` method returns the first response it matches.

The `matchAll` method is useful when you need to match responses using a route, not just a specific URL. For example, if you want to get a list of all a podcast's banner images, you could do something like this:

```
caches.open("podcasts").then(function(cache) {
  cache.matchAll('/images/').then(function(response) {
    response.forEach(function(element, index, array) {
        //do something with each response/image
    });
  });
});
```

[171]

Cache add and addAll

If you want to retrieve an asset and immediately cache the response, the `add` and `addAll` methods manage this process. The `add` method is equivalent to the following code:

```
const precache_urls = [...]

caches.open(preCacheName).then(function (cache) {
  return cache.addAll(precache_urls);
})
```

Both the `add` and `addAll` methods have a single parameter: a `request` object. Like the `match` method, you can also supply a valid URL and the method will convert it into a `request` object.

Both methods return a promise, but do not resolve a value. As long as there were no exceptions making and caching the requests, you can use the resolution to continue the application workflow. If there was an exception, you can catch and handle it appropriately.

The add methods are useful in the install and activate life cycle events because you can provide a list of URLs to precache. You are not limited to these scenarios, as they can be called anytime.

They are not helpful during most caching strategies, which are initiated by the fetch event handler. We will go over many of these strategies in the following chapter. When handling real-time fetches, the network response is typically needed to render a page. These methods do not return access to the responses.

cache.put

Despite what you might think, the `add` method do not let you cache a response directly. If you receive a network response from a fetch call, you would need to explicitly handle its caching. This is where the `put` method gives you the control needed to cache a response with the flexibility to use the response in parallel to the caching process.

As you will learn in the next chapter, there are many different caching strategies where a network response is cached once the network request resolves.

The `put` method has two parameters, `request` and `response`. These are the same `Request` and `Response` objects that were covered in the *Fetch* section.

The `put` method uses these two objects to catalog the assets in a key value fashion, sort of like localStorage, just specialized for caching page assets.

The `put` method returns a promise, but does not resolve a value.

If you need to use the response, you should clone it before caching. A response body can only be used once, but the `response` object has a `clone` method that creates a copy. I typically cache the copy and return the original, but it does not matter.

The following code demonstrates how to fetch a resource, clone the response, cache the clone, and return the original response:

```
fetch(request).then(function (response) {
   var rsp = response.clone();
   //cache response for the next time around
   return caches.open(cacheName).then(function (cache) {
       cache.put(request, rsp);
       return response;
   });
});
```

Deleting Cached items

You are also responsible for periodically purging cache entries. The browser will not invalidate cache for you. It might purge items if available space becomes limited. However, I would not worry about this scenario. Instead, you need a plan to delete cached assets so that you can control how long an item is cached for.

The best way to manage or invalidate cached assets is to apply a set of rules to control your cache. Chapter 8, *Applying Advanced Service Worker Cache Strategies*, goes into more detail about invalidation strategies. Before you reach that level, it's important to know how to remove an asset or delete an entire cache.

The `delete` method returns a promise that resolves true if a matching response was found and deleted, otherwise it returns false:

```
cache.delete(request,{options}).then(function(true) {
  //your cache entry has been deleted
});
```

This method has two parameters, a request and an optional options object. The options are the same ones that are used in the match method. This is because you can cache multiple responses to a URL if there are different request variations using those options.

cache.keys

The cache object's `key` method returns a promise that resolves an array of requests that are stored in the cache. The method has two optional parameters, request and options. These are the same two types we have seen for the other methods.

When supplying these parameters, the `keys` method works much like the match and `matchAll` methods.

The array of keys or requests can then be used to update your cache. For example, you could loop through and delete all matches or maybe do a silent background update:

```
caches.open(cacheName).then(function(cache) {
  cache.keys().then(function(keys) {
    keys.forEach(function(request) {
      fetchAndUpdateCache(cacheName, request);
    });
  });
})
```

The keys are returned in insertion order. This can come in handy if you want to manage cache invalidation by removing the oldest pair(s) first. We'll review some cache invalidation strategies in the later chapters. You will see how this can be done along with some other strategies.

Summary

In this chapter, we saw how the Fetch and Cache APIs are critical for the service workers. To get the most out of service workers, you need to be able to intercept and manipulate requests and the server responses. Because service workers rely on asynchronous functions (Promises), you must use Fetch, as a new replacement for `XMLHttpRequest`.

The Cache API provides a new storage medium in the browser, which is highly specialized for request/response pairs. The API is a rich platform, providing the maximum amount of control over network resources.

Your goal is to use the best logic and platform resources to make your website load quickly and work offline. Now that you know how the Fetch and Cache APIs work, it's time to start crafting the best caching system you can.

In the next chapter, we will review different caching patterns and start seeing how they can be applied so that you can determine what strategy you should employ in your applications.

Service Worker Caching Patterns

The internet is great, until you are offline or have poor connectivity. Then it becomes an act of futility as you wait for a page to load that never seems to materialize. Eventually, the request times out and the browser displays a message letting you know you're offline—Chrome is known for its cute offline dinosaur.

Most web traffic comes from smartphones, and many of those connections are made over a cellular connection (GPRS). Cellular networks are great when they work, but often a clean connection to the internet is not guaranteed.

Even in the United States, reliable LTE networks are not ubiquitous. There are several locations near my house where I have no cell coverage. Imagine what it might be like in a less developed area.

This is where service workers and the Cache API can help you out. The combination of these two features enables you to make the network optional. A service worker has several events that you can leverage to craft a web server in the browser.

The topics that will be covered in this chapter are as follows:

- How the service worker cache works
- Common service worker caching strategies

How the service worker cache works

The service worker sits between the browser and the network. By adding a `fetch` event handler, you can determine how the request is handled. All network requests pass through the service worker's fetch event handler:

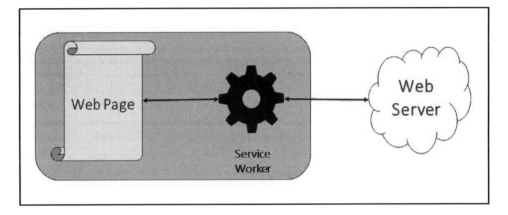

This gives you a hook, or way to inject logic into the workflow, to intercept requests and determine how and where the response is returned.

With the service worker, you can do the following:

- Pass the request to the network, the traditional method
- Return a cached response, bypassing the network altogether
- Create a custom response

When the network fails, you can program the service worker to return a response from the cache, even if it is a *fallback* response. Because the service worker can return responses from the cache, your pages can load instantly if they are cached:

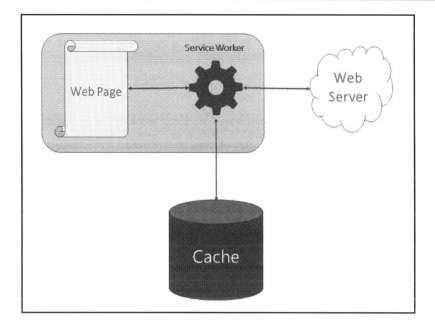

In the preceding diagram, the service worker is programmed to intercept all network requests, and can return a response from either the cache or the network.

Because the service worker runs locally, it is always available. It can decide the best way to return a response based on the conditions.

The following diagram illustrates the service worker living within the context of the browser, providing a proxy to handle requests, even when the network is unavailable:

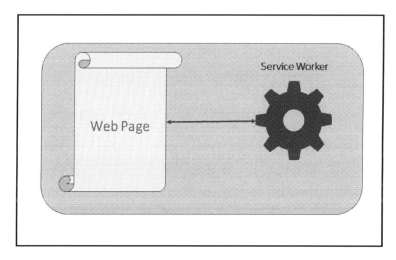

Service Worker Caching Patterns

When utilizing a service worker and the network is unavailable, your website can still function if you have valid cached responses. Even if a page is not cached, you can create a response so that the customer has something relevant to interact with. Later in the book, I will go over how you can queue the user's actions and update the server when the network is available.

The following diagram shows how the service worker can use cached resources when the network is unavailable:

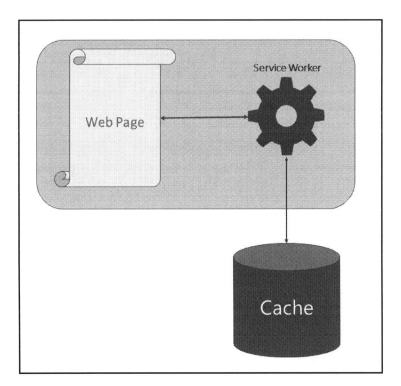

Service worker events

A service worker has several events. You can use these to manage your application's cache. We have already looked at using the *install* and *activate* events to precache responses in Chapter 5, *The Service Worker Life Cycle*.

The all-star service worker event is `fetch`. This event fires each time a network-addressable asset (URL) is requested. By adding a `fetch` event handler to your service worker, you can intercept all network requests, triggering a workflow to determine how to respond:

```
self.addEventListener("fetch", event => {
    //process request and return best response
});
```

As you learned `Chapter 6`, *Mastering the Cache API – Managing Web Assets in a Podcast Application*, you can use the Fetch API's custom `request` and `response` objects to inspect requests and create or clone network responses.

The event variable supplied by the `fetch` event handler has a request property. This property is a `request` object. You can use the `request` object to determine how you will return the response. In this chapter, you will learn several caching strategies that you can apply to make your progressive web application work faster, and offline.

Knowing how to use the `fetch` event to maximize performance using the application's cache is the key to providing the best user experience possible.

Caching patterns and strategies

Service worker events give you gateways to the service worker life cycle in order to apply your caching strategy. But there is more to this than just checking whether a valid response has been cached or is passing the request to the network. You should have a plan of how your application will use the service worker cache, events, and the network to deliver the best experience.

This means that you need to have a collection of common patterns and strategies to build your application logic upon. The rest of the chapter will review common caching patterns that you can use to build your applications.

Strategies are the combination of guidelines and example code that you can use to build your applications. As you continue through this book, you will see these strategies used in the PodStr and PWA Tickets applications.

Precaching

One of the key aspects of the PRPL pattern, which we will learn more about in a later chapter, is to store application assets when the application is installed. When a user accesses an initial entry point to a web application, a background process is triggered that will automatically load additional assets that will later be needed as different aspects of the site are rendered. This is known as precaching, or priming your application's cache for better performance in the future.

Service workers make this practice easy to manage. You can take advantage of the `install` and `activate` events, as well as when a service worker is initially triggered. The common practice is to use the `install` event when a new service worker is registered to precache a list of well-known assets:

```
self.addEventListener("install", event => {
    event.waitUntil(
        caches.open(cacheName(PRECACHE_NAME)).then(cache => {
            return cache.addAll(PRECACHE_URLS);
        })
    );
});
```

There are two types of precache strategies you need to understand: precaching as a dependency and not as a dependency.

Installing as a dependency

When precaching application assets, there are certain assets you know will be used rather quickly or frequently. You can consider these mission-critical. And while the initial page load or app shell load may trigger network requests for these assets, causing them to be cached, there will probably be other assets that you want to ensure are cached early in the application-loading process:

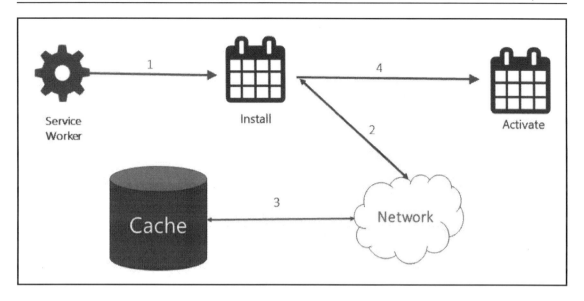

These assets should be precached as a dependency of the install event completing. In other words, these assets must complete caching before the install event closes, which means you should use the event.waitUntil method to hold the process open. By doing so, you delay any active events from triggering until these assets are completely cached:

```
self.addEventListener('install', function (event) {
    event.waitUntil(
    //pre-cache
    //on install as a dependency
    return caches.open(preCacheName).then(cache =>{
        return cache.addAll(PRECACHE_URLS);
    });
});
```

Installing not as a dependency

Precaching is not limited to mission-critical assets. You can most likely identify many assets that will be commonly used, but are not mission-critical to your application's success. You can still use the service worker install event to cache this set of assets, but choose not to make them dependent on the event completing. This is known as precaching assets without dependency.

In this scenario, you will also trigger the precaching of these network assets, but you will not return the `cache.addAll` method in the `event.waitUntil` call. The assets will still be added to the cache, but will not hold the `install` event open until all of the assets are cached.

This technique gives you the ability to minimize the latency of precaching assets that might hold the service worker installation up. One of your goals when registering a new service worker is to make it available as quickly as possible. Requesting assets that may take a little while can hold that process up. This means that your service worker cannot take control of any clients until all this caching, including the `activate` event, is done, as shown in the following diagram:

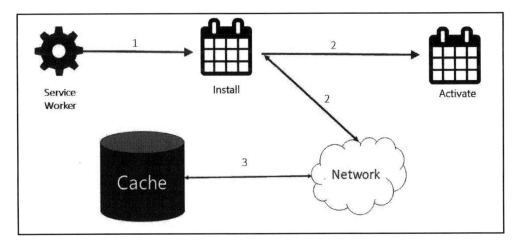

While you trigger this request in the `install` event, the event is not delayed. The request will still be cached, but outside of the `event` loop:

```
self.addEventListener('install', function (event) {
    event.waitUntil(
        //won't delay install completing and won't cause installation to
        //fail if caching fails.
        //the difference is as dependency returns a Promise, the
        //no dependency does not.
        //on install not as dependency (lazy-load)
        caches.open(preCacheNoDependencyName).then(cache =>{
            cache.addAll(PRECACHE_NO_DEPENDENCY_URLS);
            return cache.addAll(PRECACHE_URLS);
        }));
});
```

On activate

The `activate` event is the next part of the service worker life cycle chain that you can leverage to manage cached assets. It can also be used to cache assets, but is more commonly used to perform cache model cleanup.

Instead of focusing on caching assets, the `activate` event is better suited to clean up legacy caches. This can eliminate version mismatch issues that can break your application:

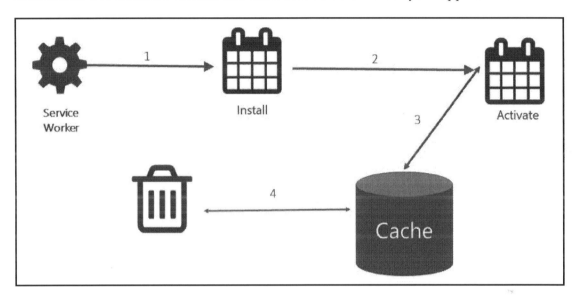

To implement this strategy, you need to have a discernible version cache-naming convention. I recommend adding a version number to all of your named caches. This gives you a simple pattern that you can match to determine whether a named cache should be removed. Just be aware that any assets that are cached in those named caches will also be removed. This is okay, as the new version of the service worker typically caches updated versions of these assets:

```
self.addEventListener('activate', function (event) {
    //on activate
    event.waitUntil(
caches.keys().then(function (cacheNames) {
            cacheNames.forEach(function (value) {
            if (value.indexOf(VERSION) < 0) {
                caches.delete(value);
            }
        });
        return;
```

```
            })
        );
    });
```

The preceding example code loops through all the named caches and checks whether the cache belongs to the current service worker. The version variable has the version number pattern we are looking for. My personal preference is to declare a `const` value at the beginning of the service worker:

```
const VERSION = "v1",
```

I add a `v` to the value to further indicate that it is a version number, but that is more of a mental tool to appeal to my personal preferences. Feel free to use any sort of versioning pattern you like. Semantic versioning or even a random hash or GUID would also work well here.

The main point is to have a unique pattern that you can identify in your cache names. Creating a variable is useful because it can be appended to the cache name to make cleanup easier to manage.

Real-time caching

Caching does not need to be limited to the service worker installation events. While you should precache your common assets, there are probably many resources that are dynamic in nature. Some example in podcast applications are the individual podcasts and podcast episode pages.

Each podcast contains unique properties, such as a title, description, and logo. Each episode also has a unique title, description, possibly an image, and, of course, the audio file.

These are very dynamic and fluid pieces of data that create many opportunities for new pages and page assets, as well as updates to these same pages and assets. The service worker `fetch` event handler gives you the hook to intercept all requests to the network so you can determine whether those assets are properly locally cached before hitting the internet.

This basic pattern gives you the ability to instantly load assets that were previously cached without worrying about network connectivity. There are many variations of this pattern, as you will see in the following sections.

On user interaction

The first dynamic caching strategy is in response to a user interaction, such as clicking a button. Instead of this being explicitly caught by the service worker `fetch` event, it can be managed from the client JavaScript. This takes advantage of the client's (browser) access to the Client API:

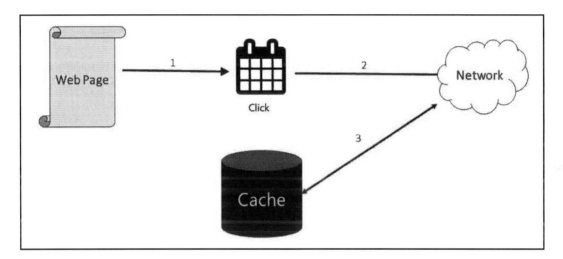

The podcast application episode page has a button that the user can select to cause the episode's MP3 file to be stored offline. This is part of the listen-later functionality, something I love to use in the Stitcher app!

The following example code is a function that is executed when the user clicks the **Listen Later** button on an episode page. A `fetch` is made to the API and the response is cached in the `LISTEN_LATER` cache:

```
function saveEpisodeData(guid) {
    var episodeSource = "api/episodes/" + guid + ".json";
    fetch(episodeSource)
        .then(function (response) {
            if (response && response.ok) {
                caches.open("LISTEN_LATER").then(
                    cache => {
                        cache.put(episodeSource, response);
                    });
            }
        });
}
```

Service Worker Caching Patterns

To make this feature complete, a similar method would be used to cache the episode's MP3 file. You would also want to persist something you can use to visually indicate that the episode is saved for later if the user opens the episode page later. You would also want to maintain a local list of saved episodes. This can be done using `IndexedDB`.

On network response

When a request returns from the network, you can intercept this part of the `fetch` process and handle it based on your application's logic. The most common thing to do is to cache the response while returning a copy to the client.

This also extends the core pattern of on-demand asset caching. It's important to note that when you intercept a request from the network, you should clone the response before caching it. A response can only be used once:

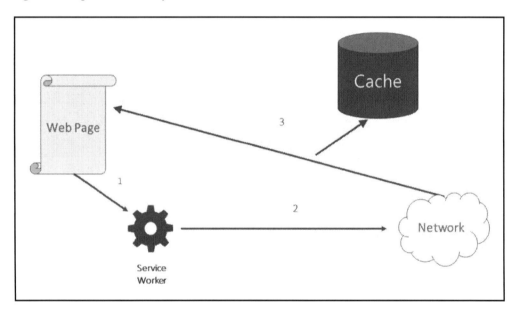

The `clone` method creates a deep copy of the response, allowing you to do something else with the response. The most common use of the `clone` method is to create a copy so that one can be cached and the other returned to the client, as shown in the following code:

```
self.addEventListener('fetch', function (event) {
    event.respondWith(
        caches.open(cacheName).then(cache =>{
            return cache.match(event.request).then(function (response)
```

```
                {
                    return response || fetch(event.request).then(
                        function (response) {
                            caches.open(cacheName).then(
                                cache =>{
                                    cache.put(event.request,
                                    response.clone());
                                });
                            return response;
                        });
                });
            })
        );
    });
```

Stale while revalidating

The next phase of our basic network-caching strategy is to return a previously cached version to the client while making a network request for the latest version.

This strategy is very helpful when you need to return a response quickly, but the freshness of the data is not the biggest requirement. For example, a podcast episode does not change its details much, if at all. Returning a cached version of the page and its images would not mean that the user is missing out on fresh data. The following diagram shows the interactions involved in this process:

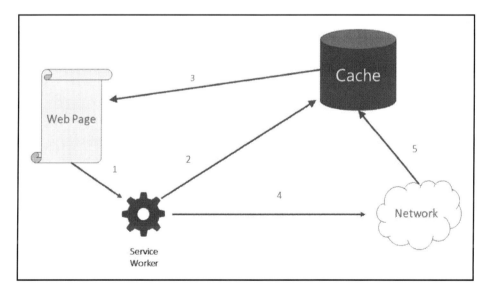

Service Worker Caching Patterns

But maybe you want to make sure that the user has the latest content. You can return the cached response instantly, while making a new request to the network and caching that response. This will replace any previously cached data for the next time the page is requested, as shown in the following code:

```
self.addEventListener('fetch', event => {
    event.respondWith(
caches.open(dynamicCacheName).then(cache =>{
        return cache.match(event.request).then(function
        (response) {
            var fetchPromise = fetch(event.request)
            .then(function (networkResponse) {
             cache.put(event.request,
             networkResponse.clone());
             return networkResponse;
              });
             return response || fetchPromise;
            })
        })
    );
});
```

On push notification

User activity and network requests are not the only times you can cache a network resource:

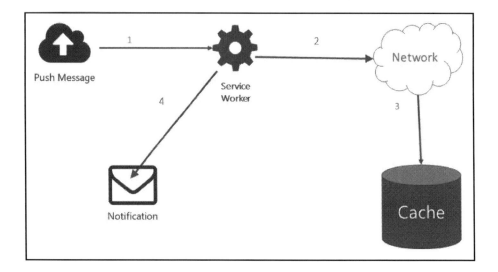

You can also use a push message to initiate caching responses, as shown in the following code:

```
//On push message
function parsePushMessage(message){
    //parse the message
    If(message.update){
    //notify user of background update process here
     caches.open(preCacheName).then(cache =>{
         return cache.addAll(message.urls);
     });
  }
}

self.addEventListener('push', event => {
   parsePushMessage(event.data);
});
```

In this strategy, the push event handler determines the type of message action. If it is a notice to update the application, it initiates the process. The preceding code example is a bit of an oversimplification, but it shows the important parts.

The push message body should have some sort of property indicating the action that should be taken. In this case, it triggers an update workflow. Included in the message is a property, urls, which is an array of all the URLs that should be updated or cached.

The cache.addAll method makes the code simple, since it will perform all the fetch requests and cache the responses for you.

You should always notify the user that a push notification has been received and the application is being updated. In this situation, you may also want to prompt the user to reload the app if they are currently using it. You can check to see whether there are any active clients while you are updating the cache, and notify them of the updating process. You will learn more about push notifications in a future chapter.

On background sync

A more advanced caching pattern would be to use the Background Sync API. We'll talk about this in more detail in a later chapter.

Service Worker Caching Patterns

The core idea is to wrap all of your network request in a background sync wrapper. Here, you would create a request tag and cue it up to be processed as soon as the network is available.

This adds a new layer of complexity to using the service worker fetch, but can be very valuable if you need to maintain an asynchronous dataset with the server.

If you are connected to the network, any request passed to the Background Sync API will immediately be executed as normal. If you are not connected, it's added to a queue and executed when the device regains connectivity. The following image shows the interactions involved in this process:

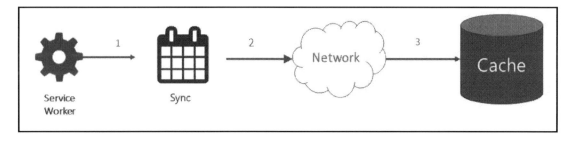

At that point, a `sync` event triggers, which could be used to initiate a cache update, as shown in the following code:

```
self.addEventListener('sync', function(event) {
  if (event.id === 'update-podcast-XYZ') {
    event.waitUntil(
      caches.open(DYNAMIC_CACHE_NAME).then(function(cache) {
        return cache.add("podcast/xyz/");
      })
    );
  }
});
```

In this example, a `background sync` tag has been created for a specific podcast. If that tag triggers the `sync` event, the corresponding podcast details page is added to the dynamic cache.

Cache only

When a network resource is precached, you can choose to implement a policy of only using a cached version of the asset. This is known as the cache-only strategy.

When you know a resource can be safely cached long term, you can reduce more overhead in your application by eliminating unnecessary network chatter.

Retrieving these resources from the cache also means that the application can load faster and, of course, load offline. Just make sure they don't become too stale.

Here, any request for a network resource will be retrieved only from the cache and no network response will be used. This can be very valuable for long-term static resources, such as application core JavaScript and CSS files. You could also apply it to images such as your site's logo and font files.

If you are employing the cache-only strategy, I advise having a routine automatically triggered when your service worker is executed. This routine should periodically check for new response versions to ensure that you have the most up-to-date data.

Also, make sure that these resources are static or they could potentially break your application. If you choose to make them static, I advise adding these resources to a service worker version change before deploying them to your server. The following image shows the the interactions involved in this process:

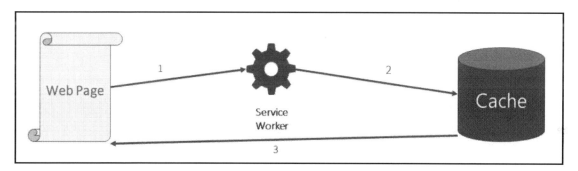

The cache-only strategy pairs well with either of the precache strategies discussed earlier in the chapter. Precaching cache-only resources should ensure that they are available from the cache, as shown in the following code:

```
self.addEventListener('fetch', event => {
  // If a match isn't found in the cache, the response
  // will look like a connection error
  event.respondWith(caches.match(event.request));
});
```

In this code example, the `fetch` event handler only responds with a match from the cache. If one does not exist, the client will receive a `not found` (404 status code) response.

Network only

The complete opposite of cache-only is to only request a resource from the network. In this scenario, you will identify network resources that should always be requested from the server.

The strategy should be employed on data that changes very frequently. For example, a stock ticker application would want to make sure that the request to update stock prices is made immediately and not from a local cache. Stale data in this scenario can cost you a fortune. The following image shows the interactions involved in this process:

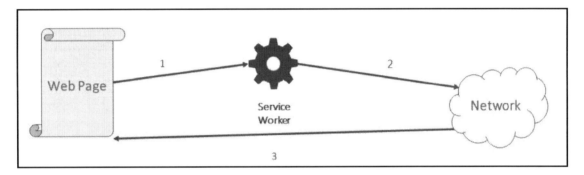

You should identify the nature of any file or network resources you might need to access, and ensure that the data is constantly being updated. You can intercept these requests and apply the proper strategy based on routes and patterns. To do so, I would advise you to have some unique identifier in these assets' URLs, as shown in the following code example:

```
self.addEventListener('fetch', event => {
  event.respondWith(fetch(event.request));
  // or simply don't call event.respondWith, which
  // will result in default browser behaviour
});
```

Cache falling back to network

The most common pattern I see employed in service workers is the cache falling back to the network. It's very popular because checking for an asset's presence in your cache means that it can return immediately. If it does not, you still have the network fallback retrieving it as fast as possible.

Any asset that is not precached or previously cached from the same pattern would be accessible, assuming you are online. The following image shows the interactions involved:

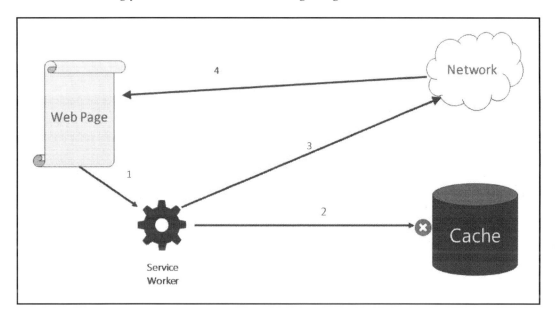

I say that this is probably the most common pattern used because any asset that is not precached could comfortably fit into this pattern. The podcast application uses this pattern for all the individual podcast and episode pages. This makes them accessible as soon as possible, but we don't want to precache every single file and image ahead of time, only on-demand.

The following is an example of this pattern being executed:

```
self.addEventListener('fetch', event => {
  event.respondWith(
    caches.match(event.request).then(function(response) {
      return response || fetch(event.request);
    })
  );
});
```

It seems pointless to execute this pattern without caching the network response. The following code shows how I recommend you apply this strategy; I call it "cache falling back to the network", caching the result:

```
self.addEventListener('fetch', event =>{
        caches.match(event.request).then(
```

Service Worker Caching Patterns

```
            function (response) {
                return response || fetch(event.request).then(
                    function (response) {
                        caches.open(dynamicCacheName).then(
                            cache =>{
                                cache.put(event.request, response.clone());
                            });
                        return response;
                    }
                )
            })
        });
```

This is the more complete version of this pattern. Now, the next time the resource is requested, it will come from the cache. But if it was not previously cached, it can be retrieved from the network.

Cache and network race

Another interesting caching pattern, of the variation of the cache falling back to the network pattern, is a cache and network race pattern. This is where you will simultaneously request the resource from the cache and the network. The fastest response wins. While the cache should be the winner, it may not always win. This pattern also gives you the opportunity to retrieve the network version a little bit faster if there is no cached version. The following image shows the interactions involved in this process:

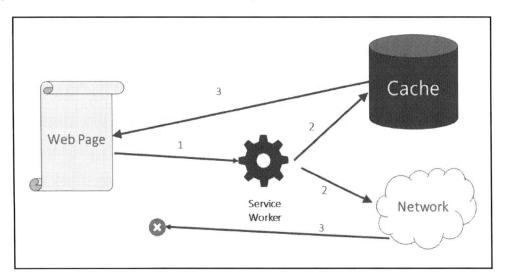

The drawback to this pattern is that you will always make a network request even if it's not needed. This will increase your network traffic. But you could also look at it as a way to ensure you've got at least some of the freshest content cached every single time. It can also be viewed as a variation of the stale while revalidating strategy. The following code shows how to implement the cache and network race pattern:

```
self.addEventListener('fetch', event =>{
        promiseAny([
            caches.match(event.request),
            fetch(event.request)
        ])
});

// Promise.race is no good to us because it rejects if
// a promise rejects before fulfilling. Let's make a proper
// race function:
function promiseAny(promises) {
    return new Promise((resolve, reject) => {
// make sure promises are all
        promises = promises.map(p => Promise.resolve(p));
// resolve this promise as soon as one resolves
        promises.forEach(p => p.then(resolve));
// reject if all promises reject
        promises.reduce((a, b) => a.catch(() => b))
            .catch(() => reject(Error("All failed")));
    });
};
```

Note that there is a custom `promiseAny` function. This is because of a limitation of the `Promise.race` method. When a `Promise.race` method is used and any of the supplied promises throws an exception, the entire process fails.

This pattern depends on at least one promise resolving a response. The `promiseAny` function is a modification to the `Promise.race` method, except it will not fail if a supplied promise fails. It assumes that one of the promises will succeed and return the winner.

Network falling back to cache

If you have a time-sensitive network resource that you always want to hit the network, you should also consider using the network falling back to cache strategy. Here, you will always try to access the network, but if the network is inaccessible, then you have the built-in option to retrieve the most recently cached version of the file.

Service Worker Caching Patterns

If it is critical that the resource is fresh, I advise that you visually alert the customer of the time that is associated with that response. The following image shows the interactions involved in this process:

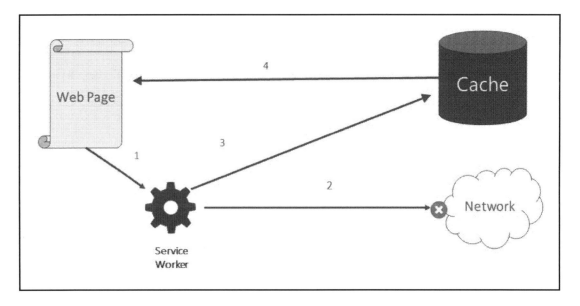

This pattern can also be to provide a fallback for any asset that is inaccessible over the network, which we will see in the next pattern. The following code shows how to implement the network falling back to cache pattern:

```
self.addEventListener('fetch', event => {
    event.respondWidth(
        fetch(event.request).catch(function () {
            return caches.match(event.request);
        })
    );
});
```

Generic fallback

The next step from the network falling back to the cache is to have a generic fallback for all requests. You should use this when no response was available either in the cache or from the network.

You can see this pattern employed across the Podstr application for podcast episodes and their associated images.

Chapter 7

The trick here is to precache a fallback response for these particular network assets. I also advise that you apply this strategy by matching route variations and not individual URLs.

In the Podstr podcast application, there are generic fallbacks for the podcast pages, episode pages, and podcast logos. I identified each of these as dynamic resources that cannot be precached.

Typically, if you can't access the resource, that means that it is not found or the device is offline. I think it's important that you have some logic in place to determine the difference. If the application is offline, you want to visually indicate that somehow, but if the resource is truly not found, you may want to return a slightly different response.

I think Flipkart does a fantastic job of this. When the application is offline, they greyscale the entire UI. This is a very clear indication to the end user that the device is offline, which means that they may not necessarily be able to access the information, and that any information they receive may not be current. The following screenshot shows an example of this greyscaling:

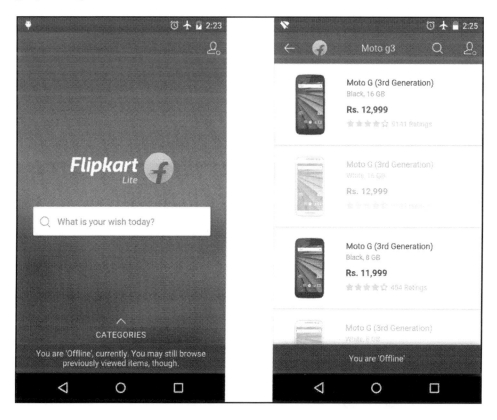

Service Worker Caching Patterns

If you receive an error 404 message, then you can return a Not Found page and use that to your advantage as well. The following image shows the interactions involved in this pattern:

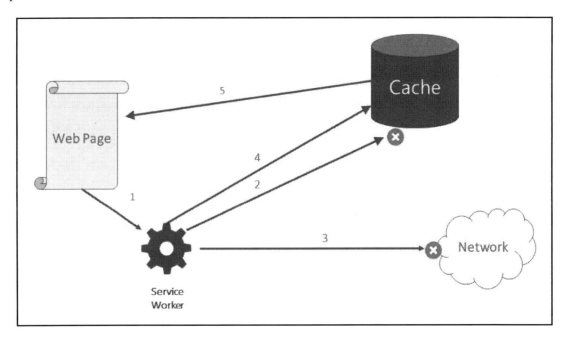

Maybe you will choose to direct them to a related resource, or provide a sitemap, as shown in the following code:

```
self.addEventListener('fetch', event =>{
    event.respondWidth(
        caches.match(event.request).then(response => {
            // Fall back to network
            return response || fetch(event.request);
        }).catch(function () {    // If both fail, show a generic
          fallback:
            return caches.match("fallback/").then(function(response){
                return response;
            });
            // However, in reality you'd have many different
            // fallbacks, depending on URL & headers.
            // Eg, a fallback images for podcast logos.
        })
    );
});
```

[200]

Service worker templating

A concept you should embrace about service workers is that they can act like a web server in the browser. Traditionally, web servers have used runtime rendering platforms, such as ASP.NET, PHP, Ruby on Rails, and content management systems such as WordPress, Drupal, and Joomla!. These systems are rendering engines more than anything else. You can perform HTML rendering inside of a service worker.

Single-page applications have become very popular this decade. They effectively take ownership of this rendering process from the server. Today, it is popular to preload application templates, whether you're using mustache, handlebars, or larger frameworks such as Angular and React. All of these are essentially just HTML rendering systems. The difference between the server side and the client side is where the rendering takes place. Because you can intercept network requests in a service worker, the rendering process can be moved from the client UI or the server to the service worker.

In this pattern, you will most likely precache the page or component templates ahead of time and make network requests to an API to return data, typically formatted in JSON. When you retrieve the new JSON, you will then render the markup in the service worker and return the HTML to the client. The following image shows the interactions involved in this pattern:

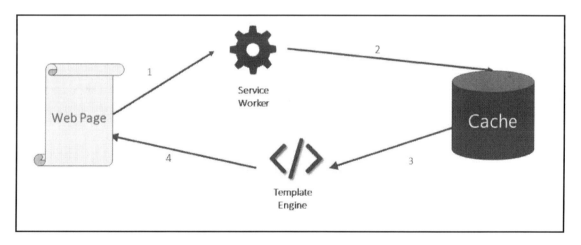

My personal technique is to use mustache because it is simple and fast. The overall technique is a little bit advanced, but once you have a working pattern, I think you'll see that it's easier to implement.

Service Worker Caching Patterns

In this example, the `fetch` event handler looks for any request to the podcast episode routes. When an episode request is made, it is intercepted and a new custom request created. Instead of requesting the HTML from the server, the service worker will create a request to an API to retrieve the JSON.

In theory, the request for the JSON should be smaller than a request for the HTML. The smaller packet should be loaded slightly faster. The real question is can the small request be retrieved and rendered faster than a request for prerendered HTML? This is an answer I cannot give you. It will require some experimentation with your application's pages and API to determine which one is the best solution.

For small pieces of data, such as the episode page, chances are that the service worker rendering will be slightly slower. But if your page contains a lot of information that is repeatable—such as the kind of information that you often see in line-of-business applications—this technique could improve your overall performance. The following code shows how you can implement this pattern:

```
self.addEventListener('fetch', event => {
    event.respondWidth(
        Promise.all([
            caches.match("/product-template.html").then(
                response => {
                    return response.text();
                }),
            caches.match("api/products/35.json").then(
                response => {
                    return response.json();
                })
        ]).then(function (responses) {
            var template = responses[0];
            var data = responses[1];
            return new Response(Mustache.render(template, data), {
                headers: {
                    "Content-Type": "text/html"
                }
            });
        })
    );
});
```

Once the API request returns the service worker logic, it then loads the content template and renders it to HTML. This HTML is then returned to the client in a custom `response` object.

An even more advanced way to use the strategy is to use it in concert with caching a response. This way, you render the response once, cache it, and check to see whether it's cached the next time.

This pattern may not be optimal for every scenario, but it should be considered if you have pages with large, repeating datasets and wish to take advantage of any speed gains.

The scenario I believe this pattern offers the most benefit for is dynamically rendered markup where data changes frequently. Progressive web apps, such as the Podstr application, may not realize performance gains, but a line-of-business application can.

Summary

These strategies should serve as your service worker fetching and caching workflow. The reason there are so many strategies is that there are many scenarios for application assets. How you apply these strategies is up to you, and they may require some experimentation to determine the best strategy for each asset type.

These strategies may not be the exact patterns you need for your application, but they will serve as the foundation for all your caching needs. You can use these as starting points that you can extend, mix, and match to create the best strategies for your application.

8
Applying Advanced Service Worker Cache Strategies

It's time to take our progressive web app capabilities up a notch. So far, you have learned how to add to the home screen experience, core service worker concepts, and how to make your site secure. In this chapter, we will dive into advanced service worker concepts and a brand new progressive web app, PWA tickets.

The following topics will be covered in this chapter:

- What is PWA tickets?
- How to run a local, mock API server
- PWA application architecture
- Importing utility libraries to a service worker
- A service worker response manager
- Advanced caching strategies and techniques
- Caching invalidation techniques

What is PWA tickets?

The PWA tickets application is an example hosted service application designed to resemble an online ticket purchasing solution. While there are many aspects of this application I could have focused on, this book focuses on the consumer app.

Applying Advanced Service Worker Cache Strategies

The following screenshot is the PWA ticket home page, which displays a list of cards for upcoming events that the customer can purchase tickets for. Card refers to the UI metaphor that is used to style the block representing items in a list:

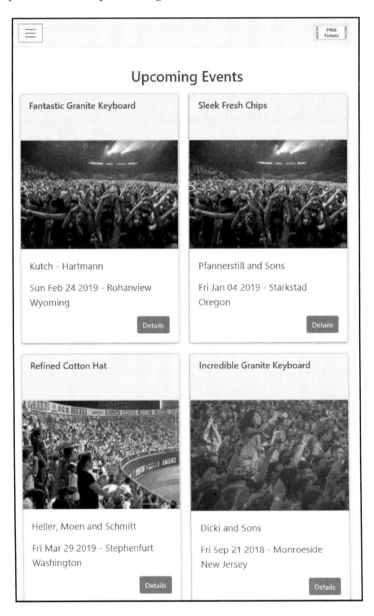

A real ticket service application would be a suite of apps including an administrative application and an app for ushers to validate tickets. For this book, I will focus on the consumer client experience.

The consumer version of the application features user login, profile management, access to a list of future events, the ability to buy tickets, and the user's ticket purchase history.

The application itself consists of a live API and static web pages, but the real area of focus for this chapter is some of the advanced service worker concepts.

The service worker evaluates each `fetch` request and processes it differently. The service worker pre-caches critical assets, but also defines custom rules for different routes.

Another new advanced concept is the idea of cache invalidation. This is where you define a rule that applies to cached responses and determines if a network request should be made and the cache invalidated. This is an important concept to understand because it gives you full control over your applications, caching rules and allows you to manage how much is stored in the cache.

The PWA tickets application will demonstrate some new concepts and tactics, which will help you create professional progressive web apps, such as the following:

- Service worker templating
- Cache invalidation
- Triggering different cache strategies based on a requested URL
- Using `importScripts`

Reviewing the PWA ticket application

Let's take look at the different sections that our application will consist of. There are eight main page areas of the application:

- Home
- User Profile
- Events
- Tickets
- Cart
- Contact
- Configure
- Login

Applying Advanced Service Worker Cache Strategies

Tickets and events both consist of two pages: one for a list and another for an item detail. The application also features our first pages, which make POST requests to an API rather than just a GET request. This introduces a new `fetch` method that our service worker must handle correctly

The homepage lists 10 future events, followed by a list of user purchased tickets. Each item utilizes a card, which is styled using the bootstrap card classes. Each ticket card also has a button to show the item's details.

The user profile page list the user's contact information and some of their most recently purchased tickets. It also features a button to update the user profile. This will toggle the view from read-only to edit mode.

The application's navigation consists of **Events**, **Tickets**, **Profile**, **Logout**, and a **Search** field:

A user can enter a search term and whatever page they are on will automatically update to show any matching events without making a round trip to load a new page. It does this by making an AJAX call and rendering the results in the browser and service worker.

The application's API is not representative of a production quality search feature, but serves our purpose. It will match any event that contains the phrase entered in the search box.

The events page will list all future events that are available in the system. Again, each event is a card with a button to view the event's details. The event's details page shows a little more information and includes a list of tickets that are available to purchase:

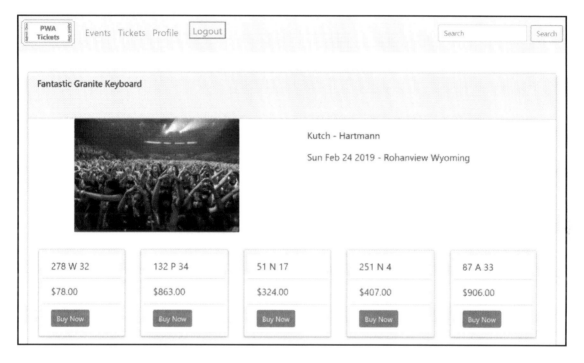

A true ticket service app would offer a more sophisticated way to find tickets, but I wanted to keep this simple for demonstration purposes.

When a user buys a ticket, they must confirm the purchase and then it is added to their profile

Applying Advanced Service Worker Cache Strategies

Selecting the **tickets** link in the **Now** bar takes the user to a list of their purchased tickets. From here, they can view the details of any ticket, which includes a QR code. The QR code is meant to simulate what modern E-ticket solutions use for ushers and gate agents to scan when you enter a venue or when you need to find your seat:

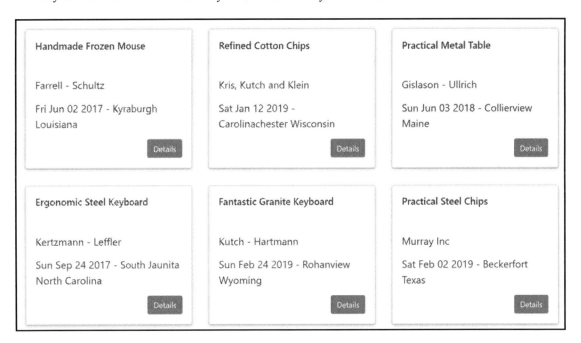

This is where the usher's app would come into play. They could use their phone to scan the QR code to confirm the ticket and allow the customer into the venue.

There is also a contact page where a user could submit a message to the system administrators. It is mostly used to demonstrate how to handle post messages using fetch and the service worker.

Finally, the entire application requires a user to be authenticated. Each page does a quick verification if the user is logged in, and if not, loads the login page:

The user logs in by entering a username and password. The credentials are sent to the API for verification. The API returns the user's profile, which simulates an authentication token. The authentication token is persisted and `IndexedDB` (using `localForage`), and verified before each page load.

The user does not yet have a profile they can select. They can use the create new profile link and add themselves to the system.

The following function is the application's API call to log a user into the application:

```
login: function (credentials) {
    return fetch(api +
        "users/?userName=" +
        credentials.username +
        "password=" + credentials.password)
        .then(function (response) {

        if (response.ok) {
            return response.json()
            .then(function (token) {
            if (token.length > 0) {
                return saveAuthToken(token[0]);
            }
        });
```

```
            } else {
              throw "user tickets fetch failed";
            }
        });
}
```

Notice that the username and password are passed to the API using the `queryString`. I would not do this normally, but I needed a way to work with json-server and it did not seem to offer a way to match without a custom function using a POST.

You would not want to do this in production because it exposes credentials. When posting the credentials as part of the request body, they are shielded behind HTTPS.

The PWA ticket application includes a minimal feature set, which I feel will help demonstrate the concepts covered in the last three chapters. This introduction to how the application works does not quite cover everything. I invite you to clone the source code (`https://github.com/docluv/pwa-ticket`) and run it locally.

Using the JSON server for an API

When you build modern applications, the frontend almost always communicates with an API to interact with a date source. The API is the gateway to the backend application and can be consumed by any client application, such as a Progressive Web App.

Developing against an API can be rather tricky when you don't want to develop the entire API first. In the podcast application, we simply loaded a pre-rendered JSON to simulate an API. The podcast application only made a GET request and did not do any post requests or attempts to update the underlying data model.

The PWA ticket application does make post requests and attempts to update the underlying data model, but rather than building out an entire infrastructure for this, I found a nice solution: json-server (`https://github.com/typicode/json-server`). This is a node module that works much like the http-server we used for the previous applications.

The real advantage of json-server is its built-in ability to create a fully functioning API based on a JSON data model. You must install the module like any other node module: by using `npm install` and including a reference to it in your `packages.json` file.

Before you execute the server, you must create a data source. This is just another JSON file. Rather than manually creating the data and the data model, I chose to write a script that uses the faker module (https://github.com/marak/Faker.js/). This can also be installed using the standard NPM tasks.

faker is a pretty cool node module that allows you to dynamically generate massive amounts of fake data for you to build your application around. This is one of the more troubling aspects of front and web development in my opinion, because you need large amounts of data to validate your application logic. However, that takes a long time to create. Faker eliminates this problem.

Combining json-server and faker together allows you to create a very complex and deep API and data source. You can emulate just about every aspect of your potential API and backend with these two modules.

As I created the PWA ticket application, I modified the data model numerous times trying to get things just right. Rather than hand coding all of the data, I was able to write a script to rebuild the database from scratch.

The project source repository includes a top-level folder called `utils`. In this folder, there are a couple of scripts: one to generate fake data and another to render the pages. The fake data script utilizes a combination of faker and some fixed data sources.

Faker has the capability to generate data of all kinds, including images. However, I found the images that it generates and uses to be a slow, random image generation service. Rather than rely on those images, I chose to fix a small set of 8 venue images and 8 headshot images. The 16 images are stored under the website's `img` folder.

You will also notice a method to generate QR codes. This is also done with a pair of node modules: one to generate a QR code image and another to save that image to disk.

A QR code is generated for each ticket and represents the ticket's unique identifier. Each barcode image that is generated is saved to the website in the barcodes folder. Each barcode image is a `.gif` file and has the extension appended to its name.

While these node modules are critical to running the PWA ticket application, they are not directly related to service workers and progressive web apps. I do want to take a little time to explain how they work so that you can use the source code locally.

Making a database and the API

The JSON server allows you to host a local REST API by supporting basic CRUD operations without writing any code. The node module works by reading a source file with a complete JSON object. The PWA ticket app relies on a JSON data structure, which is outlined here:

```
{
    tickets: [],
    users: [],
    futureEvents: [],
    pastEvents: [],
    contact: []
}
```

You can configure the data source to include methods to return data based on supplied parameters. I chose not to do this in order to keep things simple. Hence, this explains the use of both the `futureEvents` and `pastEvents` arrays instead of creating these lists on demand.

To execute `json-server`, run the command-line utility with the `--watch` switch. The watch switch causes `json-server` to update when the source data file updates:

```
json-server --watch db.json
```

The PWA ticket source code has the `db.json` data source file in the root folder. The server creates RESTful end points that map to the names of the top-level objects. It also doubles as a static file server. You just need to watch out for overlapping paths between the objects in the data file and pages.

I ran into a scenario where I duplicated routes in the same site using `json-server` while creating this demonstration application. This forced me to run two instances of the web server: one for the API and one for the website.

For localhost-based servers, you can specify different port numbers to run multiple local servers. You can define the port number by adding the `-port` switch to the command-line interface:

```
json-server --watch db.json -port 15501
```

I ran into some frustration trying to launch a static web server-only instance, so I chose to launch the API using `json-server` and the static website using `http-server`.

You can run both local web servers from a command line, one console instance each, since they are running a server:

```
>npm run api-server
>npm run web-server
```

Another advantage of running the API server on a different port is that it helps emulate cross-domain access, or CORS.

CORS stands for **cross origin resource sharing** and was created to allow browsers to more securely request resources on external domains. It relies on the browser using extra headers to manage access to the external resource, typically via AJAX.

CORS-specific headers are added by the server to tell the browser which domains are allowed to access the resource.

To retrieve the data, you can load a URI that corresponds to the API server and the name of the object:

```
http://localhost:15501/users/
```

This example URL returns an array of user objects:

```
[
  {
    "id": "891ad435-41f3-4b83-929b-18d8870a53a4",
    "firstName": "Catharine",
    "lastName": "Cormier",
    "mugshot": "avtar-2.jpg",
    "userName": "Clay.Parker",
    "password": "93gQtXaB0Tc3JM5",
    "streetAddress": "401 Kassulke Square",
    "city": "Cronintown",
    "state": "Vermont",
    "zipCode": "09904-5827",
    "email": "Bradly_Fahey56@gmail.com",
    "phoneNumber": "400.748.9656 x0600",
    "tickets": [...]
  }, {...}
]
```

There are more advanced features available with json-server, but this should be enough for you to understand how to run the site locally.

Using faker

Before you can host the API using json-server, you need the source data file. This is where the faker module is helpful. Creating enough data for a realistic test environment has always been one of my top challenges. Today, it seems like there are libraries or tools like faker available for most platforms.

Since I use Node.js for the majority of my projects, faker stands out as a powerful tool. It just requires a script to generate the data. This script is in the /utils folder, generate-fake-data.js:

This script helped me not only generate the file data set, but also allowed me to continually modify the source data as the overall model evolved.

This script generates a random number of users, events, and tickets, and maps them randomly together to create a complete database.

I won't go into all of the details of possible data types available from faker. This is how the script generates a new user:

```
let user = {
    "id": faker.random.uuid(),
```

```
        "firstName": faker.name.firstName(),
        "lastName": faker.name.lastName(),
        "mugshot": mugshots[mugshot],
        "userName": faker.internet.userName(),
        "password": faker.internet.password(),
        "streetAddress": faker.address.streetAddress(),
        "city": faker.address.city(),
        "state": faker.address.state(),
        "zipCode": faker.address.zipCode(),
        "email": faker.internet.email(),
        "phoneNumber": faker.phone.phoneNumber()
    }
```

The `faker` object has different top-level data types with various methods to generate properly formatted, random data.

The data values generated by faker are in the correct or expected format. I love some of the text values it generates. I encourage you to read through some of them because they create some rather humorous values and combinations! For example, *Generic Plastic Cheese*.

The script is self-contained and will create a fresh database each time it runs. Plus, when you launch json-server using the `-watch` switch, the API will automatically update for the new data.

The next aspect of the database remains: QR codes!

Generating QR codes

Modern ticketing solutions are more about barcodes and QR codes than the physical ticket. To create a life-like ticket application, I needed to create custom QR codes for each ticket. Again, a pair of node modules made this very straightforward: `qr-encode` (http://cryptocoinjs.com/modules/misc/qr-encode/) and `ba64` (https://www.npmjs.com/package/ba64).

qr-encode converts strings into one of a variety of QR code options. The following code shows you how to use the `qr` method to generate `dataURI`:

```
let dataURI = qr(id, {
    type: 6,
    size: 6,
    level: 'Q'
});
```

Applying Advanced Service Worker Cache Strategies

The `qr` method returns a `base64` encoded data buffer. You still need to convert this into a physical file. This is where `ba64` helps. It converts the `base64` encoded buffer into a file:

```
ba64.writeImageSync(qrCodePath + "/" + id, dataURI);
```

The `qrCodePath` points the local path to the `public/qrcodes` folder. The script will delete the existing QR image file and create the new QR codes as each ticket is generate:

The QR code encodes the ticket's unique identifier, which is a GUID generated by faker. This ensures that each ticket can be identified by scanning the QR code.

Now that the data is generated, and we have a way to serve both the API and website, we just need one more thing: the website.

Rendering the website

The 2048 and Podstr apps were based on static websites. While the Podstr app used some dynamically rendered pages, most of it was pre-rendered. It also had a script to create the HTML pages, but this was not as integral to the demonstration as the PWA ticket application.

The PWA ticket application has a script to render the core pages by combining an app shell and the individual pages markup for the actual page. This is handy because it allows you to update the app shell and the pages independently as well as customize the rendering script for different environments.

For example, before deploying to production, you will want to bundle and minify some style sheets and scripts. As you will see in the next chapter, you will also want to reduce the assets, such as styles using tooling.

The source markup files are in the site's HTML folders, `/public/html` and `/public/html/pages`, respectively. The rendering script loops over these files and loads a corresponding data file defining page-specific configuration data:

```
{
    "name": "events",
    "slug": "events",
    "scripts": ["js/app/pages/events.js"],
    "css": []
}
```

The PWA ticket application has some simple configuration objects. The properties are used to define components in each page, like the route or folder to save the final rendered file to. These properties are used in the rendering pipeline to produce the final page based on a common template.

The script is run from the command line:

```
>node render-public
```

The console will log each page as it is rendered.

The PWA ticket application is more advanced than the Podstr app because most of the pages are rendered on the client, not as a full static website. The reason the ticket application relies on client-side rendering is due to each page being tied to the user's profile and ticket purchase.

This chapter will explore these scenarios and how the service worker can enhance the overall experience.

The PWA ticket rendering architecture and logic

We introduced the concept of an app shell earlier in this book. As a quick recap, this is where the application uses a common markup file to manage the common HEAD and layout features. This shell is then combined with individual pages to compose each page.

The concept has a mass adoption due to the recent rise of single page applications. Progressive web apps can benefit from this concept, but do not need to rely on rendering the markup in the UI thread.

Instead, the markup can be rendered in the service worker. The technique is similar: it uses `Mustache`, a JavaScript template library, to merge the data into the markup template. The rendered page markup is returned to the client. I will review the code for this later in this chapter.

This technique is the practical application of the final caching strategy, *Service Worker Templating*, which was discussed in the `Chapter 7`, *Service Worker Caching Patterns*.

The PWA ticket JavaScript architecture

Similar to the Podstr application, the PWA ticket app utilizes a combination of third-party libraries and application-specific JavaScript.

The following screenshot shows how the JavaScript files are organized in the source code:

The custom service worker logic or workflow utilizes different libraries to render content on the client. The two third-party libraries are `localForage` for `IndexedDB` interactions and `Mustache` to render markup.

`localForage` (https://localforage.github.io/localForage/) is another `IndexedDB` wrapper. It provides a simple interface that mimics `localStorage`. The main difference is that `localForage` supports promises, making it asynchronous.

There are three `polyfils`, and these are `Object.assign`, `Promise`, and `Fetch`.

Each page uses a few application-specific libraries: `api` and `push-mgr`, and common application modules. Each page has a page-specific script to drive the user experience.

The application module handles the common UI components, which are hamburger menu toggle, logout, search, and authentication validation. It also registers the service worker and manages the push notifications at a high level.

Because the common user interface is simple, I combined these components in single script to keep things simpler to manage. Notice that there is no reference to jQuery or more complex frameworks to drive the UI. The entire app script is roughly 200 lines of nicely spaced code. Individual page scripts are much shorter, so there is not a lot of application-specific code.

The `api.js` file is a module that contains methods to interact with the application's API. Because the application is small, I placed all the methods in a single module. For a more complex application, you would want to refactor to separate modules to make the code easier to maintain:

```
var pwaTicketAPI = (function () {

    var api = "http://localhost:15501/",
        authToken = "auth-token";

    function saveAuthToken(token) {

        return localforage.setItem(authToken, token)
            .then(function () {
                return token;
            });
    }
```

Applying Advanced Service Worker Cache Strategies

```
        return {
          //API wrapper methods go here
        };

})();
```

This method creates a global variable, `pwaTicketAPI`, which can be accessed by individual page controller modules to interact with the API.

Each method wraps a fetch call to an API endpoint:

```
    getUser: function (userId) {

        return fetch(api + "users/" + userId)
            .then(function (response) {

                if (response.ok) {
                    return response.json();
                } else {

                    throw "user tickets fetch failed";
                }
            });
    },
```

Most of the API methods make GET requests, but a few make POST requests to update or create new records:

```
    updateUser: function (user) {

        return fetch({
            "method": "POST",
            "Content-Type": "application/json",
            "body": JSON.stringify(user),
            "url": api + "users/"
        });
    },
```

Each page controller uses an **Immediately Invoked Function Expression (IIFE)** to isolate the page logic from the global scope:

```
    (function () {

    //no need to render if service workers are supported
    //unless the service worker is not in control of the page yet.
    //test if the loader element exists. If so then fetch the data to //render
    if (_d.qs(".loader")) {
            pwaTicketAPI.loadTemplate("templates/event.html")
```

```
            .then(function (template) {
              if (template) {
                pwaTicketAPI.getEvent(pwaTickets.getParameterByName("id"))
                  .then(function (event) {

              var target = _d.qs(".content-target");

              target.innerHTML = Mustache.render(template, event);
                });
              }
            })
            .catch(function (err) {
                console.log(err);
            });
      }
    })();
```

Each of the pages follows a common pattern of retrieving data from the API and rendering markup to build the page. Most pages have a placeholder with a spinning disc. This is replaced when the markup is rendered:

```
<div class="loader"></div>
```

The main app-shell has a main element with the `content-target` class. This class name is used as a reference to select the element and set the inner HTML with the dynamically rendered text:

```
<main class="page-content content-target">
    <%template%>
</main>
```

You should have noticed how I used `_d.qs()` to select the target element. This is a simple utility object that I created to eliminate the need to write `document.querySelector()` and the related selector methods. I don't know about you, but I get tired of typing that out everywhere and it's sort of long for the simplicity of jQuery's selector syntax:

```
var _d = {
    qs: function (s) {
        return document.querySelector(s);
    },
    qsa: function (s) {
        return document.querySelectorAll(s);
    },
    gei: function (s) {
        return document.getElementById(s);
    },
```

```
    gen: function (s) {
        return document.getElementsByName(s);
    }
};
```

This utility provides a simple shorthand to select elements, but without the overhead of jQuery.

The PWA ticket service worker architecture

The 2048 and Podstr apps have relied on a single script. The PWA ticket app uses more complex techniques like importing libraries to drive the logic.

Service workers can load external scripts using the `importScripts` method. This function is available in the global scope and accepts an array of URLs. These are additional scripts and work much like the node.js `require` system:

```
self.importScripts("js/libs/localforage.min.js",
    "js/app/libs/api.js",
    "sw/response-mgr.js",
    "sw/push-mgr.js",
    "sw/invalidation-mgr.js",
    "sw/date-mgr.js"
);
```

The first two scripts are also used in the client code. `localForage` is an `IndexedDB` wrapper and the API script manages access to the API and authentication token. The `Mustache` library file is imported in the `ResponseManager` module and I will cover how it is used later.

The remaining scripts are common service worker libraries to help with caching strategies, such as cache invalidation and push management. Each service worker library contains a JavaScript class with methods to manage an aspect of the cache strategy and life cycle.

Importing scripts is a great way to refactor your service worker logic into smaller units that can be reused and easier to maintain. I have reviewed several service workers that were over 10,000 lines of code. Any time you have a large code file, you tend to introduce unwanted maintenance issues.

The first problem large code files create is navigating the code. Even with modern development environments and nice keyboard shortcuts, it is very easy to get lost in the code. If you have ever wasted time looking for functions and coordinating variables, you know what this is like.

Another common problem is managing team access to the code. When you have two or more developers with their hands in a single file, this introduces too many opportunities for code merges. Code merging is one of my least favorite developer activities, especially when someone else wrote the other version.

The last problem I see when large files are created is no code reuse. When you refactor your code into smaller modules, not only are they focused on a single responsibility, the classes, modules, and so on, can be reused in other areas of the application or across different applications.

This is why I like importing scripts in service workers. The 2048 service worker was very simple and did not warrant this tactic. The Podstr app could use the `importScripts` capabilities, but I chose to save this till now. For a true production version of Podstr, I would have to refactor the code to import different scripts.

One drawback of importing scripts to your service worker is regarding updating the scripts. They are not updated when the service worker is updated. Unfortunately, I am still not clear on when these files will update from the server. I have read references saying that the imported scripts should following normal browser cache or cache-control invalidation, and others claimed that this is not working as expected.

There are some open discussions about this problem in the specification chats, but at this point, I think a true solution has not been adopted.

Either way, during development, this issue can be very frustrating. You need to update these files frequently as you update the code. The best way I have found to force these files to update is to manually unregister the service worker.

After unregistering the service worker, reloading the page registers the service worker again and it will execute the `importScripts` method.

Applying Advanced Service Worker Cache Strategies

There is one *bug* with this technique that I am currently seeing in the Chrome developer tools, and this is that each unregistered service worker leaves its footprint in the tools:

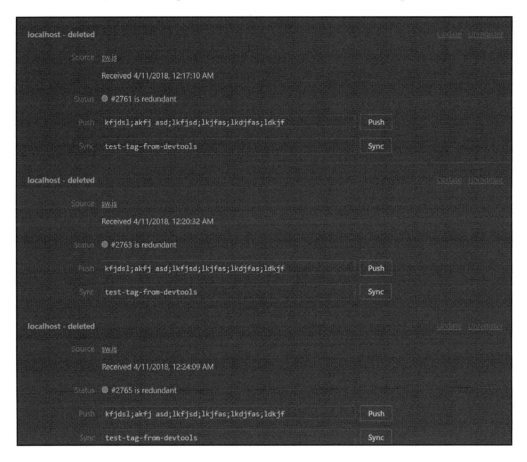

You can close the tools to reset the service worker panel. If you can tolerate scrolling down to the current, active service worker, you can avoid this step. I think this is just an issue with the developer tools UI not properly refreshing when a service worker is unregistered manually.

`importScripts` can also be used in any script that is imported by the service worker. In fact, the service worker's global scope is available to these scripts. Any variable declared in the service worker's global scope is available in the scripts. This also refers to any objects exported from the other imported scripts.

The node request system is similar to the `importScript` method. They both load external scripts to create methods and objects you can use in your script, which in this case is the service worker.

The ResponseManager

The `ResponseManager` contains common logic that correlates to some of the caching strategies covered in Chapter 7, *Service Worker Caching Patterns*. The `ResponseManager` class contains a condensed set of cache strategies and the corresponding methods for five caching strategies:

- Cache only
- Network only
- Cache falling back to network
- Cache falling back to network and caching response
- Cache falling back to network, render result, and cache

This is the `ResponseManager` class definition with method signatures:

```
class ResponseManager {
    fetchText(url) {...}
    fetchJSON(url) {...}
    fetchAndRenderResponseCache(options) {...}
    cacheFallingBackToNetwork(request, cacheName) {...}
    cacheFallingBackToNetworkCache(request, cacheName) {...}
    cacheOnly(request, cacheName) {...}
    networkOnly(request) {...}

}
```

The `cacheOnly` and `networkOnly` method do exactly what their name implies, returning a response either from just the cache or just the network:

```
cacheOnly(request, cacheName) {
    return caches.match(request);
}


networkOnly(request) {
    return fetch(request);
}
```

[227]

`cacheFallingBackToNetwork` checks if a response has been cached and if not, makes a network request to fetch the response. The response is not cached.

`cacheFallingBackToNetworkCache` repeats that logic, but caches the network response.

There are two additional helper methods, which are `fetchText` and `fetchJson`. These two methods specifically help the render result strategy to retrieve HTML templates and fetch JSON from the API.

`fetchText` is used to retrieve HTML files. `fetchJSON` makes an API call to get data. The `fetchAndRenderCache` method utilizes a supplied option parameter to execute the API call.

I covered the core concepts around these caching strategies in previous chapters. However, I do want to review the `fetchAndRenderCache` strategy because it was not covered in detail.

The goal of this strategy is to dynamically render a response in the service worker and cache the rendered result for the next request. This works great in applications like the PWA ticket app, which are highly dynamic.

While you could pre-render all the HTML pages on the server for any app, it may not be as efficient or cost-effective as rendering on demand. In the past, we have relied on run-time rendering systems such as ASP.NET, PHP, and so on, on the server and large single page app frameworks on the client.

It does not matter how you render the markup; the process is always the same. You merge data with a markup template. The engine you are using utilizes some sort of merge field syntax and replaces those fields with the matching values in the source data.

I prefer to use `Mustache` (http://mustache.github.io/) because the syntax is relatively simple:

```html
<div class="card ticket-card" id="{{id}}">
    <div class="card-header">
        <h5 class="card-title">{{event.title}}</h5>
    </div>
    <div class="row">
        <div class="col-md-6 text-center">
            <img class="card-img-top ticket-barcode"
            src="qrcodes/{{barcode}}"
             alt="{{id}}" />
        </div>
        <div class="col-md-6">
            <div class="card-body">
```

```
                <p class="card-text">{{event.venue}}</p>
                <p class="card-text">{{event.date}} - {{event.city}}
                {{event.state}}</p>
                <p class="card-text">{{id}}</p>
            </div>
            <ul class="list-group list-group-flush">
                <li class="list-group-item">Section {{section}}</li>
                <li class="list-group-item">Row {{row}}</li>
                <li class="list-group-item">Seat {{seat}}</li>
            </ul>
        </div>
    </div>
</div>
```

`Mustache` gets its name from the use of two curly braces to denote the merge field. The render method will merge a JSON object's properties with the matching field name. It can do single records or create a repeated list using the same template. It also supports basic `if...else` logic and a few other features.

The PWA ticket application uses `Mustache` templates for most pages, both for single records and lists. The application templates are stored in the `/templates` folder:

The JavaScript `Mustache` library can be used on the client or as a node module. I use it on both the server and client in many applications. It's great because you can make a single template and use it anywhere in the application and not worry about the rendering library being different.

If you are following any of the mainstream JavaScript frameworks, they all have mature server-side rendering components. I think this is an important trend because these frameworks have caused a lot of performance issues and made many sites impossible to index in search engines.

The rise of these server-side components should give these frameworks a longer lifespan and help them to produce better quality user experiences by moving their heavy logic to the server. This is also good since so many developers have invested many hours learning their proprietary syntaxes.

The `fetchAndRenderResponseCache` method executes service worker level run-time rendering. It accepts an options parameter that contains different properties which are required to drive the strategy.

I highly recommend pairing this method with a call to cache to see if the response is available. The `ResponseManager` has a `cacheOnly` method you can utilize:

```
responseManager.cacheOnly(request, runtimeCache)
  .then(response => {
    return response ||
            responseManager.fetchAndRenderResponseCache({...});
});
```

The method uses a JavaScript object as its only parameter. It should have the following properties:

```
{
    request: //the request that triggered the fetch
    pageURL: "url to core page html",
    template: "url to the data template",
    api: //a method to execute that makes the API call,
    cacheName: "cache name to save the rendered response"
}
```

These values are used to drive the logic and make it flexible enough to be reused by different pages and components in any application:

```
fetchAndRenderResponseCache(options) {
    return fetchText(options.pageURL)
        .then(pageHTML => {
            return fetchText(options.template)
                .then(template => {
                    return pageHTML.replace(/<%template%>/g, template);
                });
        })
}
```

The first step in the sequence is to retrieve the page's HTML. This is done by passing the `pageURL` value to the `fetchText` method. This should resolve the page's core HTML.

Next, the template is fetched using the same method. This time, the resolved template HTML is injected in the `pageHTML`. It does this be replacing a custom token, `/<%template%>/g`, in the HTML page. Again, this is to make the page template more flexible. You could prerender the entire page with the template included.

I do this because I want the application to be able to fallback to using classic client-side rendering if service workers are not supported.

At this point, you should have the page's full HTML, short of rendering with the data. The following step retrieves the data from the API using the supplied method. This method should return a promise, which means you can just return the fetch you use to call the API:

```
        .then(pageTemplate => {
            return options.api()
                .then(data => {
                    return Mustache.render(pageTemplate, data);
                });
```

The API method should resolve the response to JSON. The data is then rendered with the `pageTemplate` using the `Mustache.render` method. This creates the final HTML we want!

Now for some cool magic. The logic creates a new `Response` object and clones it. The clone is saved to the named cache and the new response is returned so that it can be rendered for the user:

```
        }).then(html => {

            //make custom response
            let response = new Response(html, {
                    headers: {
                        'content-type': 'text/html'
                    }
                }),
                copy = response.clone();

            caches.open(options.cacheName)
                .then(cache => {
                    cache.put(options.request, copy);
                });

            return response;

        });
    }
```

[231]

This may seem like a lot of work, but it can be done pretty quickly assuming that the call to the API is fast. I do recommend pre-caching the page and the data template markup ahead of time. The pre-cache is a good place to do this.

You might also consider caching these responses in a special template cache so that you can apply appropriate invalidation rules to ensure that they do not become too stale.

Using the request method to determine the caching strategy

One of the magical aspects of HTTP is its use of different properties to trigger actions. The HTTP method provides a descriptive way to trigger a response. There are a variety of possible HTTP methods, with PUT, GET, POST, and DELETE being the most common methods.

Those methods correspond to **create**, **retrieve**, **update**, and **delete** (**CRUD**) actions. Cache is a powerful tool to make your application respond faster, but not all responses should be cached. The HTTP method can be a primary signal to trigger an appropriate caching strategy.

The first two applications, 2048 and Podstr, use only GET requests. The PWA ticket application utilizes POST methods, which should not be cached. When a user registers, *buys* a ticket, updates their profile, or submits a contact request, a POST request is made to the API.

The API response is typically used to determine success or some sort of failure state. These responses should not be cached. If they were, your request might not be sent to the server:

```
if (!responseManager.isResponseNotFound(response)
    request.method.toUpperCase() === "GET"
    request.url.indexOf("chrome-extension") === -1
    responseManager.isResponseCacheable(response)) {

    //cache response here
}
```

Matching routes with caching strategies

Utilizing different caching strategies involves some way of triggering specific strategies for different response types or routes. The more complex your application is, the more potential routes and media types you may need to manage.

This can be done by defining an array of rules driven by URL routes. I recommend using regular expressions to match routes, especially when the route has a common base with a large variety options. A good example would be an e-commerce site's product details page. This could be a URL to a pre-rendered page or might involve a `QueryString` value.

For the PWA tickets application, I am demonstrating how to define a dynamic route for event details using a regular expression and another for the QR code images.

A QR code request triggers the cache falling back to the network and then cache the response pattern. An event request triggers the service worker rendering strategy. This involves an extra property with values to drive the strategy:

```
routeRules = [
{
    "url": /event?/,
    "strategy": "fetchAndRenderResponseCache",
    "options": {...},
    "cacheName": eventsCacheName
},
{
    "url": /qrcodes?/,
    "strategy": "cacheFallingBackToNetworkCache",
    "cacheName": qrCodesCacheName
}
];
```

Instead of having a complex fetch event handler, you should refactor the logic to a separate method. Pass the event object to your handler:

```
self.addEventListener("fetch", event => {
    event.respondWith(
        handleResponse(event)
    );
});
```

The magic happens by testing the requested URL against the array of rules. This is done by testing the URL against each one of the rules `url` values. This testing is done using JavaScript's regular expression `test()` method:

```
function testRequestRule(url, rules) {

    for (let i = 0; i < rules.length - 1; i++) {

        if (rules[i].route.test(url)) {
            return rules[i];
        }
    }
}
```

This method returns the matching rule object. If no matching rule has been defined, you can coalesce the rule value to an empty object:

```
function handleResponse(event) {

    let cacheName = getCacheName(event.request.url);
    let rule = testRequestRule(event.request.url, routeRules);

    rule = rule || {};

    switch(rule.strategy){
        //
    }
}
```

After identifying a matching rule, the strategy can be executed using a JavaScript switch statement. The `responseManager` has the logic for each strategy. Make sure you pass the `request` object and the target `cacheName`:

```
        case "cacheFallingBackToNetwork":

            return responseManager.cacheFallingBackToNetworkCache(event.request,
            cacheName);

            break;
```

I like to make the cache falling back to the network caching the response my default strategy. By stacking this strategy in the case expression, the code only needs to be included once:

```
case "cacheFallingBackToNetworkCache":
default:
    return
    responseManager.cacheFallingBackToNetworkCache(event.request,
    cacheName)
        .then(response => {

            invalidationManager.cacheCleanUp(cacheName);
            return response;

        });

    break;
```

This approach relies on configuring routes and their corresponding caching strategy. This is similar to the WorkBox approach. I will explore Workbox, a node module to help you scaffold complex service workers, in the next chapter.

Cache invalidation strategies

Just like there are caching strategies, there are cache invalidation strategies you can employ to keep your cache from getting out of control. The PWA tickets application uses a maximum items strategy to control how many responses are cached, but there are other strategies you can use.

Unique hash names and long time-to-live values

A popular technique to make updating assets easier with long time to live values is using hash values in the file name. This is because a hash which is generated based on the file's contents means that the algorithm generates a relatively unique value.

The unique name creates a new URL for the asset and assigns a new Cache-Control value to the asset. This works well with style sheets, scripts and images, and other static resources.

MD5 hash values are the most common way to create these unique values. Node.js has a built-in `crypto` module with MD5 hash capabilities:

```
function getHash(data) {
    var md5 = crypto.createHash('md5');
    md5.update(data);

    return md5.digest('hex');
}
```

The data parameter is the contents of the file. For a style sheet or script, it is the data is the text in the file. The digest is a unique value you can use to name the file:

Name
bootstrap.min.30bb9255f4.css
css?family=Oswald:300,400
font-awesome.min.5fae804c4d.css
css?family=Open+Sans:400italic,700italic,400,600,700,800
css?family=Open+Sans+Condensed:700
site.86c77e8de9.css

This technique works great, but requires a somewhat complicated build process to update file names in all the referencing files. I don't encourage this technique for a local development environment, but for production, this is a very powerful cache busting technique. Just keep in mind that you need to update references in all HTML files and potentially in your service worker or other files that may reference these unique file names.

I think this might be a bit complex for many sites, especially without a formal system underlying the site that supports this technique. It's best if the hash technique is transparent to the developer and more or less automatic.

Unfortunately, this is not common today. There are other techniques you can utilize that provide more granular control and possibly more control over how much data you cache. The following techniques can be used in your service worker to manage how long responses are cached.

Maximum items in a cache

A simpler cache invalidation strategy is limiting the number of items persisted. I call this **Maximum Item Invalidation**.

This requires service worker logic to check how many items are saved in a specifically named cache. If the cache has saved the maximum number of responses, at least one response is removed before adding a new item.

This strategy requires multiple named caches, which correlate to different types of responses. Each named cache can have a different item limit assigned to manage the different types of responses. You can also assign a difference cache invalidation strategy, which will be discussed shortly.

The ticket application has named caches for events, which are dynamically rendered as they are requested. I arbitrarily chose a limit of 20 events to make it easier to demonstrate the strategy. It also has a QR code named cache with a limit of five responses, again, somewhat arbitrary.

You will need to choose an appropriate value for your application and types of responses. Remember, your storage quota is a combination all the different storage mediums and varies by device and capacities.

I typically use more liberal values for text responses and smaller values for binary files like images. Until you know how your site is used by your customers, you may need to adjust this value.

If you managed a site like Amazon.com, you would have access to data that tells you how many products a user visits in an average session. So, maybe you make sure you can cache that many product pages and associated images. I would probably cache most of their watch list products and everything in their shopping cart.

Every site and application is different, and within those sites there are unique page and data types that need a varied cache limit:

```
maxItems(options) {

    self.caches.open(options.cacheName)
        .then((cache) => {

            cache.keys().then((keys) => {

                if (keys.length > options.strategyOptions.max) {

                    let purge = keys.length -
```

```
                        options.strategyOptions.max;

                    for (let i = 0; i < purge; i++) {
                        cache.delete(keys[i]);
                    }
                }
            });
        });
    }
```

Just like there is not a magic number of total items you should cap a named cache capacity, not all caches should be limited by a maximum number of items. You should also consider limiting based on time.

Purging stale responses using time to live

The next cache invalidation strategy is based on how long a response can be cached. If you don't have access to the Cache-Control header, it may be challenging to determine how long to cache the response.

The good news is that the Cache-Control header is not the only way to determine a response's cache lifespan. When responses are added to a named cache, a `"date"` value is added. You can use the cached date value to apply a timeout rule to the cached responses:

```
let responseDate = new Date(response.headers.get("date")),
  currentDate = Date.now();

if(!DateManager.compareDates(currentDate,
  DateManager.addSecondsToDate(responseDate, 300))) {
    cache.add(request);
}else{
    cache.delete(request);
}
```

When a cached response becomes stale, you can delete it. The next time the asset is requested, the default caching strategy triggers.

Executing ResponseManager

Instead of writing a complex routine to fetch and cache a response directly in the service worker's `fetch` event handler, you can use the `ResponseManager`. Because the caching strategy logic is contained within the module, you can pass the request and `cacheName` to have it execute:

```
self.addEventListener("fetch", event => {

    let cacheName = getCacheName(event.request.url);

    event.respondWith(

        responseManager.cacheFallingBackToNetworkCache(event.request,
        cacheName)
        .then(response => {
          invalidationManager.cacheCleanUp(cacheName);
          return response;
        })
    );
});
```

In this example, the response is returned as a result of the promise chain. It also executes the cache's `InvalidatationManager.cacheCleanUp` method to make sure that the cache does not contain too many items or stale items.

The Invalidation Manager

The Invalidation Manager is a special module that handles implementing the maximum items and time to live invalidation strategies. The script is imported to the service worker using the `importScripts` method:

```
invalidationManager = new InvalidationManager([{
      "cacheName": preCache,
      "invalidationStrategy": "ttl",
      "strategyOptions": {
        "ttl": 604800 //1 week }
       },
     { "cacheName": qrCodesCacheName,
       "invalidationStrategy": "maxItems",
       "strategyOptions": { "max": 10 }
     }]);
```

This module has a method called `cacheCleanup`, which loops over the set of invalidation rules that are supplied in the constructor, as shown earlier. As it loops through the rules, it executes each strategy against a named cache. The invalidation rules are defined when the class is instantiated by passing an array of rules.

The class can process two invalidation strategies, which are `maxItems` and `ttl` (time to live). Each item in the rules array is an object defining the named cache, the strategy to apply to the cache, and the options for the strategy.

The `ttl strategyOptions` is the maximum time frame a cached item can remain cached. In the preceding example, the `preCached` items can remain for a week before they will be purged. Once they are purged, a network request is made, which updates the asset.

The `maxItems strategyOptions` has a `max` property, which defines the maximum number of cached items a named cache can persist. In this example, I chose an arbitrarily low number of 10 items to help demonstrate the principle.

The `strategyOptions` property is an object, even though right now there are only single properties for each strategy. By using an object, it allows additional properties to be added later and for potential future strategies to have different property options:

```
cacheCleanUp() {
    let invMgr = this;
    invMgr.invalidationRules.forEach((value) => {
        switch (value.invalidationStrategy) {
            case "ttl":
                invMgr.updateStaleEntries(value);
                break;

            case "maxItems":
                invMgr.maxItems(value);
                break;
            default:
                break;
        }
    });
}
```

The `cacheCleanUp` method can be invoked at any time. It is always executed when a new `InvalidationManger` is created, or when your service worker first wakes up.

This may not be good enough for your application. You could periodically execute this method based on a timer or after items are cached.

maxItems strategy

The `maxItems` strategy limits how many items can be stored in a named cache. It works by opening the named cache, and then retrieving an array of requests using the keys method.

The routine then compares the number of stored items (`keys.length`) to the maximum number of items allowed in this cache. If there are more items than the quota, the number of items exceeding the quota is calculated.

A `for` loop is then executed to delete the first item from the cache and repeats until the number of items to purge have been deleted:

```
maxItems(options) {
    self.caches.open(options.cacheName)
        .then(cache => {
            cache.keys().then(keys => {
                if (keys.length > options.strategyOptions.max) {
                    let purge = keys.length -
                    options.strategyOptions.max;

                    for (let i = 0; i < purge; i++) {
                        cache.delete(keys[i]);
                    }
                }
            });
        });
}
```

You may be wondering why you could not use the Array `pop` or `slice` methods to remove the cache items. This is because caches do not provide an array interface, and thus there are no native array methods.

Instead, you must create a loop or custom routine to individually delete cached items.

The time-to-live invalidation strategy

Like the `maxItems` strategy, the `updateStaleEntries` strategy opens a reference to the named cache and gets a list of the cached requests. This time, individual requests must be retrieved from the cache.

Applying Advanced Service Worker Cache Strategies

This requires calling the cache's match method by passing a request object (key). This will return the stored response with a `date` header. This is added when the item is added to the cache and can be used to determine if the response is stale:

```
updateStaleEntries(rule) {

    self.caches.open(rule.cacheName)
        .then(cache => {

            cache.keys().then(keys => {

                keys.forEach((request, index, array) => {

                    cache.match(request).then(response => {

                        let date = new
                        Date(response.headers.get("date")),
                            current = new Date(Date.now());

                        if (!DateManager.compareDates(current,
                                DateManager.addSecondsToDate(date,
                                    rule.strategyOptions.ttl))) {

                            cache.delete(request);

                        }
                    });
                });
            });
        });
}
```

After retrieving the cached date, the `DateManager` can be used to test if the response is stale or past its expiration time. If the item has expired, it is deleted from the cache.

Using a real-time asset manifest

A more complex technique I have used to manage service worker caches is the manifest file. This technique involves maintaining a file with a JSON object with caching rules:

```
[{
    "url": "/",
    "strategy": "precache-dependency",
    "ttl": 604800
}, {
    "url": "/privacy",
```

```
            "strategy": "genericFallback",
            "fallback": "fallback/",
            "ttl": 604800
    }, {
            "url": "/product/*",
            "strategy": "cacheFirst",
            "ttl": 1800
    },
    ...
]
```

To leverage this technique, you would process the dynamic requests by testing their URL against the supplied routes. This can be done using a regular expression.

This process is very similar to the way the routes and caching strategies were defined and triggered earlier. The request URL is tested against a regular expression to identify the caching strategy to use:

```
processDynamicRequest(request) {

    var routeTest = new RegExp(this.routes),
        result = routeTest.exec(request.url);

    if (result) {

        var match = result.shift(),
            index = result.indexOf(match);

        //return request handler. Should be a promise.
        return strategyManager[this.strategies[index - 1]](request);

    } else {

        //default to pass-through
        return fetch(request);

    }
}
```

The manifest file is dynamically loaded when the service worker is first instantiated. The way I manage when the manifest is updated is by persisting a series of values in `indexedDB`:

```
canUpdateCacheManifest() {

    let cm = this,
        now = new Date();
```

```
            //retrieve persisted list of precached URLs
            return cm.idbkv.get(this.CACHE_UPDATE_TTL_KEY).then(ret => {

                if (!ret) {
                    return true;
                }

                return cm.dateMgr.compareDates(ret, Date.now());

            });

    }
```

The reason I chose to control the manifest file's time to live manually is to avoid potential issues with the browser cache. It is important that you set the manifest's cache headers to not allow the resource to be cached by the browser or proxy servers.

I set the default time to live to 24 hours, just like the built-in service worker's time to live. This keeps the service worker from loading the manifest too often, but not so long that it could get out of sync from the server.

The ticket app does not use this technique, but I did include an example manifest file and some of the additional support modules you might need. I reserve this technique for more complex applications, and it does require some investment to maintain. Specifically, you would need a utility to keep the manifest file updated that I feel is outside the scope of this book.

How much should you cache?

I mentioned earlier that you need to determine how your application's data should be cached. The type of data and how it will be used should be used as guidelines as to how it is managed in your service worker.

I want you to also consider your user. Not everyone has access to an unlimited high-speed connection or a large disk. Many smartphones still come with just 8 GB of storage, which after the operating system and all the photos and videos consumers record, there is not much room left.

Just because you could cache your entire application, including images and data, does not mean you should. Nicholas Hoizey (https://nicolas-hoizey.com/2017/01/how-much-data-should-my-service-worker-put-upfront-in-the-offline-cache.html) demonstrates that that tactic could have a negative impact on your application.

You might want to consider adding an experience where the user can configure your application to control how resources are persisted. Just like we saw with push notification management, you might want to add the ability for the user to determine how many events or tickets (in the example application) are cached and how long ticket QR codes are available:

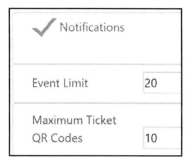

You can still use the helper modules covered in this chapter. The caching and invalidation strategies wont change, just the settings they use to execute the actions.

Summary

This has been a very long chapter with some advanced concepts being covered. You learned how to trigger different caching strategies based on the request URL, modularizing the service worker logic, and employing cache invalidation strategies. Plus, you got to play with a new progressive web app!

There was a lot of valuable information and source code covered in this chapter, but these examples should only serve as a base reference for your applications. Not only should you be a good steward of the storage your application is allocated, but you should be mindful of your users' data plans.

In the next chapter, we'll continue to review how to use service workers and caching to make applications perform better. You will also see how to use available tools to evaluate and diagnose performance issues so that you can make a better application.

9
Optimizing for Performance

Performance is one of the key aspects of user experience. In fact, many experts argue that web performance creates a good user experience. There are different aspects of web performance that you should consider when you are delivering an online experience, such as:

- **Time to first byte (TTFB)** and server-side latencies
- Rendering processes
- Interactions

One of the primary attributes of a **Progressive Web App (PWA)** is speed. That's because people like pages to load fast and respond to actions or input even faster. Making fast, interactive websites is as much of an art as it is a science.

Before diving into making fast PWAs, I want to define what this chapter is designed to help with:

- **Goals**: Defining key performance indicators to measure performance
- **Guidelines**: Defining ways for you to achieve these goals
- **Demonstrate**: Applying these guidelines to the PWA ticket app so that you have a reference code and workflow

This chapter will go deep into how the browser loads and renders pages. You will also learn details of how TCP works and how you can take advantage of this knowledge to create pages that load within 1 second.

You will learn different intermediate and advanced **web performance optimization** (WPO) techniques and how they relate to PWA design. These techniques are woven into the natural fabric of the PWA ticket application. As this chapter evolves, you will learn techniques which rely partially on an automated build script. This automation will be carried over to the following chapter, where I will be reviewing different tools to help you build PWAs.

The importance of WPO

DoubleClick and others websites have shown that 3 seconds is all you have. If the perceived page hasn't loaded within 3 seconds, 53% of mobile visitors abandon the page (https://www.doubleclickbygoogle.com/articles/mobile-speed-matters/). Additionally, DoubleClick reported that sites loading within 5 seconds enjoyed 70% longer sessions, 35% lower bounce rates, and 25% higher advertisement viewability.

Those examples are just a small sampling of the numerous case studies and reports available, demonstrating how important page load and interaction are for a website's success. You can find many more statistics at https://wpostats.com. This is one of the reasons web performance is continually emphasized by Google as a key ranking signal.

Human psychology is an important aspect of performance. We know how the brain perceives performance and can correlate the science to our web pages:

- **0 to 16 ms**: Users perceive animations as smooth, so long as 60 new frames are rendered every second or 16 ms per frame. This leaves about 10 ms to produce a frame after considering browser overheads.
- **0 to 100 ms**: Users feel like the response to an action is immediate.
- **100 to 300 ms**: Slight perceptible delay.
- **300 to 1000 ms**: Things feel part of a natural and continuous progression of tasks.
- **>= 1000 ms**: (1 second), users loses focus on the task.

Put a mental pin in those numbers because they serve as a primary benchmark for this chapter. The goal of this chapter is to modify the PWA ticket application to load within 1 second over an average 3G connection.

Loading fast gives you a competitive advantage because the average web page takes 15 seconds (`https://www.thinkwithgoogle.com/marketing-resources/data-measurement/mobile-page-speed-new-industry-benchmarks/`) to load on mobile devices, a 7 second improvement over the 2017 standard. Not only has this improved the user's engagement, but also stats that were commonly reported when site performance is optimized. Such sites enjoy higher search rankings.

The majority of web traffic comes from mobile devices. Some businesses see as much as 95% of their traffic coming from smartphones. This is why Google is switching their primary search index from desktop to mobile by June 2018.

The Google search team has stated on multiple occasions that speed is a key ranking factor. They know that we want fast sites and that fast sites provide better user experience, which makes customers happy. Their goal is to provide the best resource to answer the user's question, which means that you need to provide a fast experience.

One of the most troubling stats is the growing size of web pages. In 2015, the average web page passed the 2.5 MB mark, which is larger than the original installation disks for the game DOOM. Consequently, website performance has suffered.

Google research found the following, disturbing stats about the average web page's size:

- 79% > 1 MB
- 53% > 2 MB
- 23% > 4 MB

This is important because it takes about 5 seconds just to download a megabyte over a good 3G connection. That is not the end of the overhead, all the resources still need to be processed and the page has to be rendered.

If you consider the numbers reported by Google, this means that 79% of web pages don't even start the rendering cycle until 5 seconds after the initial request is made! At that point, the probability the user has bounced is 90%.

Reducing image payload size

Many point to images as being the root cause and to a certain degree they are, but images do not block rendering. Images can and should be optimized, which reduces the overall page size.

Optimizing image file sizes can reduce the overall payload size by an average of 25%. If the page is 1 MB, 25% equals a 250 KB payload reduction.

Responsive images should also be used. This is where you use the srcset image and sizes attributes, or the picture element to reference images that are sized appropriately for the display:

```
<img srcset="img/pwa-tickets-logo-1158x559.png 1158w,
     img/pwa-tickets-logo-700x338.png 700w,
     img/pwa-tickets-logo-570x276.png 570w,
     img/pwa-tickets-logo-533x258.png 533w,
     img/pwa-tickets-logo-460x223.png 460w,
     img/pwa-tickets-logo-320x155.png 320w"
     src="img/pwa-tickets-logo-1158x559.png"
     sizes="(max-width: 480px) 40vw,
     (max-width: 720px) 20vw, 10vw"
     alt="pwa-tickets-logo">
```

Client device viewports vary widely. Instead of trying to be exact on every device, I recommend focusing on four viewport classes: phones, mini-tablets, tablets, and desktops. I will borrow the breakpoints from the Twitter bootstrap project that correspond to these viewports.

Any images above the different viewport width thresholds should be an array of images maintaining their aspect ratios at smaller widths.

The cost of CSS and JavaScript

The real culprit behind delaying page load time is the overuse of CSS and JavaScript. Both are rendering blocking, which means that when they are being processed, nothing else happens.

Remember from the chapters on service workers, the browser uses a single thread to manage all the rendering tasks, including processing CSS and JavaScript. While this thread is doing that processing, no rendering can take place.

Developers are often naïve about the impact CSS and JavaScript has on their pages loading. Often, this comes down to forgetting what devices real users load web pages with, that is, mobile phones.

Developers generally work on high end workstations and laptops. They also load their work on those devices while developing. Therefore, they perceive their pages as loading instantly.

The discrepancy is a combination of no network latency, high speed processors, and ample memory. This is not the case in the real world.

Most consumers use cheaper phones, typically a $200 handset, not a $1,000 iPhone or a workstation. This means lower powered devices with constrained and limited network conditions do not load and render pages as fast as desktops.

To compound these limitations, when mobile devices are using battery power, they often slow down processors and even turn off cores to reduce power consumption. This means the time to process JavaScript and CSS takes much longer.

Numerous reports have demonstrated how much JavaScript affects how well a page loads. *Addy Osmani* published a canonical study (`https://medium.com/dev-channel/the-cost-of-javascript-84009f51e99e`) showing how JavaScript gets in the way of a page loading.

A common misconception is that the primary performance impact is loading a script or style sheet over the network. This has some affect, but the bigger impact is once the file is loaded. This is where the browser must load the script in memory, parse the script, evaluate, and then execute the script.

> "Byte-for-byte, JavaScript is more expensive for the browser to process than the equivalently sized image or Web Font"
>
> —Tom Dale

Optimizing for Performance

If you use browser profiling tools, you can identify this phase of JavaScript by the presence of a yellow or a golden red color. The Chrome team calls *this a giant yellow slug*:

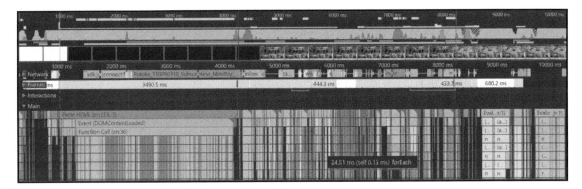

In recent years, **single-page applications (SPAs)** have become very popular. This has given rise to large frameworks that abstract the native APIs and provide an architecture developers and teams can follow.

You should determine if a SPA is the right solution for your needs. The primary reason SPAs have enjoyed so much popularity is that they enable seamless page transitions, similar to a native app experience.

If you have a service worker and utilize service worker caching, you can achieve the desired instant load and smooth page transitions SPAs offer. As a bonus, you won't need to load as much client-side JavaScript.

You can also learn the native APIs instead of framework abstractions, such as jQuery. For example, `document.querySelector` and `document.querySelectorAll` return references to DOM elements much faster than jQuery.

Other native APIs I leverage, replacing most of what I used jQuery for, include:

- `addEventListener`
- `classList`
- `setAttribute` and `getAttribute`

I have tried to give you simple architectures which you can follow with the Podstr and PWA tickets applications. The benefit of not being a SPA is that you can reduce the amount of JavaScript needed to run a page.

The PWA ticket application relies on very little JavaScript. localForage and Mustache accounts are used for most of the JavaScript. The application and individual pages lean on next to no script. After applying gzip compression, the typical page needs less than 14 KB of JavaScript.

Proper test devices and emulation

I do recommend having realistic test devices. This does not mean buying an iPhone X, a Pixel 2, or Samsung 9. You should have an average phone, which can mean different things for different areas. A baseline recommendation is:

- North America and Europe: Motorola G4:
    - *Regular 3G* in Devtools Network Throttling
- India and Indonesia: Xiaomi Redmi 3s
    - *Good 2G* in Devtools Network Throttling

The general rule is that with network constrained devices, those with slow and poor cellular connections, payload is important. Lower power, CPU, and memory constrained devices have more problems parsing and evaluating scripts and style sheets.

This is amplified when a lower powered device is using a constrained network. This is why you should architect your site as if all users have this bad combination. When you do, your site will always load quickly.

Fortunately, we have numerous tools available to measure our pages' performance profiles and improve them. Different browser developer tools provide device emulation that provides a reasonable simulation of network and device constraints. WebPageTest is an example of a free online resource that can test real devices and conditions.

Key areas to focus on are server-side factors and how your pages load in the browser. The most important goal is to make your pages render as fast as possible and respond quickly.

Optimizing for Performance

In this chapter, we will look at different key performance indicators and how you can apply techniques and patterns to ensure that you provide a great user experience. We will also look at how these techniques relate to progressive web applications.

Testing poor conditions using developer tools

The good news about testing for poor connectivity and average user devices is that it can be emulated. The Chrome, Edge, and FireFox developer tools all include some capacity to simulate slower connections and even lower powered devices.

Chrome has the best developed conditional testing tools. In the **Developer Tools**, you need to toggle the device toolbar. The keyboard shortcut is *Ctrl + Shift + M* and the button is located in the top left corner. It looks like a phone overlaying a tablet:

This changes the browser tab to render the page in a frame. The frame simulates the viewport of a target device. It also renders the device toolbar above the content frame:

The device toolbar consists of different drop-downs, allowing you to configure what device and connection scenario you want to emulate. The left most drop-down is a list of pre-configured devices. It contains some of the more popular devices and can be customized.

When you select a device, the width and height values are adjusted to match the device's viewport. I love this because it allows me to have a close proximity to the real device, without needing the real device.

I do recommend having a few real handsets to test your sites, but that can get expensive real fast. Personally, I have a couple of Androids, one high end and one low end, and an iPhone. Right now, I have an iPhone 6. I recommend buying either refurbished hardware or cheap, pre-paid phones, which are available at most retailers for about $50 US.

Chapter 9

The Chrome device emulator does a fair enough approximation of real devices to allow me to complete my responsive design work. You should note that you are still using desktop Chrome, which is not exactly Android Chrome and certainly not iOS Safari.

The device emulator also has several popular Android tablets and iPads configured. Plus, you can also create your own viewports.

You can also adjust the zoom. This can be helpful if the content is too small for you to fine tune:

Optimizing for Performance

The last option is bandwidth. This is the far right drop-down. It includes options to simulate offline, middle-tier, and lower-tier connections. They try not to label these speeds by common cellular connections because that opens them up to issues of not being an exact match.

3G, 4G, and LTE all vary by location, even in the same country. Labeling these speeds by cellular speed could be very misleading.

Since the vast majority of development occurs on high powered computers on a localhost site, developers often forget that their pages are loaded on cellular connections on phones. This leads us to assume that our pages are much faster than they actually are. Instead, you should always try to experience your site as close to real world scenarios as possible.

A big reason I encourage developers to not use JavaScript frameworks is after experiencing a mobile first application on 3G days before launching. It took about 30 seconds for each page to load. I found not only was the poor 3G connectivity to be a problem, but the amount of JavaScript to be the bottleneck.

If I had not started using our application on my 3G handset, I would not have known how poor the user experience was. Back then, browser developer tools did not have these simulation features, which made the real device mandatory. So, be thankful that these tools exist, which can save you hours of time rearchitecting your sites.

I utilize these emulation features to develop my sites, especially for responsive design work. The speed emulation helps me feel issues my customers may experience, which allows me to have more empathy for them.

Performing performance and PWA testing with Lighthouse

Chrome includes a powerful tool to test how well your site performs and meets progressive web application criteria. This tool is called **Lighthouse**. The tool is integrated into the developer tools **Audit** tab and is available as a node module and command-line utility:

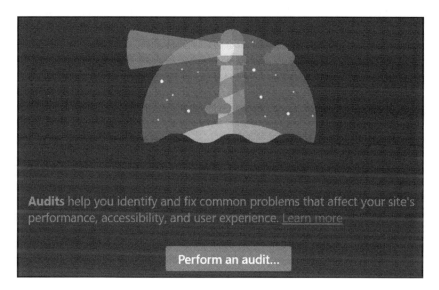

I will focus on using Lighthouse in the developer tool here and follow up with command line usage in the following chapter.

To perform an audit, press the **Perform an audit...** button, as seen in the preceding screenshot. You will then see a dialog that gives you high level configuration options.

There are five areas Lighthouse audits:

- Performance
- PWAs
- Best practices
- Accessibility
- SEO

Optimizing for Performance

You can run tests in all of these areas or only execute tests in selected areas. Lighthouse runs the audit and produces a scorecard and report:

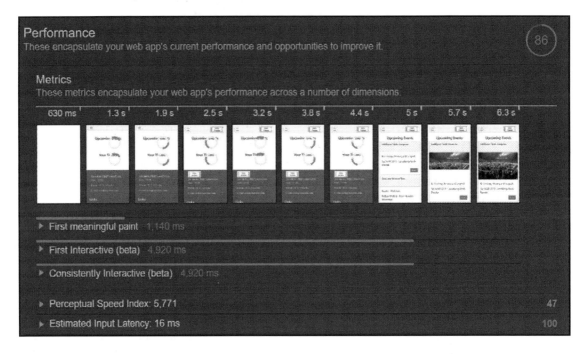

The report highlights specific areas where you can improve the page. In the preceding screenshot, I ran just a performance audit and you can see some of the specific areas to improve, including the perceptual speed index. I also had the tool take screenshots as the page loaded, so you can see how the page renders over time.

The developer tools make it easy to run Lighthouse audits on a single page. You can run them from any Chrome instance, but I recommend opening an incognito instance. When you do this, you load the page in a clean browser, with no cache, cookies, or extensions.

Because Chrome extensions run in the same process as the browser tab, they often interfere with pages and tools, such as Lighthouse. I found a page that normally loads fast and scores well suffers when extensions are included. They delay page loads and often execute well after the page completes loading.

It takes between 30-90 seconds to run a full audit. It depends on how many tests are being executed and the response time of your site.

Chapter 9

The battery of performance audits that are run are very thorough, covering not only a desktop and high speed connection, but use emulation to simulate low powered phones over 3G connections. It is these conditions that expose your weaknesses.

You can use the report to pinpoint specific areas to correct, many of which are discussed in this chapter.

Each test has online documentation to explain what the test is and the actions you can take: https://developers.google.com/web/tools/Lighthouse/audits/consistently-interactive.

Because the PWA ticket application is fairly optimized, there are not many areas to address. This test was run on the home page, after the user was authenticated. The one area that presents a delay is the perceptual speed index.

This measures how long the page content takes to load. In this example, we scored 47, which is very low. This is because the UI thread is unresponsive while making the API call and rendering the markup for the upcoming events and the user's tickets.

We can improve this score by passing the API call and rendering to the service worker or even a web worker. This would take the work out of the UI thread and place it in a background thread. This will require a shift in page and site architecture.

Another recommendation is to use next generation image formats such as WebP and JPEG 2000. While these image formats are more efficient, they are not broadly supported. This is partially due to their young age and partially due to licensing concerns by different user agents. So, for now, I tend to ignore these recommendations and hold out hope that these formats will be commonly supported in the near future.

You could leverage a complex solution using the PICTURE element, but I find that it requires more management and responsibility than the payoff warrants.

It was announced at the recent Google I/O that Lighthouse version 3 will be available soon. They previewed an updated UI and a few new tests. You can read more about those announcements on the Google Developer's site: https://developers.google.com/web/tools/Lighthouse/v3/scoring.

As a word of caution, Lighthouse is an opinionated tool. This means that it looks for things Google and the Chrome team think are important. It is not a test running tool you can add custom tests or rules to based on your specific requirements.

Optimizing for Performance

At the 2017 Microsoft Edge Web Summit, they announced a similar tool called Sonar (https://sonarwhal.com). It is also a node module and command-line tool that exercises tests against a supplied URL. The difference with Lighthouse is the ability to expand the test suite as you want. Not only can you add publicly available tests or rules, you can author your own.

Sonar can perform and does use the same test suites as Lighthouse, but allows you to add more. At the time of writing this book, it is not available in the Edge developer tools like Lighthouse. They do offer an online instance where you can test public URLs and of course run it locally as part of your test suite.

You should make Lighthouse and Sonar part of your routine developer work flow. You can quickly spot not only performance issues, but missing progressive web application requirements, best practices, basic SEO issues, and bad server configurations.

Using WebPageTest to benchmark performance

WebPageTest (https://webpagetest.org/) is a free tool you can use to give you web performance details. It works much like developer tools, but adds even more value:

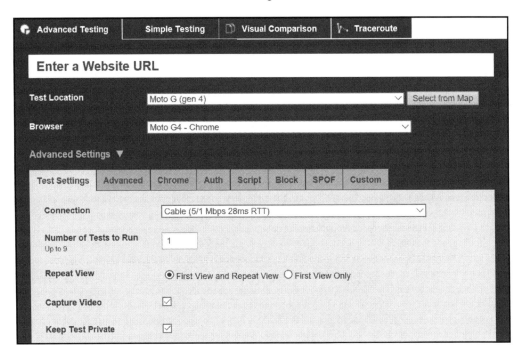

Chapter 9

Not only does it provide a detailed waterfall, it provides testing from different locations, varying speeds, and devices. Sometimes, the truths it reveals can be hard to swallow, but it provides you with targeted areas so that you can improve your performance:

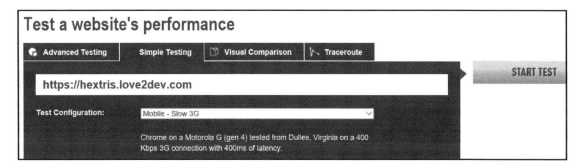

To perform a test, visit `https://webpagetest.org`. If your site has a public URL, enter it in the form and select a location, device/browser, and a speed to test. Once you submit the request, your site is evaluated using real hardware. After a minute or two, assuming it is not added to a queue to be processed, you receive a report:

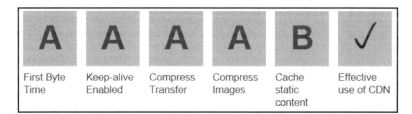

Optimizing for Performance

Just like the browser developer tools provide a network waterfall, WebPageTest can too, but with even more details:

A key metric I always check is the speed index. This is a performance indicator created by Patrick Meenan, the mind behind WebPageTest, that measures how visually complete a page is over its load time:

	Load Time	First Byte	Start Render	Speed Index	First Interactive (beta)	Document Complete			Fully Loaded		
						Time	Requests	Bytes In	Time	Requests	Bytes In
First View	1.403s	0.347s	0.900s	1122	> 1.350s	1.403s	45	310 KB	1.575s	46	328 KB
Repeat View	0.527s	0.330s	0.400s	613	> 0.356s	0.527s	5	213 KB	0.588s	6	213 KB

It measures how much white space is visible compared to the final render. The goal is to minimize the time to a complete render. Speed Index is a way to measure the time to the first interaction or perceived rendering.

A good number to target is 1,000 or less. This indicates that it took 1 second or less to render the page. For reference, most pages I evaluate score well over 10,000, indicating that it takes at least 10 seconds to render. These poor scores are over a broadband connection, so the value is much worse for cellular connections:

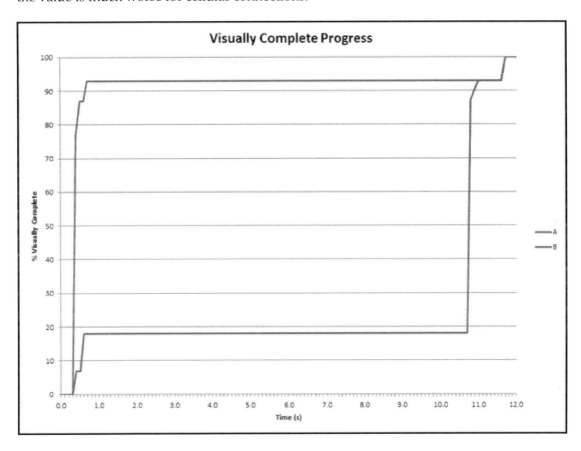

There are many advanced features and settings that can be used to execute WebPageTest, including custom scripts. You can even stand up your own virtual machine either locally or in Amazon AWS. This is helpful when you have an enterprise application that's hidden behind a firewall.

Key performance indicators

The first step to creating a fast site or improving an existing site is to use tools to measure your performance and knowing what to measure. You should create a performance baseline and make iterative changes to improve your performance profile.

In this section, I will review different metrics you should measure, why you need to track them, and how to improve them.

Time to first byte

The time it takes to retrieve the first response byte is the time to first byte. This moment starts the response download. The most important network request is for the document. Once downloaded, the rest of the network resources (images, scripts, style sheets, and so on) can be downloaded.

You can break down the time to first byte process into different steps:

- Time to create a connection between the browser and server
- The time it takes to retrieve and possibly render the file on the server
- The time it takes to send the bytes to the browser

The easiest way to measure time to first byte is by opening the browser developer tools by pressing *F12* or *Ctrl + Shift + I*. Each browser's developer tools have a **network** tab. Here, you can see a page's waterfall. You may need to refresh the page to generate the report.

I recommend performing both a primed and unprimed request. The difference is when loading the page as if this is the first time you have visited the site, which is called unprimed. In this state, there is nothing being persisted in the browser cache. You should also clear or bypass your service worker.

You can trigger an unprimed request by doing a hard reload, *Ctrl + F5*.

If you look at the following waterfall example, you will notice that the first request, the one for the document or HTML, completes first. The browser then parses the markup, identifying additional assets to load. This is when those requests begin.

You should be able to notice this pattern for all pages, even when assets are locally cached. This is why there is a slight time gap between the initial document request and the supporting resources:

Name	Protocol	Method	Result	Content type	Received	Time	Initiator	0ms
https://love2dev.com/	HTTP/2	GET	200	text/html	4.81 KB	238.59 ms	document	
https://love2dev.com/	HTTPS	GET	200 OK		(from cache)	0 s		
bootstrap.min.css https://love2dev.com/css/libs/	HTTP/2	GET	200	text/css	19.88 KB	457.98 ms		
font-awesome.min.css https://love2dev.com/css/libs/	HTTP/2	GET	200	text/css	6.77 KB	487.44 ms		
animations.css https://love2dev.com/css/	HTTP/2	GET	200	text/css	287 B	434.86 ms		
animate.css https://love2dev.com/css/	HTTP/2	GET	200	text/css	3.77 KB	460.35 ms		
style.css https://love2dev.com/css/app/	HTTP/2	GET	200	text/css	13.23 KB	395.08 ms		

A primed request assumes that you have visited the site or page before, and the browser and possibly the service worker cache contain valid responses. This means those requests are made locally, with no network activity. In theory, the page should load faster thanks to the cache.

The waterfall is composed of each file request required to compose the page. You should be able to select an individual request (double click the request in the waterfall) to see how much time each step took:

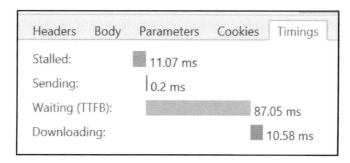

Chrome, FireFox, and Edge let you visualize the time to first byte. Each have a **Timings** panel that breaks apart the different parts of the request and the time allocated. It refines the parts a little more, showing you time to perform DNS resolution, creating the connection to the server, and the time it took the server to send the bytes to the browser.

Optimizing for Performance

Before a network request is made, it is added to a browser queue. This queue is a collection of requests the browser needs to make. Each browser determines how this queue is processed, which depends on available resources, HTTP/2 versus HTTP/1 support, and so on.

Next, if needed, the browser triggers a DNS resolution. If the device has a cache domain resolution or IP address, this step is skipped. You can speed this up by using the `dns-prefetch`, which I will cover a little later.

The browser then makes the network request. At that point, it is up to the server to send a response. If the server has any bottlenecks, you should address those issues.

Don't forget TLS negotiation. There is a slight performance hit for HTTPS, but when using HTTP/2, this hit is typically washed out by additional performance enhancements offered by HTTP/2.

You can reduce your time to first byte by optimizing your server configuration. You should look for opportunities to reduce disk I/O by caching responses in memory. In ASP.NET, this is done by implementing the Output cache. Other web platforms provide similar capabilities.

Database queries are another common bottleneck. If you can eliminate them, you should. Evaluate the page's data and find the data that could be retrieved ahead of time. I like to create JSON data files or objects in memory to avoid these expensive queries.

This is the main reason no-SQL, document databases such as MongoDB and ElasticSearch, and cloud services such as DynamoDB have grown in popularity. These databases as designed to have pre-selected and formatted data ready to go on demand. These solutions have helped popular online sites such as Twitter, Facebook, and so on grow and scale very quickly.

Another tactic is to avoid on-demand rendering as much as possible. Most websites are rendered by a server process such as ASP.NET, PHP, Ruby, Node, and so on. These all add overhead to the request process. By pre-rendering markup where possible, you reduce the opportunities for these processes to slow down the response.

I try to use a static website solution when possible because they offer the fastest response pipeline. Static sites have the advantage over runtime rendering because the rendering cycle is removed. You can create your own engine to pre-render content or use a tool like Varnish to manage the task. You don't have to abandon your existing processor, but instead add a static engine on top to maintain the static files so that your pages load faster.

The only remaining point of friction is the speed of the networks. Unfortunately, these are typically out of your control. Routers, proxies, and cell towers can all cause issues.

At this point, the response bytes start streaming into the browser for processing. The larger the file, the longer, typically, the delay.

The PRPL pattern

We have looked at both the time to first byte and runtime performance issues. The best way to make sure that your site is performing its best is by implementing architecture best practices. The PRPL pattern was created to help modern web applications achieve top performance values.

The Google Polymer team developed PRPL as a guideline to follow to help websites perform better. It should be considered an architecture you can implement, but it is not all about technical specifics. To quote the PRPL documentation:

> "PRPL is more about a mindset and a long-term vision for improving the performance of the mobile web than it is about specific technologies or techniques."

PRPL goes back to the principle of putting performance as a first-class feature of any website.

PRPL stands for:

- **Push** critical resources for the initial URL route using `<link preload>` and HTTP/2
- **Render** initial route
- **Pre-cache** remaining routes
- **Lazy-load** and create remaining routes on demand

Even though PRPL was created with modern single page apps in mind, progressive web applications can benefit from following the PRPL pattern. Service workers are a valuable tool for implementing the PRPL pattern because you can leverage the Cache API to implement the pattern. You just have to adjust how the different principles are applied to improve your apps' performance.

The primary goals of the PRPL pattern are:

- Minimum time-to-interactive:
    - Especially on first use (regardless of entry point)
    - Especially on real-world mobile devices
- Maximum caching efficiency, especially over time as updates are released
- Simplicity of development and deployment

Implementing push with browser hints and the service worker cache

The first concept of push relies on implementing the HTTP/2 server-side push. I have found this to be difficult to configure as most servers have not yet implemented HTTP/2 push.

This is where service workers can offer a solution I feel is even better. We looked at how to implement pre-caching, an excellent alternative to using HTTP/2 Push. By using pre-caching, you are effectively pushing those critical assets to the browser before they are needed.

Remember that the resources you pre-cache should be critical and common application assets. These assets should mirror what you might want to configure HTTP/2 push to send.

Combining service worker caching with the preload resource hint can recreate most of what HTTP/2 push does. Browsers use preload hint to initialize resource requests before they are encountered in the code. When paired with pre-cached assets, the loading process is lightning fast.

On the surface, resource hints like preload may not seem to provide much advantage. But as a page's composition grows complex, these hints can improve page load and rendering time significantly.

The browser does not initiate a request until it is parsed from the HTML or initiated from a script or style sheet.

Custom font files are a perfect example. Their downloads are not initiated until the browser parses the style sheet and finds the font reference. If the files are included as a preload resource hint, the browser has already loaded or at least started the request, making the file available sooner:

```
<link rel="preload" href="css/webfonts/fa-brands-400.eot "
 as="font">
 ...
<link rel="preload" href="js/libs/utils.js" as="script">
<link rel="preload" href="js/libs/localforage.min.js" as="script">
<link rel="preload" href="js/libs/mustache.min.js" as="script">
<link rel="preload" href="js/app/events.js" as="script">
<link rel="preload" href="js/app/tickets.js" as="script">
<link rel="preload" href="js/app/user.js" as="script">
<link rel="preload" href="js/app/app.js" as="script">
```

Specifying the resource content type allows the browser to:

- Prioritize resource loading
- Match future requests and reusing the same resource
- Apply the resource's content security policy
- Set the resource's correct Accept request headers

You can also add the resource MIME type. When you do this, the browser can determine if it supports the resource type before it attempts to download the file:

```
<link rel="preload" href="js/app/app.js" as="script"
type="application/javascript">
```

The idea is to make the page or application's assets available before the DOM parsing triggers a request. Since these assets are available in the service worker cache, they are already stored locally and can be loaded instantly.

You can notice the difference in the waterfall where `preload` hints are used. Do you remember that I pointed out a slight time gap between the initial markup being loaded and the assets in earlier waterfalls?

Optimizing for Performance

If you look at the following waterfall, you will notice that the dependencies are initiated before the markup has finished loading:

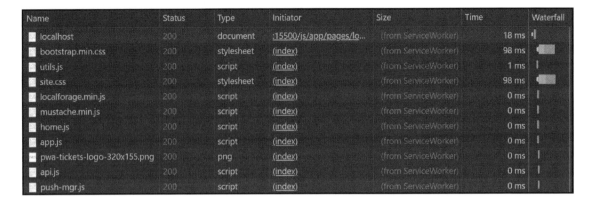

This is due to the browser identifying these assets with the preload hint applied. It starts downloading the resource as soon as the item is parsed from the markup, not after the entire document is completely parsed.

You should also note how fast these resources are loaded. This is due to them being cached using service worker caching. This eliminates the network bottleneck, which in some cases means that the files are loaded even before the markup is completely parsed.

It's a slight page load advantage, not a major improvement. Every little bit helps as milliseconds quickly add up.

Using the app shell model and service worker to render the initial route

Since the PRPL pattern was designed from a SPA first perspective, the language speaks to that architecture. But as you have seen in the previous chapters, app shells are useful for progressive web apps.

Even when you don't have a page cached, you should have at least your application's markup shell cached locally. This can serve as your initial render, giving the user a sense of response. Meanwhile, you can retrieve any assets from the network to complete the page.

The PWA tickets app uses the service worker to render pages using Mustache templates and JSON data retrieved from the API. This is an example of how you can return the app shell as a valid response to a request and then update the content once it is available.

My rule is to give the user everything I have at the moment and fill in the blanks as I have more to give. This could be a combination of supplying the app shell and replacing it later or injecting the page-specific markup once it is available.

Service worker pre-caching important routes

At this point in this book, it should be obvious how a good service worker pre-caching strategy applies to the PRPL pre-caching point, but it never hurts to review the concept.

The second P in PRPL stands for pre-caching common routes. This includes the HTML and their supporting files such as styles, images, and scripts. This is exactly how your service worker's pre-cache strategy should be designed.

Important assets are commonly visited pages, but can also be the markup templates required to render the pages in the service worker. The common styles, scripts, images, and other support assets should be pre-cached.

Lazy-loading non-critical and dynamic routes

Not every page in every website can or should be cached ahead of time. As you saw in `Chapter 5`, *The Service Worker Life Cycle*, you should also have cache invalidation logic in place to ensure that you supply the freshest content.

Dynamic content, like the available ticket events or even an updated list of podcast episodes, is difficult to cache long-term. But you can provide a better experience than just waiting to download all of the page's resources.

This is where employing one or more of the common caching strategies is helpful. You can also combine your rendering strategy with the app shell concept and build the page as assets are loaded or updated.

You can also pre-cache and update common support assets as needed. This is one of the underestimated powers of the web, dynamically updating what is rendered and how it is rendered. You can update not just the markup in a page, but change style sheets and scripts on the fly too.

As you have also learned, you can cache assets in the service worker without affecting the UI thread. This can be used to pre-cache non-critical assets and update previously cached content.

As you can see, service worker caching makes implementing the PRPL pattern very natural. Its ability to cache resources makes all four PRPL principles easy to implement. If you have followed the examples and guidelines in the previous chapters, then you have seen how to design PRPL compliant progressive web applications.

I think the number one PRPL principle is to cache as much of your application's assets in the client as possible. This makes the network nice to have and not a potential source of delay and uncertainty. This is exactly what service worker caching was designed to do: make your assets close to the user's glass.

The RAIL pattern

The RAIL pattern is an acronym used by the Google Chrome team to define one of the many WPO patterns you should try to follow. Its goal is to ensure your user experience is responsive:

- **Response**: How quickly there is a response when there is any input
- **Animation**: Includes visual animation, scrolling, and dragging
- **Idle**: Background work
- **Load**: How quickly a page can achieve the first meaningful paint

Where the PRPL pattern is concerned with resource loading, RAIL is about the runtime user experience or what happens once the resources are loaded.

The pattern is designed to be user centric, focusing on performance first. The four aspects that make up the acronym are distinct areas of a web application and page's life cycle, or what happens once the bytes are loaded.

Consider the different areas where performance is important: loading, rendering and responding to actions. There is more than just the page load phase. Page load is how fast the browser can load the assets, but many forget it still needs to process those assets and render the content. Then, once rendered, you can respond to user interactions.

You also need to consider how quickly the page response is to a click or tap. Is scrolling smooth? Are notifications prompt? What about any background activities, are they efficient?

The first critical factor to the average user is how long it takes for a page to become interactive, not how long it takes to download the files.

At the recent Google I/O, the team announced new metrics that Lighthouse will report, specifically **First Contentful Paint** (**FCP**). This is the point at which the browser renders the first pixel of a new page's DOM. The measurement starts from the time of navigation to the point that the first pixel is rendered.

The reason this is a key performance indicator is that this is the first visual queue to the user where their requested action or navigation is being handled. I like to translate that into saying that this is the point where the user knows the page is coming and was not lost in the ether, causing them to try and reload the page or give up.

The FCP is available from the Paint Timing API (`https://w3c.github.io/paint-timing/`), one of the modern performance APIs available in modern browsers.

The next KPI you should focus on is **Time to Interactive** (**TTI**). This is the point where the page is fully rendered and capable of responding to user input. Often, even though the page appears to be rendered, it cannot respond to the user due to background processing.

For example, the page is still processing JavaScript, which locks the UI thread and the page cannot be scrolled.

RAIL focuses on the user; the goal is not to necessarily make the site perform fast on a specific device, but to make your user happy. Any time a user interacts with your content, you should have a response within 100 ms. Any sort of animation or scrolling should also respond within 10 ms.

Because modern web pages tend to do a lot of background processing, you should maximize idle time to perform these tasks, not blocking interaction and rendering.

If you need to perform any non-UI processing, such as data transformations, service workers or web workers provide a channel for you to offload those processes to background threads. This frees the UI thread to focus on UI tasks, like layout and painting. It also frees the UI to immediately respond to user interaction.

Focus on delivering interactive content within one second. This can be very difficult to achieve over cellular networks and average mobile devices, but not impossible.

As I mentioned before, server load time is not the majority of your web performance profile, it's the resource processing that creates the bigger bottlenecks. That's because scripts and style sheets block the critical rendering path, leaving your page partially rendered or appearing to be hung.

If you have never heard of the critical rendering path, it is the workflow that browsers use to compose and render a page:

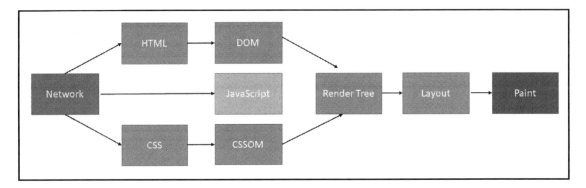

These are the main steps:

1. **Document Object Model (DOM)**
2. **CSS object model (CSSOM)**
3. Render Tree
4. Layout
5. Paint

To compose the DOM, the browser must complete these substeps:

1. Convert bytes to characters
2. Identify tokens
3. Convert tokens to nodes
4. Build the DOM Tree

Similar to building the DOM, the browser follows a similar series of steps to compose the CSSOM or process styles:

1. Convert bytes to characters
2. Identify tokens
3. Convert tokens to nodes
4. Build CSSOM

The important takeaway for CSS is just like JavaScript: it is rendering blocking. The browser must process the page's styles before it can be rendered. Multiple large CSS files cause the CSSOM process to repeat. The larger the style sheet, the longer this step takes.

Once the DOM and CSSOM are created, the browser then combines the two to compose the render tree. This is followed by the layout step, where all the size and color attributes are calculated for all the page elements.

Finally, the pixels are painted to the screen. This is not always 'instant', as different styles and style combinations take different amounts of processing to render.

How JavaScript clogs the pipeline

The DOM and CSSOM processes work together to produce what is rendered on the screen, but there is a third part of the rendering cycle, that is, processing JavaScript. Not only is JavaScript a render blocker, it is also a parser blocking process.

This is the primary reason we add script references at the end of the HTML. By doing so, the browser has a chance to parse the HTML and CSS before attempting to load scripts, which blocks the parsing process:

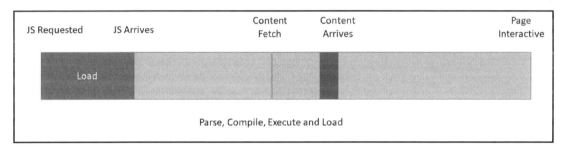

When the browser encounters a script, it stops the DOM and CSS parsers to load, parse, and evaluate the JavaScript. This is one reason I make intentional efforts to minimize my JavaScript size.

There are some tricks you can employ to minimize this behavior. The first is to mark any script you can as async. This causes the browser to casually load the script file.

This sounds great at first, but most of the time, I have found this to be a more optimistic than practical. There always seems to be at least one critical script that requires execution as the page is being rendered.

You can mark all your scripts as asynchronous and see if there are any issues when running your application. Just be thorough with your testing to flesh out any edge cases:

```
<script src="js/app/pages/config.js" async></script>
```

Another solution is to minify your scripts and then inline them in your markup. This can also help your rendering cycle. One of the main benefits is not waiting on an additional file to download.

However, if you are using HTTP/2, the multiplexing capabilities will probably offer more benefits. With HTTP/2, you are often better off using small files that can be individually cached than large file bundles.

When you inline scripts, the size of your HTML grows, which can delay its processing. However, as you are about to learn, inlining CSS is highly beneficial. It is a matter of testing to see what works best for your page and application.

Why 14 KB is the magic number

In an effort to control network traffic, TCP implements a pattern called slow start. It does this to keep the network from being overwhelmed with requests. The details are specified in RFC 5681 (`https://tools.ietf.org/html/rfc5681`).

The protocol works where the sender or initiator sends an initial, small packet. When it receives a response, it then doubles the packet size. This volley is repeated until the sender receives a congested response.

The initial packet size is 14 KB. This back and forth is a series of round trips. If you can fit an entire page or response within 14 KB, it only needs one round trip to be completely downloaded:

```
▼ Response Headers          view source
    cache-control: max-age=3600
    content-length: 10539
    content-type: text/html; charset=UTF-8
    Date: Wed, 09 May 2018 00:28:51 GMT
    etag: W/"3377699721775359-10539-"2018-04-26T20:56:01.719Z""
    last-modified: Thu, 26 Apr 2018 20:56:01 GMT
    server: ecstatic-3.2.0
```

In this example, the response is 10.5 KB, so only 1 round trip is required. You should note that this example is not compressed, which would reduce the size significantly. This is another point I want you to remember as we apply resource inlining a little later.

The initial TCP data packet is actually 16 KB, but the first 2 KB are reserved for request header data. The remaining 14 KB are where your content or data are transferred. If the content is more than 14 KB, then a second round trip is initiated, and this time the packet size is doubled to 32 KB. This repeats until there is a network congestion message.

By limiting the request to a single round trip, you are able to load the entire response almost instantly. The more round trips, the longer the data takes to load.

Inline critical CSS

When you inline CSS, you eliminate the required round trips to retrieve the styles, and they are immediately available to the browser as it parses the DOM. This makes these two critical steps much faster.

To refresh, when the browser encounters external style sheets, it blocks any rendering until the style sheets are fully loaded.

As I mentioned earlier, you want to limit the size of a page's CSS to just the CSS required to render the page. By limiting the styles to just those used by the page, you can typically reduce the amount of CSS to a handful of kilobytes.

Because the amount of real CSS is minimal, you can inline those styles in the document's `head` element. Now, the browser has no external file to download and a minimal amount of CSS to load. Plus, you have the critical styles required to render the app shell.

The PWA ticket app has a very standard app shell: `header`, `body`, and `footer`. Each individual page requires a minimal amount of custom CSS to render its content.

The good news is that there are tools available to help you identify the CSS each page requires. There are multiple node modules available, but I have focused on the UnCSS module (https://www.npmjs.com/package/uncss). It was one of the first modules created to identify the required CSS.

Because these are node modules, you can include them in a build script. The PWA ticket application has a build script in the project's `utils` folder called `render-public.js`. I won't go into all of the script's details, but it runs over the site's source to produce the site's pages and support files.

Optimizing for Performance

The `extractCSS` function handles extracting a page's styles, minimizing them, and injecting them into the `head` element.

There are additional node modules being used to help. Cheerio loads HTML and creates an object with the jQuery API, just like you were using jQuery in the browser. This makes manipulating the markup much easier.

The second module is CleanCSS. This module minifies styles, removing unnecessary white space, thus making the code take up less space:

```
function extractCSS($, callback) {

    let options = {
            ignore: [".page-content .card", ".page-content .card-
            title", ".page-content .ticket-card"],
            media: ['@media (max-width:480px)', '@media (min-
            width:768px)', '@media (max-width:992px)', '@media (max-
            width:1199px)'],
            stylesheets: [path.resolve(publicPath,
            'css/libs/bootstrap.min.css'),
            path.resolve(publicPath, 'css/app/site.css')
            ],
            timeout: 1000,
            report: true,
            banner: false
        },
        html = $.html();

    let $html = cheerio.load(html);

    $html("body").append(templates);
    $html("script").remove();

    $("script").remove();

    //run uncss
    uncss($html.html(), options, function (error, output) {

        if (error) {
            console.log(error);
        }

        let minCSS = new CleanCSS({
            level: 2
        }).minify(output);

        $("head").append("<style>" + minCSS.styles + "</style>");
```

```
        callback($);
    });
}
```

UnCSS has a long list of configuration options you can use to control how the module executes. I have supplied the most common settings I use, like media query breakpoints and eliminating banner comments.

Sometimes, I find that I still need to include a list of selectors that should not be removed:

```
ignore: [".page-content .card", ".page-content .card-title", ".page-content .ticket-card"]
```

I have also found that removing any script references from the markup will help the module. When the module finds a script, it does try to load it and execute it. This is because UnCSS exercises the page in a headless browser, which loads the page just as if it were a normal browser.

UnCSS can either process raw HTML, which is how I use it, or load a page via a URL or local path. It utilizes the standard node callback pattern, so you should write your code accordingly.

Another thing I try to do is inject potential content templates in the HTML to be processed. This should help UnCSS isolate all the styles needed, even when they are dynamically rendered.

Like UnCSS, CleanCSS also uses the callback pattern. You can supply the filtered CSS and it will return a minified version.

At this point, you can inject the minified styles into the HTML `head`:

```
$("head").append("<style>" + minCSS.styles + "</style>");
```

At this point, you have the page's HTML with all its required CSS, inline in the markup HEAD. For the PWA ticket application, the typical page is around 30 KB, which does not meet the 14 KB goal.

Fortunately, we are not done.

Static resources, like HTML, should be compressed. You can use gzip or deflate compression. Brotli is another option, but is not universally supported by all browsers. Once you compress these files, they typically reduce to around 8 KB, well within our 14 KB goal!

Optimizing for Performance

Most web servers can be configured to compress text files on demand. But as you can imagine, I like to do this as part of my deploy process. This can be done with a node, but you should check with your devops team to make sure that this is being done for your site:

```
Body = fs.createReadStream(src).pipe(zlib.createGzip({
        level: 9
    }));
```

Make sure any compressed files are served with the Content-Encoding header set to gzip or deflate so that the browser knows to decompress the response.

Minifying scripts with uglify

Just like CSS, you should also minimize JavaScript files. Just like we used Clean-CSS to minify CSS, you can use uglify to do the same for your JavaScript. Instead of inlining the script, I like to keep it in individual files.

In the past, I would have also bundled multiple script files together. HTTP/2 utilizes request multiplexing to optimize content delivery. By keeping each script in individual files, you can take advantage of long term caching and make small changes without requiring a complete download.

In addition to minimizing the scripts, I am also going to show you how to create unique file names using an MD5 hash on the content. This will allow you to apply a very long caching time without worrying about browser caches retaining stale copies. This technique is advanced and does require some planning and, of course, an intelligent build or rendering process.

There are multiple uglifier node modules. I chose `uglify-js` for the PWA ticket application. The way I tend to pick modules like this is to look at popularity, but also what popular task runners such as Grunt, Gulp, and WebPack plugins rely upon.

As a word of warning, `uglify-js` does not handle ES6 syntax, like `let` and `const`, and will throw errors when encountered. But I warn against using ES6 syntax in the browser since there are still many browsers that do not support it, such as Internet Explorer.

For the build script, I chose to create a simple uglify module to reference in the overall build script. It references `uglify-js` and creates an `uglify` class:

```
const UglifyJS = require("uglify-js"),
    uglifyOptions = {
        parse: {
            html5_comments: false,
```

```
            shebang: false
        },
        compress: {
            drop_console: true,
            keep_fargs: false
        }
    },
   ...;

class uglify {

    constructor(src) {}
    transformSrc(srcFiles) {}
    minify() {}

}
```

The class `constructor` and `transformSrc` methods are used to set up before minification. They are set up to allow you to pass either a single script reference or an array of scripts to uglify and concatenate.

Just like UnCSS, uglify allows you to customize the process. This is where the options allow you to configure the module. For this, I chose some simple settings I like to use to optimize the process:

```
        minify() {

            let src = this.transformSrc(srcFiles);
            return UglifyJS.minify(src, uglifyOptions);

        }
```

The render script not only uglifies each script; it also creates a unique hash name:

```
    function uglifyScripts() {

        scripts.forEach(script => {

            let ug = new uglify(path.resolve(publicPath, script));
            let min = ug.minify();

            if (min.code && min.code !== "") {

                let hashName = utils.getHash(min.code);

                fs.writeFileSync(path.join(publicPath,
                    path.dirname(script), hashName + ".min.js"), min.code);
```

Optimizing for Performance

```
            scriptsObjs.push({
                src: script,
                hash: hashName + ".min.js"
            });
        } else {
            console.log("uglify error ", min.error);
        }
    });
}
```

The file is calculated by passing the script's contents to the nodejs crypto object. The crypto object makes calculating hashes simple. In this case, I want an md5 hash value, so when the `createHash` method is called, you supply the `'md5'` value.

If you are not familiar with md5 hashes, they are a cryptographic way of generating a checksum to verify data integrity. They are not good for cryptography, but provide a unique value based on the data. That unique value is helpful for creating a unique file name:

```
function  getHash(data) {
    var md5 = crypto.createHash('md5');
    md5.update(data);

    return md5.digest('hex');
}
```

The uniqueness is good enough to have faith that the script file name won't be duplicated within your application. The build script needs to not only generate unique hash values, but save the file with the hash name. It could also just rename the source file.

Even after you create the file with the unique file name, you still need to integrate it into the HTML files. The render script takes care of that task. The product looks something like this:

```
<script src="js/libs/470bb9da4a68c224d0034b1792dcbd77.min.js"></script>
<script src="js/libs/ca901f49ff220b077f4252d2f1140c68.min.js"></script>
<script src="js/libs/2ae25530a0dd28f30ca44f5182f0de61.min.js"></script>
<script src="js/libs/aa0a8a25292f1dc72b1bee3bd358d477.min.js"></script>
<script src="js/libs/470bb9da4a68c224d0034b1792dcbd77.min.js"></script>
<script src="js/app/libs/e392a867bee507b90b366637460259aa.min.js"></script>
<script src="js/app/libs/8fd5a965abed65cd11ef13e6a3408641.min.js"></script>
<script src="js/app/512df4f42ca96bc22908ff3a84431452.min.js"></script>
<script src="js/app/pages/bc8ffbb70c5786945962ce782fae415c.min.js"></script>
```

I also added .min to each one of the files because the scripts have been minimized. This is done out of convention rather than a requirement. The benefit is for tools, like browser developer tools, that understand that the script is minimized. Edge allows you to choose to bypass the script when you are debugging because .min is appended to the file name.

Because each page also sets a preloaded hint for the script files, those references must also be updated:

```
<link rel="preload" href="js/libs/470bb9da4a68c224d0034b1792dcbd77.min.js"
as="script" type="application/javascript">
<link rel="preload" href="js/libs/ca901f49ff220b077f4252d2f1140c68.min.js"
as="script" type="application/javascript">
<link rel="preload" href="js/libs/2ae25530a0dd28f30ca44f5182f0de61.min.js"
as="script" type="application/javascript">
<link rel="preload" href="js/libs/aa0a8a25292f1dc72b1bee3bd358d477.min.js"
as="script" type="application/javascript">
<link rel="preload"
href="js/app/pages/bc8ffbb70c5786945962ce782fae415c.min.js" as="script"
type="application/javascript">
<link rel="preload" href="js/app/512df4f42ca96bc22908ff3a84431452.min.js"
as="script" type="application/javascript">
```

So, why did I add this complicated renaming step to the build and render processes? To enable long cache time frames. This tells the browser to attempt to cache the response locally in the built-in browser cache, not the service worker cache.

The recommended time to live is at least a year. Most scripts can and will be updated in that time frame and the hash name technique gives you a guaranteed cache busting technique. Other techniques, like appending a unique QueryString parameter, may not always work.

You can set the long time to live by setting the cache-control header. This needs to be done in your web server, so that it will be part of your devops workflow:

```
cache-control: public, max-age=31536000
```

I won't dive into the art of configuring Cache-Control headers, but you can use the preceding example as a reference. Files such as scripts, style sheets, and even images are candidates for the hash naming trick. Just be sure to update any references to the files to the new name.

Using feature detection to conditionally load JavaScript polyfils

The PWA ticket application uses many modern APIs, but some are not supported by older browsers. There are two browser scenarios you should be most concerned with: Internet Explorer and older Android phones. UC Browser is another popular browser that does not support all newer features yet.

Internet Explorer is the now deprecated Microsoft Browser. The only supported version is IE 11, and right now only lives on Windows 7 and in enterprises. Enterprises use many line of business applications, and many were created against old and obsolete web standards. Often, it is expensive for them to update or replace these applications.

Internet Explorer provides a legacy browser channel for them to continue running these applications. However, when they upgrade to Windows 10, they should configure these line of business applications to trigger Internet Explorer from Edge as needed and not as a default browser.

This means that the default behavior you should expect is Edge, not Internet Explorer on Windows 10. However, human nature and habits often override recommended practice, which means IE is still a very popular browser.

Fortunately, most of the modern APIs PWA tickets use can be polyfiled. This is where a script can be loaded, on demand, to implement the new API. Other APIs can be safely used behind a feature detection gate, like we do before registering a service worker, or be trusted to be gracefully ignored. The latter is how modern CSS properties are handled.

Loading a feature polyfil can be done as needed using feature detection and a simple technique I call toggling a script.

The PWA tickets application uses 4 polyfils:

- `Object.Assign`
- Promises
- The Fetch API
- `IntersectionObserver`

The trick relies on these script references applying a type attribute other than script. This tells the browser that even though it is a script element, the src is not a script. Of course, the src files are scripts, but by setting the type to something else, the browser does not download the scripts.

The `toggleScript` method takes a supplied ID to reference the polyfil's `script` element. It then toggle's the script's type from `script-polyfil` to text/JavaScript. When this toggle happens, the browser downloads and processes the polyfil script:

```
<script type="script-polyfil" id="polyfilassign"
    src="js/libs/polyfils/object.assign.js"></script>
<script type="script-polyfil" id="polyfilpromise"
    src="js/libs/polyfils/es6-promise.min.js"></script>
<script type="script-polyfil" id="polyfilfetch"
    src="js/libs/polyfils/fetch.js"></script>
<script type="script-polyfil" id="polyfilintersection"
    src="js/libs/polyfils/intersection-observer.js"></script>
<script>
    //wrap in IIFE to keep out of global scope
    (function () {
        function toggleScript(id) {
            var target = document.getElementById("polyfil" + id);
            target.setAttribute("type", "text/javascript");
        }

        if (typeof Object.assign != 'function') {
            toggleScript("assign");
        }

        if (typeof Promise === "undefined" ||
        Promise.toString().indexOf("[native code]") === -1) {
            toggleScript("promise");
        }

        if (typeof fetch === "undefined" ||
        fetch.toString().indexOf("[native code]") === -1) {
            toggleScript("fetch");
        }
    }());
</script>
```

Optimizing for Performance

All this depends on the polyfil being needed. Each API or feature support can be detected with a simple test. If the test fails, the feature is not supported, and the toggleScript method is called to load the polyfil.

You should put this code before you load any of the application-specific code or any code that might depend on these APIs.

Dynamically loading polyfils is important because it means you will use the native APIs when present and avoid loading these expensive files when the native API is present.

Any time you need to load these polyfils, the page load suffers. however, I think that this is a reasonable trade off because these older browsers will run slower in the first place and the user may not have the same expectations as someone using a modern browser.

Lazy loading images

Images can delay your overall page load experience due to image numbers and their size. There are different strategies for optimizing image delivery. The first one you should consider is lazy loading images below the fold.

This could be a very tricky technique to execute. Modern APIs can help you, the `IntersectionObserver` (https://developer.mozilla.org/en-US/docs/Web/API/Intersection_Observer_API) API in particular gives you the ability to detect when elements are entering the viewport. You can designate the distance and time estimated threshold for an element to appear.

The `IntersectionObserver` API will trigger an event to let you know when an element is about to be displayed. At this point, you can initiate an image download if necessary. This means that your pages images will not be loaded in the initial render process, but be loaded as needed. This can conserve valuable bandwidth and network connections in that initial page load:

```
        lazyDisplay: function () {

            var images = document.querySelectorAll('.lazy-image');
            var config = {
// If the image gets within 50px in the Y axis, start the download.
                rootMargin: '50px 0px',
                threshold: 0.01
            };

            // The observer for the images on the page
            var observer = new IntersectionObserver(this.showImage, config);
```

```
        images.forEach(function (image) {
            observer.observe(image);
        });

    }
```

Instead of using the images `src` attribute, you can designate the image source as a data attribute (`data-src`). You should also do the same thing for the `srcset` attribute:

```
<img class="lazy-image" data-src="img/venues/venue.jpg"
    data-srcset=" img/venues/venue-1200x900.jpg 1200vw, img/venues/venue
-992x744.jpg 992vw, img/venues/venue -768x576.jpg 768vw, img/venues/venue
-576x432.jpg 576vw"
    sizes=" (max-width: 577px) 90vw, (max-width: 769px) 45vw, (max-width:
769px) 30vw, 20vw" >
```

The `showImage` function handles toggling the `data-src` and `data-srcset` values to the corresponding `src` and `srcset` values. This causes the browser to load the images just before they come into view, or on demand:

```
showImage: function (entries, observer) {
    entries.forEach(function (io) {
        if (io.isIntersecting) {
            var image = io.target,
                src = image.getAttribute("data-src"),
                srcSet = image.getAttribute("data-srcset");

            if (srcSet) {
                image.setAttribute("srcset", srcSet);
            }

            if (src) {
                image.setAttribute("src", src);
            }
        }
    });
}
```

If you're worried about legacy browsers supporting `IntersectionObserver`, don't worry: there is a polyfil (https://github.com/w3c/IntersectionObserver/tree/master/polyfill). Right now, Chrome, Firefox, and Edge have native `IntersectionObserver` support. The polyfil allows you to use this technique in other browsers.

You should use feature detection to determine if you need to load the polyfil and the polyfil technique that was described previously.

The PWA ticket application uses the `IntersectionObserver` pattern to lazy-load images. I also want to point out a key aspect of this technique, which is specifying the images' render size as a placeholder.

Summary

This chapter has focused on improving your progressive web app's performance. You have learned about key performance indicators you can measure as well as tools to measure your application.

Once you have identified items to improve, you can attack them to improve your page load time and response times.

You have also been given some techniques and been exposed to code to help you build your pages to provide a better user experience. You have seen how to minimize the amount of code each page needs, improve caching, and reduce the initial page payload.

In the next chapter, you will see how to automate your progressive web application workflow to ensure that you have a consistently performing and qualifying PWA.

Service Worker Tools 10

Web development has become complicated today with so many options, steps, and tools. **Progressive Web Apps (PWAs)** require a new model but that can produce many opportunities for errors to creep into the code. The good news is that there are several tools that you can integrate into your workflow to improve your application code's integrity.

In this chapter, I will review several tools I have found invaluable in helping me ensure that my applications meet a level of consistent quality before I ship them. These include **PWABuilder**, **Lighthouse**, **Sonar**, and **WorkBox**.

Lighthouse and Sonar are *linting tools* you can use to audit your web pages to ensure that a minimum criteria is met, including PWA, performance, hosting, and SEO requirements. PWABuilder and Workbox are very helpful in scaffolding important aspects of progressive web apps including the manifest, icons, and service workers.

As a bonus, all of these tools are available as node modules which you can execute as part of a script and from the command line. This means that you can include much of this functionality as part of your automated workflow and build processes.

The following topics will be covered in this chapter:

- Scaffolding PWA assets with PWABuilder
- Auditing web pages using Lighthouse
- Auditing web pages using Sonar
- Making complex service workers with WorkBox

Using PWABuilder to scaffold your PWA

PWABuilder is a progressive web application scaffolding tool built by the Microsoft Edge team and publicly hosted at `https://pwabuilder.com`. I love this tool because you can quickly scaffold the assets you need to upgrade any website to a progressive web app in less than a minute.

There are three steps to scaffolding the PWA components, which are generating a web manifest file, picking a simple service worker, and downloading the assets:

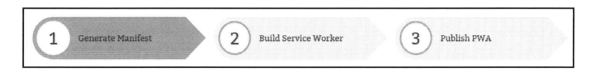

Let's check each of these steps in detail.

Generating a valid web manifest file

A valid web manifest file is one of the primary PWA requirements, but you would be surprised at how many sites miss this simple step. Most of them just forget an important field or to supply values that don't meet the guidelines, such as a long and short name value.

The biggest mistake is not including the minimum set of icons required by all the different browsers and operating systems.

To use the online tool, you need to supply a public URL, two primary application colors, and a logo or image you want to make application icons:

Chapter 10

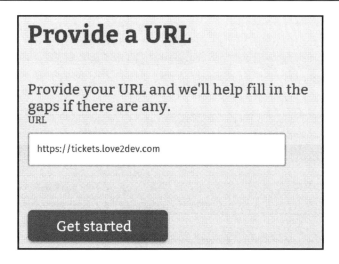

The wizard will try to parse values to supply properties, such as full name, short name, and description. If your site already has a web manifest file, it will use those properties. Don't worry: you can supply or change any value in the online form, as well as specify display orientation and language, as shown in the following screenshot:

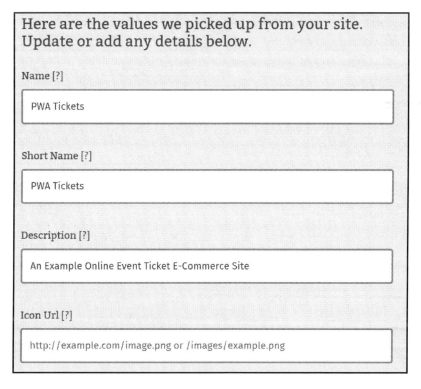

Service Worker Tools

The next step in the PWABuilder wizard is to generate a set of application icons, and there are over 100 at the time of writing this book. You can either supply a URL to a public image or upload a base image. The image generator will create a set of images to meet the criteria of each major platform: iOS, Android, and Windows. It also covers Chrome and FireFox requirements.

My favorite feature is how it includes proper references for each image in the generated web manifest file. I can't emphasize how much time this saves and how it eliminates potential errors. The fact that the service creates a complete set of images also means that you won't miss an important icon size that could keep your PWA from qualifying as a progressive web app on different platforms. Check out the following screenshot:

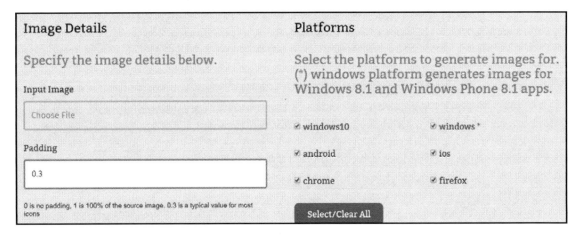

When you click the **Input Image** input field, you are greeted with a form so that you can upload an image. You can choose a file on your hard drive:

When the wizard completes, the product is a package containing all the icons and a manifest file with the icons referenced:

```
"theme_color": "#000066",
"icons": [{
        "src": "meta/windows10/Square71x71Logo.scale-400.png",
        "sizes": "284x284"
    },
    {
        "src": "meta/windows10/Square71x71Logo.scale-200.png",
        "sizes": "142x142"
    },
    {
        "src": "meta/windows10/Square71x71Logo.scale-100.png",
        "sizes": "71x71"
    },
    {
        "src": "meta/windows10/Square71x71Logo.scale-150.png",
        "sizes": "107x107"
    },
    {
        "src": "meta/windows10/Square71x71Logo.scale-125.png",
        "sizes": "89x89"
    },
```

Building a service worker

After uploading a source image to make the application icons, the service worker step displays. Here, you are given a selection of premade service workers. These are all basic service workers that can work with most sites so that you can start the progressive web application journey.

There are five starter service worker options:

- **Offline page**: Initializes the service worker cache with an offline fallback page
- **Offline copy of pages**: As the user visits pages on your site, they are cached, making return visits fast and offline capable
- Offline copy with a backup of offline pages
- **Cache-First Network**: Checks the cache for a valid response before hitting the network, which adds network responses to the cache
- **Advanced Pre-Caching**: Currently under development, but designed to give you more control over site assets that are cached when the service worker is installed

Downloading your site's PWA assets

After selecting a starter service worker, PWABuilder provides links to download packaged versions of your PWA and native apps. You have the option to download just the progressive web app assets, a pre-packaged Windows appx file, and native apps for the Google Play and iOS App stores.

In most cases, the native app versions won't be needed, but can be handy just in case you need access to platform-specific APIs and integrations.

You can click the buttons corresponding to the package you need. PWABuilder will then generate a package, a ZIP file, containing the assets you need. The site also provides instructions for integrating the scaffolded code into your site and submitting the app store packages to the various stores.

This is an example of the generated web manifest file:

```
{
    "name": "PWA Tickets",
    "short_name": "PWA Tickets",
    "icons": [ ...
    ],
    "start_url": "https://tickets.love2dev.com/",
    "display": "standalone",
    "background_color": "#7E040E",
    "theme_color": "#DFD6D9",
    "lang": "",
    "description": "An Example Online Event Ticket E-Commerce Site"
}
```

Scaffolded PWA images

I think the best part to PWABuilder is how it quickly generates all the application icons as the web manifest file that properly references each image. It generates over 100 images, and I don't know about you, but I don't have the time or patience to create that many variations, much less add the code to my web manifest file.

This is part of the PWABuilder wizard, but you may have already created a valid web manifest file and a service worker and only need a collection of icons.

This is where you can access the image generation service directly at `https://www.pwabuilder.com/imageGenerator`. You'll see the same form that's included in the wizard interface. The only difference is that once you provide the base image, you can directly click the **Download** button to get just your PWA icons and the web manifest JSON.

You are not limited to just using the online image generator. The source code is an open source ASP.NET project, `https://github.com/pwa-builder/App-Image-Generator`. You will need to stand up a web server that's capable of servicing an ASP.NET site, which you could do using Docker. I don't think this version is built on .NET Core, which means you will need an instance of IIS on Windows.

The tool does not modify any files in your site, so you still need to update your pages to register the service worker and web manifest file. You will also need to copy the icons, manifest, and service worker files to your site's folder.

Running PWABuilder locally

If your site is not public, don't worry: you can still take advantage of PWABuilder by running it locally. PWABuilder is actually the second generation of PWA tools produced by Microsoft. In its previous life, it was called Manifold JS, and still uses that engine.

Manifold is a collection of node modules, used by the PWABuilder site, that generate the files needed for your PWA. The Manifold JS components are available both on GitHub (`https://github.com/pwa-builder`) and npm (`https://www.npmjs.com/package/manifoldjs`).

You can run PWABuilder directly from the command line. Since it is a node module, you will need Nodejs installed, and so on.

I recommend installing the PWABuilder node library globally:

```
npm install -g pwabuilder
```

Now, you can execute `pwabuilder` from any command line. In the following example, I added a couple of options, one to specify the target directly to save the generated assets and another to designate what platform to generate assets:

```
C:\>pwabuilder http://localhost:15500/ -d "C:\Source Code\PWA\pwa-ticket" -p web
[warn ] general    : Manifest validation WARNING   - The short name contains invalid characters (it will be sanitized)(member: short_name).
[warn ] general    : Manifest validation WARNING   - The target website must be served from a secure origin (i.e. moved to HTTPS) to be compliant with Progressive Web Apps requirements(member: start_url).
```

If you want to get even more ambitious, you can build your own node script to execute the PWABuilder libraries directly. You can clone the PWABuilder projects and examine the source code and how the command-line utility executes to see how you can incorporate parts of the library in your own scaffolding routines.

Auditing web pages using Lighthouse

Lighthouse (`https://developers.google.com/web/tools/lighthouse/`) is an automated tool managed by the Chrome team that can help you audit your site to identify problems that need attention. The tools audits more than just progressive web app requirements, as it checks for many best practices including performance, accessibility, and SEO.

 Lighthouse is an open source project, and contributions are welcome.

As mentioned earlier in this book, Lighthouse can be executed two different ways:

- Built-in to the Chrome Developer tools' **Audit** tab
- Node Module (`https://www.npmjs.com/package/Lighthouse`)

The Chrome extension was the original implementation, but this is being phased out. Today, the extension is redundant since Lighthouse is built-in to the Developer tools.

Lighthouse will exercise a given URL in Chrome and run it through a battery of tests. These tests cover different scenarios emulating mobile cellular network and desktop versions.

It runs a battery of test against the URL in these different scenarios, looking for potential issues. It can establish a baseline for your application's performance and how well it meets minimum requirements, like being a PWA.

Lighthouse produces a score/report card, listing how a page has performed against the battery of tests. Over the course of a minute or so, an audit will reload the page several times under different conditions, with loads capturing traces each time. How long it took to load pages, become interactive, how well it worked offline, and so on are all logged.

The primary categories the Lighthouse audits are for progressive web application features, web performance optimization, accessibility, and general best practices. Recently, the tool added an SEO audit section, but this functionality is still limited at this time.

After you run a Lighthouse audit, you will see a report card. This is an example of the five top level audit type scores. These scores are based on a 0-100 scale, with 100 being perfect. The score is comprised of a weighted score for each point in the audit group:

Each one of these top-level audits runs granular tests and provides a very detailed report. Lighthouse can produce a report as either JSON or the default HTML. You can also save the data collected during a Developer tools test so that you can review and compare it with a later test.

The HTML report will automatically highlight areas you either failed on or need to address. It also provides helpful links to documentation that will help point you to a solution:

From time to time, I like to run Lighthouse from the Chrome Developer tools, just to see where I'm at in my development process. It's a quick and automated tool that can help me get insight into where I may have missed something mundane that can have a measurable impact.

For progressive web apps, it runs through a set of checklist items to be a full-blown progressive web app. Most can be automatically tested, but a few must be manually evaluated. The Lighthouse report list items should be manually verified.

The big two are obvious, HTTPS, web manifest file in a service worker, but it goes to a deeper level. It also looks at your performance and if you can load in under three seconds over a cellular connection. It does this by simulating slower network conditions and CPUs.

Service Worker Tools

It also checks to make sure that you have valid icons for the different viewports and that you can prompt the Homescreen banner.

All tests are run, emulating a 3G connection and throttle down your CPU 4x from its default speed. This last part can obviously skew your test results from device to device based on the available CPU. I work on a very new i7 Surface Laptop, which runs much faster than a more seasoned i3 or i5 processor. You will also see variability as you use different virtual machines with different CPU power allocated.

Collectively, all these little things will help you know if your website will provide a good user experience or not. It's not the only way to test, but it does give you a good baseline that covers most of the areas that you need to audit.

Running Lighthouse from the Chrome Developer Tools

The easiest way to use Lighthouse is from the Chrome Developers Tools. By now, you should know how to open these tools. All desktop browsers contain Developer tools and they can be opened by pressing *F12* or *Ctrl + Shift + I*.

Once the Developer tools are open, you have multiple options. Lighthouse is one of those options. It is labeled **Audits** and is presented as the last native tab. If you are like me, you may have an extension that has parked a custom tab in the tools as well. They are listed after the **Audits** tab:

Initially, there is not much to the **Audits** tab when you open it, just the Lighthouse dialog.

The dialog has a list of the five current audit categories, and the **Run audit** and **Cancel** buttons. Each category can be toggled on or off. Pressing the Run audit button starts the audit process:

[298]

Chapter 10

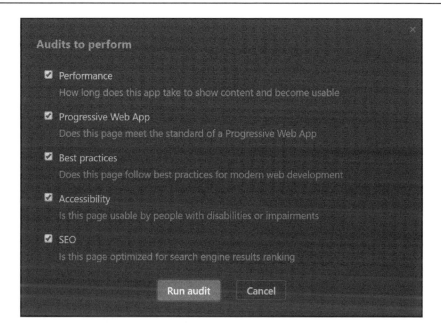

During the audit process, you will see a new dialog, assuring you that the audit is running and sharing useful web development facts and stats to keep you entertained. Meanwhile, the corresponding browser tab is being exercised by Lighthouse.

If you watch the browser tab, you will see it use the built-in emulation tools to load the target page in different virtual devices and under different network conditions, including offline.

Based on how the page behaves and loads, the different tests either pass or fail. In the end, Lighthouse produces a report, which you can then use to evaluate how your page stands. Use the report to identify different aspects of the page and site to improve:

Service Worker Tools

After the audit completes, you are presented with a nicely formatted report featuring a high-level grade in each category at the top. Below the scores, each category lists any failing tests or tests that you did not quite meet target numbers but should investigate. All tests that passed are grouped together and collapsed out of view but can still be viewed.

Every test should have a link with more details, indicated with a separate **Learn more** link, about what was tested and hopefully guidance to help you improve the page, so that you can pass the test:

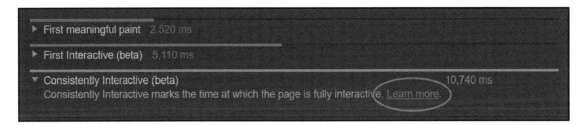

You should also consider the hosting environment you are testing against. Some tests will fail on a local site because you may not have a full production scale web server. While the node http-server makes it easy to run a local web server, it does not have HTTPS and HTTP/2 by default. This makes your page fail any tests that are looking for these two features.

In these scenarios, you can safely ignore these test results due to environment limitations. I do advise performing additional tests once the site is deployed to full scale environments like development, staging, and production.

Remember, when running in the Developer tools, you should use this as an important triage step to ensure that your code and site updates improve the overall site's experience. They are not the actual experience a real user may have, because the site is hosted in a different environment. Also remember the conditions Lighthouse emulates are just that, emulated, and may not perfectly reflect a real-world device or network conditions.

Another big issue with the Developer tools Lighthouse implementation is that there is the inability to customize the audit beyond toggling major test categories. You cannot extend the audit with your own tests and categories.

This is where running Lighthouse directly as a node module offers big benefits.

Running Lighthouse as a command-line utility

I really enjoy the ability to execute Lighthouse as a node module. The Lighthouse node module has a dependency on Chrome Launcher (https://www.npmjs.com/package/chrome-launcher), which will open an instance of Chrome to execute the test.

This means the machine executing Lighthouse should have Chrome installed. The tool uses a full instance of Chrome because it needs to render the page and use the Developer tools to emulate different modes.

Because Lighthouse is a node module, you need to install it using either npm or yarn. Like the other tools, I recommend installing it globally:

```
>npm install -g Lighthouse
```

You can run a full audit right from the command line by executing Lighthouse followed by the target URL:

```
>Lighthouse https://tickets.love2dev.com
```

This launches a new instance of Chrome and runs the test battery against the target URL. When completed, an HTML report file is created in the current folder. You can load this in a browser to review. It is the same report that's loaded in the Developer tools.

This is an example of an automated test report file loaded into the Lighthouse report viewer:

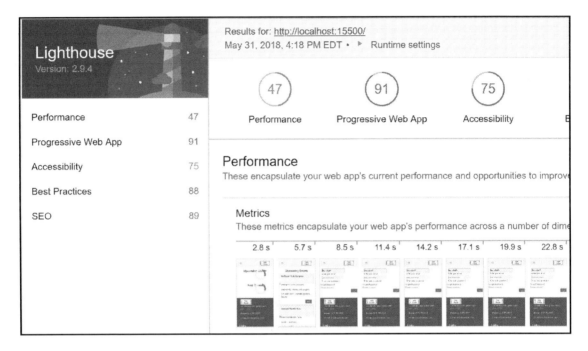

You can customize Lighthouse to perform the tests you need and report in the format you want. These are just some of the common options I use on my projects:

- `--config-path`: The local path to the configuration file you want to use for the audit.
- `--output`: The report format. Options are JSON, CSV, and HTML with HTML by default. You can designate more than one format.
- `--output-path`: The location to write the report. If multiple formats are designated, the path is ignored, but each format is saved to the current path based on the target's basename.
- `--view`: Launches a HTML report in the browser once it is written.
- `--block-url-patterns`: Forces the browser to ignore certain assets. This is good to test without third-party scripts.
- `--throttling-*`: Different options here to granularly control how network and CPU throttling is set during tests.
- `--save-assets`: Persists test assets like screenshots to disks.

In this example, a full audit is run and saved in both JSON and HTML formats:

```
>Lighthouse https://tickets.love2dev.com --output json --output html --output-path ./myfile.json
```

The report is saved locally in both output formats. I like doing this because the HTML report is easy to read and the JSON report is easy to consume into third party or custom reporting solutions.

The default Lighthouse audit may not cover the rules you need to monitor or more than you want to test. You can also create your own tests, which need to be included. You can customize the audit with your own configuration.

Custom configurations are written as JSON objects. This example extends the default configuration, but limits the tests to just the performance and progressive web app tests:

```
{
    "extends": "Lighthouse:default",
    "settings": {
        "onlyCategories": ["performance", "pwa"]
    }
}
```

To use the custom configuration file, you must supply the path as a command-line switch:

```
>Lighthouse https://tickets.love2dev.com --config-path=./custom.Lighthouse.config.js --output json --output html --output-path ./pwa-tickets.json
```

Ultimately, you can control everything Lighthouse uses to run an audit, including gathers, test groups, categories, and how different passes execute.

A custom configuration file makes it very easy for you to control how Lighthouse is exercised against your web app without fussing with extended command-line options. This also makes testing very repeatable and you can include the configuration files in your source control to easily restore and audit how tests were executed.

Lighthouse and headless testing

Recently, the Chrome team also released a tool called Puppeteer (https://github.com/GoogleChrome/puppeteer), which executes a headless instance of Chromium. This is not Chrome, but a variation in the code base upon which many popular applications such as Visual Studio Code are built.

A headless browser can execute a page, but not with the ability to view the page. Because the page is not visibly rendered, some of the tests are not run. You should keep this mind when executing an audit using a headless browser.

The ability to exercise Lighthouse against a headless browser has opened up opportunities for the tool to be integrated in different tools. For example, WebPageTest, HTTPArchive, Calibre, and others use Lighthouse to add additional test points to their reports. You can follow their lead and incorporate the Lighthouse node module in your in-house test and auditing work flows.

Because Lighthouse can be executed from a script as a node module, you can create an automated test to exercise over your entire website or a sample set of URLs in your website. You can then audit the results and find the common area areas you need to address.

I do advise running it over more than one URL in your site because there are many different types of pages that compose most applications. But a word of caution: limit the number of pages you automate testing. Each test instance will launch a new instance of Chrome, which can quickly get out of hand if you try to test an entire site.

The lightcrawler (https://github.com/github/lightcrawler) project is a possible tool you can use to automate testing your entire site. Lighthouse Cron (https://github.com/thearegee/Lighthouse-cron) allows you to audit a site at scheduled and random intervals using cron jobs to collect scores over time. These are just a couple of examples of how Lighthouse and similar tools are being used to provide valuable testing and performance audits to make web applications better.

I would also recommend running multiple test cycles to create a comparison. Any time I run a site or page audit, I find result variations. Sometimes, like any real scientific experiment, you find outliers that do not accurately reflect the overall experience.

For example, the test machine may have a high CPU background task running or one that consumes disk and memory I/O, causing performance issues. When testing against a live site, you may also encounter network issues that fall outside of your control.

These can all lead to failed tests and poor audit results. When I see poor performance results, I will typically run 3-5 more tests to see what sort of variations I may have. When I consistently see a test fail or log poor results, I then work to improve the issue. If a failed test is consistent, the problem is my site, not the environment around the site.

Running Lighthouse in a Node script

Like Sonar (which will be covered in the next section) and the other node-based utilities, you can also use Lighthouse in your own node scripts and modules. You need to create references to both the `Lighthouse` and `chrome-launcher` modules:

```
const Lighthouse = require("Lighthouse"),
    chromeLauncher = require('chrome-launcher');
```

Both the Chrome Launcher and Lighthouse modules return promises. You must create a new Chrome instance before launching Lighthouse.

Chrome Launcher resolves a reference to a Chrome instance. You need to pass the developer port number to the Lighthouse module. This is how Lighthouse communicates with Chrome to perform the tests:

```
function launchChromeAndRunLighthouse(url, flags, config = null) {

    return chromeLauncher.launch({
        chromeFlags: flags.chromeFlags
    }).then(chrome => {

        flags.port = chrome.port;
        return Lighthouse(url, flags, config).then(results => {
        // The gathered artifacts are typically removed as they can be
        //quite large (~50MB+)
            delete results.artifacts;
            return chrome.kill().then(() => results);
        });
    });
}
```

You should also supply your custom configuration to the Lighthouse method. You can leave this empty and the default audit is executed.

When Lighthouse starts, a new instance of Chrome is opened, just like from the command line. You can watch your site run through all the tests.

When Lighthouse is finished, it resolves the results in the target format.

Continuous build with Lighthouse

Another way to use Lighthouse is to embed it as part of your build and deployment workflow. For example, you may use a tool like **Travis**, which exercises a script to deploy and test applications. This way, you can make sure that the project passes the Lighthouse audits before deploying to a production server.

There is a problem running more modern sites requiring authentication like the PWA ticket application. Because Lighthouse exercises web pages using an unprimed environment and sometimes when storage is not available, persisted tokens may not be available.

In the PWA ticket application, this means the site redirects to the login page. I have seen a few mentions of potential solutions to this issue, but have not had much success.

Finally, one of the cool Lighthouse tools I found is Eric Bidel's Score badges (`https://github.com/ebidel/Lighthouse-badge`). You can include the badges as part of your project's `readme` file:

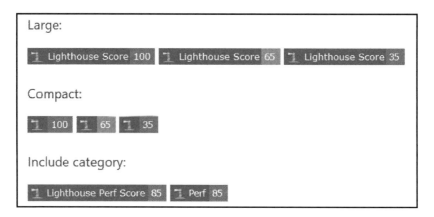

Lighthouse is a fantastic tool that can help you find and diagnose many common issues that will affect your overall application user experience. It provides valid valued insight into things like progressive web application features, web performance, accessibility, and feature acts. And as we've recently seen, the team is continually adding new test sets to Lighthouse. The SEO set is just the start of a new air area that Lighthouse will cover.

The built-in tooling gives you, the developer, or any concerned party, the ability to quickly test a page to see how well you meet expectations in the default categories. You should remember the default tests run by the Chrome tool are what the Chrome team considers important and they may not match exactly to your needs.

I do recommend starting with the default tests to benchmark your site's current state. The default tests are a great set of baseline tests that I personally think every site should use as a minimum standard.

The ability to run Lighthouse directly using node gives you the ability to not only tailor tests to your requirements, but gives you the ability to customize and extend the test battery. You can dig into the Lighthouse documentation to see how to create your own tests.

Auditing web pages with Sonar

Similar to Lighthouse, the Microsoft Edge team has also released a new site linting tool called **Sonar** (https://sonarwhal.com/). Like Lighthouse, it is an open source node module that serves as a testing harness to execute rules over a web page.

The two tools offer similar testing abilities, but also offer a different set of abilities and test batteries. Both provide a default starting point to execute a base set of tests on a page. Both can be customized with your own configurations and even extended with custom tests and reports.

Unlike Lighthouse, Sonar is not built into the browser developers tools. At least not yet, and I only say that because I could see the tool being integrated into Edge at some point, like Lighthouse is in Chrome.

Sonar also differs because it can execute tests in either Microsoft Edge, Chrome, or other testing libraries. For example, Sonar ships with a jsdom parser.

Using the Sonar CLI

Because Sonar is not part of a browser, but a node module, it needs to be executed either within a custom node script or by using its command-line interface. The CLI is the best place to start using Sonar, and like Lighthouse, you need to install Sonar first. Again, I recommend a global install:

```
npm install -g sonarwhal
```

Service Worker Tools

Before you can run Sonar, you need to create a configuration file, `.sonarwhalrc`. You can do this by hand or use the command line to initialize a configuration file:

```
> sonarwhal --init
```

This kicks off a wizard, asking you a series of questions to initialize your configuration. You can choose a predefined configuration or make a custom configuration:

```
C:\Users\clove>sonarwhal --init
Welcome to sonarwhal configuration generator
? Do you want to use a predefined configuration or create your own based on your installed packages? predefined
? Choose the configuration you want to extend from (Use arrow keys)
> web-recommended
  progressive-web-apps
```

There are two predefined configurations available at this time: `web-recommended` and `progressive-web-apps`. Depending on which configuration you choose, the wizard will install any required node dependencies. I will cover the Sonar components a little later:

```
C:\Users\clove>sonarwhal --init
Welcome to sonarwhal configuration generator
? Do you want to use a predefined configuration or create your own based on your installed packages? predefined
? Choose the configuration you want to extend from web-recommended
Installing packages...
√ Running command: npm install @sonarwhal/configuration-web-recommended -g
```

This produces a started config file, extending the built-in `web-recommended` package:

```
{
    "extends": [
        "web-recommended"
    ]
}
```

This contains a base configuration with a minimum set of rules, a formatter, and connector definition. This is what the `web-recommended` configuration file looks like. You can use the following code as a reference to see how to create your own configuration files:

```
{
    "connector": {
        "name": "jsdom",
        "options": {
            "waitFor": 5000
        }
    },
    "formatters": [
        "summary"
```

```
    ],
    "rules": {
        "axe": "error",
        "content-type": "error",
        "disown-opener": "error",
        "highest-available-document-mode": "error",
        "html-checker": "error",
        "http-cache": "error",
        "http-compression": "error",
        "meta-charset-utf-8": "error",
        "meta-viewport": "error",
        "no-bom": "error",
        "no-disallowed-headers": "error",
        "no-friendly-error-pages": "error",
        "no-html-only-headers": "error",
        "no-http-redirects": "error",
        "no-protocol-relative-urls": "error",
        "no-vulnerable-javascript-libraries": "error",
        "sri": "error",
        "ssllabs": "error",
        "strict-transport-security": "error",
        "validate-set-cookie-header": "error",
        "x-content-type-options": "error"
    },
    "rulesTimeout": 120000
}
```

I will demonstrate how to customize this configuration a little later.

You are not limited to a single configuration to extend, as you can extend multiple configurations, as mentioned in the following code:

```
{
    "extends": [
        "config1", "config2"
    ]
}
```

You are not limited to the built-in configurations and you don't need to run the initialization wizard. You can create your own configuration file, as they are just JSON documents:

```
{
    "connector": {
        "name": "edge"
    },
    "formatters": ["json"],
    "rules": {
```

```
        "rule1": "error",
        "rule2": "warning",
        "rule3": "off"
    },
    "rulesTimeout": 120000
    ...
}
```

Once Sonar has a configuration, you can execute it from the command line. Like Lighthouse, you just need to execute Sonar followed by a valid URL:

```
> sonarwhal https://tickets.love2dev.com
```

You can customize the test by creating a custom configuration file. Sonar will look for the `.sonarwhalrc` file in the current folder.

Sonar components

There are five components of Sonar you need to familiarize yourself with to understand how the tool works.

Configurations

These are the `.sonarwhalrc` files I covered earlier. These are the files that drive a specific test or audit against your site.

Connectors

The connector is the interface between the rules Sonar executes and the URL. Right now, there are three official connectors available:

- `jsdom`: A nodejs implementation of the WHATWG DOM, which means it provides a pretty good engine to test how the page renders.
- `chrome`: Executes the rules by launching Chrome, using it's debugging protocol.
- `edge`: Exercises the rules using Microsoft Edge. This requires Windows 10 because Edge only works on Windows.

Formatters

Formatters take the test results and *print* them. There are currently five formatters being maintained by the Sonar team:

- `json`: Creates a JSON formatted report
- `stylish`: Produces a table formatted report
- `excel`: Generates the report as an Excel worksheet
- `codeframe`: Produces the report in a codeframe style
- `summary`: Formats the report in a table

My personal favorite is JSON because I can then use that as a raw data source to add it to a custom report or combine it with other tools like Lighthouse's reports to complete a full site audit.

Parsers

Rules subscribe to parsers and the events they emit to perform tests. They are designed to focus on specific resource types, like JavaScript and web manifest files.

Rules

Rules are the heart of Sonar because they are responsible for exercising the page to see if the desired criteria are met. There are a number of rules included in the default Sonar installation. Like the rest of Sonar, you are free to create your own rules.

Automating site audits with the Sonar node module

The combination of being a nodejs module and the command-line interface gives you multiple ways to integrate Sonar as part of your build and deployment process.

Unlike Lighthouse, there are no command-line switches because it relies on the configuration file. If you want to execute different configurations, you need to run sonarwhal from the target folder so that the desired custom configuration is loaded.

Making complex service workers with workbox

Workbox (`https://developers.google.com/web/tools/workbox/`) is another open source project to help you create service workers. It is maintained by the Chrome team, but like the other projects, I have reviewed those open to public contributions.

The goal of Workbox is to help scaffold complete service workers or add complex components to existing service workers. Workbox allows you to build on a solid foundation, so you can configure to meet your specific needs. It gives you control over how you build your service worker. You can manually add features to existing service workers and tooling to scaffold a service worker from scratch.

A properly configured service worker uses a combination of appropriate caching strategies. The key part of that sentence is a *properly configured service worker*, which is, as you should know by now, not simple.

Workbox is a tool to scaffold the caching components in your service worker. The tool focuses on providing boilerplate code to help with the following service worker areas:

- Precaching
- Runtime caching
- Strategies
- Request routing
- Background sync
- Helpful debugging

Workbox's history is rooted in a pair of now deprecated projects, `sw_precache` and `sw_toolbox`. `sw_precache`, which are managed precaching assets and `sw_toolbox` handled dynamic caching. Workbox focuses on managing all caching and invalidation strategies.

At the time of writing this book, Workbox is currently at version 3.2 and has come a long way in the past 18 months. Its strength is its ability to abstract complex code away from you, the developer. Instead, you can focus on configuration and in some cases, customization.

For the rest of this chapter, I will focus on updating the PWA ticket application to replace most of the code covered in `Chapter 8`, *Applying Advanced Service Worker Cache Strategies*, with Workbox. I created a separate branch in the source repository called workbox.

Installing workbox

Workbox is a collection of library and node modules. To get the full breadth of the tool, you need to install the node modules globally and clone the GitHub repository. Cloning the library is not required, but I recommend it so that you can study how the library is structured:

```
> npm install -g workbox-cli
```

The Workbox node modules include command-line interfaces to help you scaffold your service worker and Workbox components. I will cover how to use the CLI as I explain the different parts of the tool.

The first step you need to take after installing the CLI is to run the Workbox wizard:

```
> workbox wizard
```

This will start a series of questions about your application:

```
C:\Users\clove\love2dev>workbox wizard
? What is the root of your web app (i.e. which directory do you deploy)? Manually enter path
? Please enter the path to the root of your web app: C:\Source Code\PWA\pwa-ticket\www\public
? Which file types would you like to precache? html, css, eot, svg, ttf, woff, woff2, png, txt, jpg, json, js, gif, manifest
? Where would you like your service worker file to be saved? C:\Source Code\PWA\pwa-ticket\www\public\sw.js
? Where would you like to save these configuration options? workbox-config.js
To build your service worker, run

  workbox generateSW workbox-config.js

as part of a build process. See https://goo.gl/fdTQBf for details.
You can further customize your service worker by making changes to workbox-config.js. See https://goo.gl/gVo87N for details.
```

This will create a configuration file that the `workbox-cli` tool can use during additional steps. This is what it generates when run and choosing the default options for the PWA ticket app:

```
module.exports = {
  "globDirectory": "C:\Source Code\PWA\pwa-ticket\www\public",
  "globPatterns": [
"**/*.{html,css,eot,svg,ttf,woff,woff2,png,txt,jpg,json,js,gif,manifest}"
  ],
  "swDest": "C:\Source Code\PWA\pwa-ticket\www\public\sw.js"
};
```

Service Worker Tools

The CLI commands use the settings in the configuration file to find all the files matching the `globPatterns` and creates an entry in the precache array. I will cover the precache list format in the next section:

```
C:\Users\clove\love2dev>workbox generateSW "C:\Source Code\PWA\pwa-ticket\www\public\workbox-config.js"
Using configuration from C:\Source Code\PWA\pwa-ticket\www\public\workbox-config.js.
The service worker was written to C:\Source Code\PWA\pwa-ticket\www\public\sw.js
604 files will be precached, totalling 10.7 MB.
```

I don't advise precaching 600 files and 11 MB like this example demonstrates. Instead, you should customize the configuration to trim the list to a proper amount. In this case, the PWA tickets app has all the ticket barcodes generated as part of the build process, so there is data to develop against.

I'll circle back around to show you how to customize the configuration file to maximize your Workbox service worker experience. The configuration file and the workbox-cli commands to compose your service worker are key to using the library.

You are free to use the Workbox library any way you see fit. The configuration is for the command-line tools. If you are not familiar with the different nuances to how Workbox works, then I suggest starting with the wizard first.

Once you have mastered or at least feel very comfortable with how the Workbox library works, you can start integrating it by hand. It all starts with importing the library to your service worker.

In previous chapters, I demonstrated how you can use `importScripts` to reference additional scripts within your service worker. You will need to reference the workbox library using `importScripts`:

```
self.importScripts("https://storage.googleapis.com/workbox-cdn/releases/3.2
.0/workbox-sw.js",
    "js/libs/2ae25530a0dd28f30ca44f5182f0de61.min.js",
    "js/app/libs/e392a867bee507b90b366637460259aa.min.js",
    "sw/sw-push-manager.js"
);
```

This example shows how I replaced some of the supporting libraries in the PWA tickets app with a reference to the CDN hosted Workbox script. The library is hosted in the Google Cloud CDN.

You can also use the `workbox-cli copyLibrary` command to copy the library to your site. The library is not a single file, but a collection of many files containing different JavaScript classes. These files are all copied to the target directory. I used the /sw folder in the PWA tickets app.

A folder with the current Workbox version number is created within the target folder. To add a reference to the library, you need to reference the `workbox-sw.js` file:

```
self.importScripts("sw/workbox-v3.2.0/workbox-sw.js",
    "js/libs/2ae25530a0dd28f30ca44f5182f0de61.min.js",
    "js/app/libs/e392a867bee507b90b366637460259aa.min.js",
    "sw/sw-push-manager.js"
);
```

In previous Workbox versions, the entire library was loaded, which is a lot of code. This has been improved, so that now only the files needed by your service worker are loaded, reducing the payload and required storage. The 3.2 version I am using for this example has 23 different files or classes.

If you look in the folder that's created by the `copyFiles` method, you will see more. There are two versions for each class, production and debug. There are also source map files as well. I will show you how to toggle which versions are used as well as how to tell Workbox how to find the local modules a little later.

The CLI tool is a great way to familiarize yourself with using Workbox to scaffold your service worker, but it is really just a library. In the next section, I will review how the library is structured and get you started with how to use Workbox in your service workers to maximize your experience.

Workbox structure

When you import the Workbox library, you are importing the root level module. The module loads additional components belonging to the workbox namespace, such as:

- `workbox`
- `workbox.core`
- `workbox.precaching`
- `workbox.routing`
- `workbox.strategies`
- `workbox.expiration`

Service Worker Tools

- `workbox.backgroundSync`
- `workbox.googleAnalytics`
- `workbox.cacheableResponse`
- `workbox.broadcastUpdate`
- `workbox.rangeRequest`
- `workbox.streams`

Each library has its own API. Some are higher level and others work within or even extend others. Routing uses the strategies classes, which in turn can be extended through plugins. The Workbox libraries can handle most scenarios out of the box, but are configurable and extensible to allow you to customize them as needed.

You are not limited to the modules included in the library. You can create your own components and add even more value to Workbox's functionality. You can also use their modules as references to build your own custom solutions.

Service worker setup

By default, Workbox uses a debug version of the library with extra logging capabilities. You can turn this off and use the production version by setting the debug flag to false in the `setConfig` method. The production version is more lightweight, which means you won't be as much of a burden on your customer's data plans. The production code is minified and has heavier logging capabilities removed:

```
workbox.setConfig({
    debug: false
});
```

By default, Workbox loads modules from the CDN. If you are hosting Workbox on your server, then you need to configure Workbox to load modules from your server. This requires using the `modulePathPrefix` in the configuration object.

To configure Workbox to use a local production version, the `setConfig` call would look like:

```
workbox.setConfig({
    debug: false,
    modulePathPrefix: "sw/ workbox-v3.2.0/"
});
```

You can let Workbox manage everything about your service worker, including life cycle events. If you want your service worker to immediately become active, you should do this for the `skipWaiting` (in Chapter 5, *The Service Worker Life Cycle*) and `clientsClaim` methods:

```
workbox.skipWaiting();
workbox.clientsClaim();
```

If you are integrating Workbox components in your service worker and are not outsourcing all life cycle management to Workbox, then you can still manage this within the install and active events, as you learned earlier in this book.

Pre-caching with Workbox

Earlier in this book, I covered the concept of pre-caching assets within the install event. The standard pattern used is to create a list of URLs to cache and pass those to the `cache.addAll` method. This is great when your application is very stable and rarely changes assets. But what if you only need to update a handful of the pre-cached responses?

Instead of using the `cache.addAll` method, you need to create more sophisticated routines to check revisions against cached assets and perform updates.

This is where the Workbox precaching module is helpful. It abstracts the complex logic required to manage your pre-cached assets. You can still supply a simple array of URLs, as I have demonstrated in previous chapters, and it will cache those. But you have the option of also including a corresponding hash or revision value Workbox which you can use to track the asset.

The `workbox.precaching.precahceAndRoute` method accepts an array which can contain strings, objects, or a combination of both. In this example, I have just copied the PWA tickets pre-cache list into the method:

```
workbox.precaching.precacheAndRoute([
    "/",
    "img/pwa-tickets-logo-320x155.png",
    "js/app/512df4f42ca96bc22908ff3a84431452.min.js",
    "js/libs/ca901f49ff220b077f4252d2f1140c68.min.js",
     //...the remaining URLs to pre-cache
    "cart/"
]);
```

Workbox maintains an index of cached responses with extra meta data in `IndexedDB`. It can only use this to update precached assets when needed. The change you need to make is converting your pre-cache list from just strings to objects containing the URL and a revision value.

Here, I have a modified the version of the list, showing just a few of the entries:

```
workbox.precaching.precacheAndRoute([
    ...
  {
    "url": "error.html",
    "revision": "24d4cb67d5da47a373764712eecb7d86"
  },
  {
    "url": "event/index.html",
    "revision": "7127ba50c2b316ccbc33f2fad868c6a7"
  },
  {
    "url": "events/index.html",
    "revision": "6702e4d3b1554047e8655696875b396d"
  },
  {
    "url": "fallback/index.html",
    "revision": "d03fa5c7471ec4c84ca8bf8fefaddc2b"
  },
    ....
]);
```

The most common way to generate a revision value is to calculate the file's hash. I demonstrated how to generate file hashes in Chapter 8, *Applying Advanced Service Worker Cache Strategies*. You can leverage this routine as part of your build process or you can leverage the Workbox CLI to help.

When you run the Workbox CLI wizard, it uses the glob patterns to identify your site's assets. It creates a list of files to pre-cache with a hash value assigned to the corresponding revision values. You have two options: let the wizard scaffold your entire service worker, or have it inject the precaching code into an existing service worker.

The `injectManifest` functionality allows you to inject pre-caching code using the Workbox infrastructure. This is done using the CLI and the `injectManifest` command. You need to supply the path to the configuration script:

```
> workbox injectManifest path/to/config.js
```

The CLI tool looks for the following to replace with a call to `preCacheAndRoute`:

```
workbox.precaching.precacheAndRoute([]);
```

This method allows you to maintain a source service worker you can modify as part of your build process. It also allows you to lean on the wizard to create the file hashes for you.

If you are using a file naming convention that includes a hash or revision value, you can continue to do this without supplying the hash to Workbox. For these scenarios, you can just supply the string reference.

Some files cannot use revision values in their file names, like the path to any HTML. Changing the URL changes the address, which means you either need to configure complex 301 redirect rules or worse, break links to assets.

In this example, the `precacheAndRoute` method is passed an array of both strings, URLs with revision values built into the names, and objects for the HTML files without a revisioned name:

```
workbox.precaching.precacheAndRoute([
    ...
        "js/app/libs/e392a867bee507b90b366637460259aa.min.js",
        "js/app/libs/8fd5a965abed65cd11ef13e6a3408641.min.js",
        "js/app/pages/5b4d14af61fc40df7d6bd62f3e2a86a4.min.js",
        "js/app/pages/8684e75675485e7af7aab5ca10cc8da5.min.js",
        "js/app/pages/88ea734e66b98120a5b835a5dfdf8f6c.min.js",
    {
      "url": "error.html",
      "revision": "24d4cb67d5da47a373764712eecb7d86"
    },
    {
      "url": "event/index.html",
      "revision": "7127ba50c2b316ccbc33f2fad868c6a7"
    },
    {
      "url": "events/index.html",
      "revision": "6702e4d3b1554047e8655696875b396d"
    },
    {
      "url": "fallback/index.html",
      "revision": "d03fa5c7471ec4c84ca8bf8fefaddc2b"
    },
    ....
]);
```

Service Worker Tools

You can build your list and call the `preCacheAndRoute` method, as I have shown, but you can also break the precache list into logical groups so that you can supply those individually using the `workbox.precaching.precache` method. After you have supplied all the precache references, you must call the `addRoute` method to complete the process:

```
workbox.precaching.precache([
    ...
        "js/app/libs/e392a867bee507b90b366637460259aa.min.js",
        "js/app/libs/8fd5a965abed65cd11ef13e6a3408641.min.js",
        "js/app/pages/5b4d14af61fc40df7d6bd62f3e2a86a4.min.js",
        "js/app/pages/8684e75675485e7af7aab5ca10cc8da5.min.js",
        "js/app/pages/88ea734e66b98120a5b835a5dfdf8f6c.min.js",
    ...
]);
workbox.precaching.precache([
    ...
  {
    "url": "error.html",
    "revision": "24d4cb67d5da47a373764712eecb7d86"
  },
  {
    "url": "event/index.html",
    "revision": "7127ba50c2b316ccbc33f2fad868c6a7"
  },
  {
    "url": "events/index.html",
    "revision": "6702e4d3b1554047e8655696875b396d"
  },
  {
    "url": "fallback/index.html",
    "revision": "d03fa5c7471ec4c84ca8bf8fefaddc2b"
  },
    ....
]);

workbox.precaching.andRoute();
```

If you are using the CLI to generate a list of files and hash values to pre-cache, you need to trim or limit the files it includes in the list. For example, the PWA tickets application automatically creates hashed names for style sheets and scripts, but not the templates and HTML assets.

A simple modification of the site's Workbox configuration file removes the css and js files from the automated process. Just remove those extensions from the `globPatterns` regular expression:

```
module.exports = {
  "globDirectory": "C:\Source Code\PWA\pwa-ticket\www\public",
  "globPatterns": [
    "**/*.{html,eot,svg,ttf,woff,woff2,png,txt,jpg,json,gif,manifest}"
  ],
  "globIgnores": ["qrcodes/*.gif", "img/venues/**/*.*", "img/people/*.*", "meta/**/*.*",
    "html/pages/*.*", "css/webfonts/*.*", "img/pwa-tickets-logo*.*", "sw/cache.manifest"],
  "swDest": "C:\Source Code\PWA\pwa-ticket\www\public\sw.js",
  "swSrc": "C:\Source Code\PWA\pwa-ticket\www\public\sw.src.js"
};
```

Also note that I added a `globIgnores` property to the config as well. This tells the wizard to ignore any files matching these patterns. I know that the QR codes are generated by ticket and the venue images should only be loaded as needed. I also added a few additional patterns to the ignore list. Now, those assets are not pre-cached, and instead of precaching over 11 MB of assets, the service worker will now pre-cache 886 KB in 39 files:

```
c:\Source Code\PWA\pwa-ticket\www\public>workbox generateSW workbox-config.js
Using configuration from c:\Source Code\PWA\pwa-ticket\www\public\workbox-config.js.
The service worker was written to C:\Source Code\PWA\pwa-ticket\www\public\sw.generated.js
39 files will be precached, totalling 886 kB.
```

Workbox ships with three ways you can use it to generate the revision values:

- `workbox-build`: Can be included in a task runner like grunt, gulp, or npm script
- `workbox-cli`: Can generate a list and add it to a scaffolded service worker
- `workbox-webpack-plugin`: For webpack users

You are not limited to the revision values the Workbox tools generate, and you can generate them as part of your own build process. The revision value just needs to be unique for each version of the file so that the Workbox service worker libraries can check to see if it needs to update the resource.

Workbox can manipulate requests to match variations to cached versions. For example, often, marketing tags are added in the `QueryString` and vary for many reasons. Workbox can be configured to ignore `QueryString` patterns to avoid duplicate content caching.

These are the common variation scenarios Workbox can be configured to optimize:

- **queryStrings and URL parameters**
- **Default documents**: `index.html` and `default.html`
- **Cean URLs**: Automatically appending `.html` to extension-less URLs
- **Custom manipulations**: An opportunity for you to define a callback method to return an array of possible matches

This requires using the `precaching.PrecacheController` object. To do so, you need to create a new instance of the controller and use the `addToCacheList` method. This method consumes the same array(s) used with the precaching methods.

The difference is that you must manage the service worker install, activate, and fetch events manually:

```
const precacheController = new workbox.precaching.PrecacheController();
precacheController.addToCacheList([
    "/",
    "img/pwa-tickets-logo-320x155.png",
    "js/app/512df4f42ca96bc22908ff3a84431452.min.js",
    "js/libs/ca901f49ff220b077f4252d2f1140c68.min.js",
    //... the remaining URLs to pre-cache
    "cart/"
]);

precacheController.addToCacheList([
   {
     "url": "html/pages/tickets.html",
     "revision": "11c6e0cb67409cf544b162cd6a7ebfbf"
   },
   {
     "url": "html/polyfils.html",
     "revision": "337170ad8814e7571a7b8ddb8831ae04"
   }
]);

self.addEventListener('install', (event) => {
  event.waitUntil(precacheController.install());
});
self.addEventListener('activate', (event) => {
  event.waitUntil(precacheController.cleanup());
});
self.addEventListener('fetch', (event) => {
  event.respondWith(caches.match(event.request).then(...));
});
```

Inside the service worker event install and activate handlers, you need to call the `precacheController install` and `cleanup` methods.

Pre-caching is just one of Workbox's strengths. Its pre-caching system solves a common issue encountered with pre-caching, and that is how to keep the cached assets up to date without flushing the entire cache and reloading. Now, you can update the service worker and it will only update changed assets, a big win.

The pre-caching system is also highly configurable and customizable. Even though Workbox performs a lot of work behind abstractions, you don't need to feel like you lost control.

Dynamic routes with Workbox

Up to this point, the Workbox section has focused on scaffolding, pre-caching, and configuration concerns. But as you should know by this point, the complexity of a service worker grows, managing dynamic requests or any request that does not have a pre-cached response.

This is where Workbox really flexes its muscles.

Dynamic routes, like the PWA tickets event pages, need to have custom caching logic applied to them. This is where the `workbox.routing` object comes into play. For each dynamic route, you need to register what the route is and a handler using the `registerRoute` method. Its signature looks like this:

```
workbox.routing.registerRoute(matchCb, handlerCb);
```

The method requires a match and handler callback method. Each one of these callback methods is supplied a URL and event (`FetchEvent`) object. The callback methods use these parameters to determine what to do.

The callback signatures should look something like this:

```
const routeCallback = ({url, event}) => {
  //do something here
};
```

Service Worker Tools

The match callback should evaluate the request and return back a truthy value, indicating if the request matches the pattern or not:

```
const EventsMatch = ({url, event}) => {
  return (url.pathname.includes("/event/");
};
```

You can also supply a regular expression object (`RegEx`). This gives you the flexibility to assign a route handler to multiple, related assets at the same time. This is the most common way you will use Workbox routing.

The handler callback is free to apply any caching strategy needed. Again, the method should use the URL and event objects to perform these actions, just like you learned in previous chapters.

This example shows how you might integrate the `fetchAndRenderResponseCache` functionality demonstrated in Chapter 8, *Applying Advanced Service Worker Cache Strategies*:

```
const eventsHandler = ({url, event, params}) => {
        return responseManager.fetchAndRenderResponseCache({
            request: event.request,
            pageURL: rule.options.pageURL,
            template: rule.options.template,
            api: rule.options.api,
            cacheName: cacheName
        })
            .then(response => {
                invalidationManager.cacheCleanUp(cacheName);
                return response;
            });
};
```

In most cases, you won't need to create your own custom callback methods because Workbox has strategy modules for most common scenarios.

You can also define a default handler for any route that may not have an explicit handler registered:

```
workbox.routing.setDefaultHandler(workbox.strategies.cacheFirst());
```

Notice how I used one of the caching strategies as the default, `cacheFirst`? This should help us segway to the next step in dynamic routes, using caching strategies.

You should probably have a handler any time there is an exception retrieving a response. Workbox can do this with the `routing.setCacheHandler` method:

```
workbox.routing.setCatchHandler(({url, event, params}) => {
  //create a custom response to provide a proper response for the error
});
```

Caching strategies

Workbox has the five most common caching strategies built into the library:

- Stale-While-Revalidate
- Cache-First
- Network-First
- Network-Only
- Cache-Only

Each one of these strategies is available as a method in the `workbox.strategies` namespace. You can use these strategies without any custom configuration, but as you have seen, everything in Workbox of highly configurable.

The best part is that these strategy methods return a reference to a properly configured route response handler.

If you want to use any of these strategies with your own fetch handler, feel free. Create a new instance of the desired strategy. Then, use the `event.respondWith` method, suppling the strategy's handle method. You just need to supply the `fetch event` object to the handle method:

```
self.addEventListener('fetch', (event) => {
  if (event.request.url === '/my-special-url/') {
    const staleWhileRevalidate = new workbox.strategies.StaleWhileRevalidate();
    event.respondWith(staleWhileRevalidate.handle({event}));
  }
});
```

Each strategy method lets you configure the following properties:

- The cache name
- Expiration policy
- Plugins to extend the functionality

Each caching strategy method accepts an `options` object. Here, you can specify these customizations. First, is the `cacheName`. In this example, I am registering a custom route to catch individual event page requests and cache them in the events named cache:

```
workbox.routing.registerRoute(
    new RegExp('/event/'),
    workbox.strategies.cacheFirst({
        cacheName: 'events'
    })
);
```

I like this option because it makes it easier to manage how different asset types are cached and invalidated. Workbox makes managing invalidation easier with a custom module.

Workbox cache invalidation

Cache invalidation is handled by the Workbox Expiration plugin. This plugin allows you to control how many responses, lifetime, or a combination of both can be cached for a specific rule.

The expiration plugin is applied to the route's handler or caching strategy method. This is done by adding a new expiration plugin reference to the strategy's plugins array:

```
workbox.routing.registerRoute(
    new RegExp('/event/'),
    workbox.strategies.cacheFirst({
        cacheName: 'events',
        plugins: [
            new workbox.expiration.Plugin({
                maxEntries: 20,
                maxAgeSeconds: 24 * 60 * 60  //1 day
            })
        ]
    })
);
```

If you want to limit the number of cached responses for the rule, supply a numeric value for the `maxEntries` property. If you want to limit a responses time to live, supply a numeric value matching the number of seconds a response is valid for. As the preceding example demonstrates, you can use both at the same time. In this situation when either of the conditions is true, the clean-up logic is triggered.

Adding background sync functionality

Service worker background sync is a little complicated. It requires that you wrap all network-related activities you want to include in your sync logic in tags. This means in many cases that you must modify or completely rewrite your caching logic.

Plus, most browsers do not have support for this feature yet. We are on the verge of ubiquitous support, but that has limited this important feature's appeal.

However, Workbox includes a plugin module to make background sync a breeze. Just like the Expiration plugin, you add the Background Sync plugin to a strategy's list:

```
workbox.routing.registerRoute(
    new RegExp('/event/'),
    workbox.strategies.cacheFirst({
        cacheName: 'events',
        plugins: [
            new workbox.expiration.Plugin({
                maxEntries: 20,
                maxAgeSeconds: 24 * 60 * 60   //1 day
            }),
            new workbox.backgroundSync.Plugin('events', {
                maxRetentionTime: 24 * 60 // Retry for max of 24 Hours
            });
        ]
    })
);
```

Inside the plugin, a queue is managed that works with the background sync API to make sure requests are sent to the server. You can limit how long the service worker will try to connect with the server. In this example, I limited the retry to a single day. Unlike the expiration plugin, the `maxRetentionTime` property is measured in minutes, not seconds.

The added complexity background sync adds to your service worker code, which been a big roadblock for my enthusiasm. Workbox making this feature easy to integrate means it is much easier for you and I to add an extra layer of functionality to our web apps without writing this complex code.

Service Worker Tools

Background sync is an important feature if you are expecting responses or data from end users. I know many enterprise applications rely on internet connectivity, but employees may not be on stable Wi-Fi. This gives them to the ability to be productive when there is intermittent or no connectivity.

As a word of caution, I do advise you to give the user advice about the state of the requests hanging in the background synch queue. This way, they know the form they submitted has not been submitted to the server.

Using Google Analytics, even when the user is offline

A common question I am asked and see others asking in various forums is, "how can I use analytics services like Google Analytics with a service worker?"

What they are ultimately asking is how they can use an analytics package when the device is offline, but the service worker allows the user to continue using the application. How do user activities get logged to the analytics tool?

The good news is that you can track offline activity with a service worker, but it does require extra plumbing on your part to store all the activities in a custom queue and sync those to the analytics package when the device comes back online.

Sounds simple, right?

One area I did not spend any time on in this book is the background sync API. There were a few good reasons, mostly due to limited browser support and the added complexity it brings to your service worker.

If you have ever written an application with a dependency on an analytics package like GA, Ensighten, and so on, you know things can be complex. Stakeholders use this data to know if their marketing campaigns and websites are working and where they can focus improvement activities.

The good news is that Workbox has you covered, at least for Google Analytics. Workbox is a Google project, so you should expect them to offer easy support for one of their products! Easy might be understating their solution, as it is a single line of code:

```
workbox.googleAnalytics.initialize();
```

This turns on the Workbox library that manages Google analytics. Every request and response is managed through a background sync layer. If you need to perform some advanced configurations, you have that option as well.

For instance, if you need to differentiate online versus offline activities, you can provide overrides. If you understand custom dimensions, the cd1 parameter will make sense to you:

```
workbox.googleAnalytics.initialize({
  parameterOverrides: {
    cd1: 'offline',
  }
});
```

Even though Workbox only includes a Google Analytics provider does not mean you can't create a similar handler for your analytics package. You can use the GA provider as a reference or template to create your own analytics package provider. The production code is located in the `workbox-google-analytics.prod.js` file.

Don't limit yourself to just thinking about analytics packages when it comes to synchronizing offline activities. Use this as a model for any online API you may need to interact with where the user can continue interaction, even when their device is offline. This can be very handy for companies with line of business apps for field agents.

Summary

I have always been a fan of tooling and automation to make my applications faster to code with more maintainability and hopefully fewer bugs, but it is important you have a firm understanding of what any generate code or component is doing. This is why even when you are using the progressive web application tools I highlighted in this chapter that you need to be able recognize their strengths and limitations.

You also need to have a firm understanding of how complex features like service workers function before you start using a tool like Workbox. Without this fundamental knowledge, you can quickly make a service worker that does not work as you expect. You also need to have a strong knowledge foundation to help you debug issues when these tools break.

I chose four tools I think add the most value for the developers to review in this chapter. This by no means that all the tools available to you help you build great progressive web applications.

Service Worker Tools

Pinterest has a small collection of tools you may find useful on GitHub (`https://github.com/pinterest/service-workers`). They also have a tool to generate a service worker. There is also a webpack plugin. But the most intriguing tool may be their service worker unit testing mocking environment. This allows you to write unit tests against your service worker without running a browser instance.

Most of the major frameworks have also released command-line utilities to help you generate routing logic against your single page applications. I am also very intrigued with the rapid inclusion of CLI tools to convert these rendering engines into server engines using the same logic they have shipped to the client. I think these static sites are much easier to build PWA logic around as they have real URLs.

With the increased demand for PWAs by businesses, developers are put in the position where we need to have a deep knowledge of how to create new and update existing web apps so that they can be progressive web apps with a range of service worker complexity. The tools surveyed in this chapter should help you craft those solutions. I hope this book has helped give you the firm foundation you need to make those applications.

Other Books You May Enjoy

If you enjoyed this book, you may be interested in these other books by Packt:

Progressive Web Apps with React
Scott Domes

ISBN: 9781788297554

- Set up Webpack configuration, as well as get the development server running
- Learn basic Firebase configuration and deployment
- Create routes, manage multiple components, and learn how to use React Router v4 to manage the flow of data
- Use React life cycle methods to load data
- Add a service worker to the app and learn how it works
- Use a service worker to send Push Notifications
- Configure Webpack to split up the JavaScript bundle and lazy load component files
- Learn how to use the web Cache API to use your app offline
- Audit PWAs with Google's Lighthouse tool

Hands-on Full Stack Development with Angular 5 and Firebase
Uttam Agarwal

ISBN: 9781788298735

- Understand the core concepts of Angular framework
- Create web pages with Angular as front end and Firebase as back end
- Develop a real-time social networking application
- Make your application live with Firebase hosting
- Engage your user using Firebase cloud messaging
- Grow your application with Google analytics
- Learn about Progressive Web App

Leave a review - let other readers know what you think

Please share your thoughts on this book with others by leaving a review on the site that you bought it from. If you purchased the book from Amazon, please leave us an honest review on this book's Amazon page. This is vital so that other potential readers can see and use your unbiased opinion to make purchasing decisions, we can understand what our customers think about our products, and our authors can see your feedback on the title that they have worked with Packt to create. It will only take a few minutes of your time, but is valuable to other potential customers, our authors, and Packt. Thank you!

Index

2
2048 game
  about 22, 23
  application's code structure 23, 24
  manifest, adding 28
  node modules, adding 25, 26, 27
  service worker, adding 28, 29
  source code 23

A
add to homescreen experience
  Chrome add to homescreen experience 52
  homescreen prompt, disabling 59
  responsibilities 55, 56, 57, 58
  testing, in Chrome 65, 66
  triggering 51, 52
AJAX 104
API
  JSON server, using for 212, 213
app-image-generator
  reference 295

B
ba64
  reference 217
background sync 130, 131, 132

C
cache 196, 197, 232
cache invalidation strategies
  about 235
  Invalidation Manager 239, 240
  long time-to-live values 235, 236
  Maximum Item Invalidation 237
  purging state responses 238
  real-time asset manifest 242
  ResponseManager execution 239
  unique hash names 235, 236
Cache object
  about 170
  addAll 172
  Cache add 172
  cache.keys 174
  cache.match() 170
  cache.matchAll 171
  cache.put 172
  Cached items, deleting 173
caches object
  about 167
  caches.delete() 169
  caches.has() 168
  caches.keys() 169
  caches.match 168
  caches.open 168
caching patterns
  about 181
  cache falling back to network 194, 195
  network race 196, 197
  On activate 185
  On background sync 191, 192
  precaching 182
  real-time caching 186
caching responses 166, 167
caching strategies
  about 181
  Cache only 192, 193
  determining, request method used 232
  generic fallback 198, 200
  network falling back to cache 197
  network only 194
  On network response 188
  On push notification 190, 191
  On user interaction 187, 188

routes, matching with 233, 234, 235
  stale while revalidating 189, 190
certificate authority (CA) 68
certificate signing request (CSR) 84
Chrome add to homescreen experience
  about 52, 53, 54, 55
  testing 65, 66
Chrome improved add to homescreen experience 50, 51
create, retrieve, update, and delete (CRUD) 232
cross origin resource sharing (CORS) 215
CSS
  impact 250, 251, 253

D

developer tools
  used, for testing device conditions 254, 255, 256
device emulation 253
domain-validated SSL certificate (DV certificate) 81, 82

E

Extended Validation SSL certificates (EV certificates) 82, 83

F

faker module
  about 213
  reference 213
  using 216
feature detection
  used, for conditionally loading JavaScript polyfils 284, 285, 286
Fetch API
  about 103, 104, 105
  body mixin 161, 162, 163, 164
  headers object 157
  request object 153
  response object 108, 109, 110, 164
  using 105, 106, 107, 108, 152, 153
Fetch specification
  reference 160
fetch
  polyfilling, in legacy browsers 111, 112

First Contentful Paint (FCP) 273
Flipkart PWA
  reference 12

G

Google Analytics (GA) 86
grunt-contrib-connect npm page
  reference 27
Grunt
  about 26
  reference 27

H

headers object, Fetch API
  about 157
  header value, accessing 159
  headers, adding 158, 159
  protected headers 160
homescreen installs
  tracking 59, 60
homescreen library
  reference 60
homescreen
  adding 34, 35, 36
  polyfils, avoiding 64
Hosted Web App (HWA) 62
HTML5 Cross Browser polyfill
  reference 112
HTTP (Hypertext Transport Text Protocol) 71
HTTP Push
  reference 116
HTTP/2 79
HTTP/2 push
  implementing, with browser hints 268, 269
  implementing, with service worker cache 268
HTTPS
  about 71
  adoption 79, 80
  APIs 78
  no longer cost-prohibitive 76, 77
  padlocks, in browser address bar 75
  search engine optimization 75, 76
  security properties 72, 73, 74
  versus HTTP 78
  website, migrating to 85, 86

I

image generation service
  reference 295
image payload size
  reducing 250
IndexedDB (IDB) 94
inline critical CSS 277, 278, 280
Internet Explorer 62, 64
IntersectionObserver
  reference 287
Invalidation Manager
  maxItems strategy 241
  time-to-live invalidation strategy 241, 242
iOS
  homescreen experience, polyfilling 60, 61
  iPhone to Support Third-Party Web 2.0 Applications
    reference 36

J

JavaScript polyfils
  conditionally loading, with feature detection 284, 285, 286
JavaScript
  impact 250, 251, 253
JSON server
  API, making 215
  database, making 214
  using, for API 212, 213
json-server
  reference 212

K

key performance indicators
  about 264
  first byte 264, 265, 266, 267

L

Lancôme
  reference 12
lazy loading images 286, 288
Let's Encrypt
  reference 77
Lighthouse
  about 257
  building 306, 307
  executing, as command-line utility 301, 302, 303
  executing, from Chrome Developer Tools 298, 299, 300, 301
  executing, in Node script 305
  headless browser, testing 303, 304
  performance test, performing 257, 258, 259, 260
  PWA test, performing 257, 258, 259, 260
  reference 296
  used, for auditing web pages 296, 297, 298
localForage
  reference 221

M

Manifold JS
  about 295
  reference 295
Microsoft Edge 62, 64
Microsoft Edge service worker support 96
mixed content 85
Mustache
  reference 110, 228

N

node module
  reference 296

O

one click purchasing 16
online validator
  reference 48
organization-validated SSL certificate (OV certificate) 82

P

package.json format
  reference 26
Paint Timing API
  reference 273
pay-per-click (PPC) 36
podcast application 99, 100, 101, 102
polyfills 99
precaching

about 182
installing, as dependency 182, 183
installing, not as dependency 183, 184
Progressive Web Application (PWA)
about 7, 8, 13, 14
advantages 18, 19, 20
application shell 21, 22
features 16, 17, 18
peak app 15, 16
real-world examples 11, 12, 13
technical requisites 20
PRPL (Push, Render, Pre-cache, and Lazy- load) 17
PRPL pattern
about 267, 268
app shell model, used for rendering initial route 270, 271
lazy-loading dynamic routes 271, 272
lazy-loading non-critical routes 271, 272
push, implementing with browser hints 268, 269
push, implementing with service worker cache 268, 269
service worker pre-caching routes 271
service worker, used for rendering initial route 270, 271
Puppeteer
about 303
reference 303
Push Notification specification
reference 120
push notifications
handling 123, 124, 125, 126, 127
implementing 116, 117
setting up 117, 118, 119
unsubscribing from 127, 128, 129
using 115, 116
push subscription change
handling 129, 130
PWA Builder
reference 63
PWA images
scaffolding 294, 295
PWA iOS web app
application title, setting with META tag 39, 40
capable making 36, 37, 38

PWA ticket application
logic 219
QR codes, generating 217, 218
rendering architecture 219
reviewing 207, 208, 209, 210, 211
website, rendering 218, 219
PWA ticket JavaScript architecture 220, 221, 222
PWA ticket service worker architecture
about 224, 225, 226
ResponseManager 227, 228, 230, 231
PWA tickets 205, 206, 207
PWABuilder
executing 295, 296
PWA assets, downloading 294
PWA images, scaffolding 294, 295
service worker, building 293
used, for scaffolding PWA 290
valid web manifest file, generating 290, 291, 292, 293

Q

qr-encode
reference 217

R

RAIL (Response, Animation, Idle, Load) 17
RAIL pattern
14KB packet size 276, 277
about 272, 273, 274, 275
JavaScript parser blocking process 275, 276
request method
used, for determining caching strategy 232
request object, Fetch API
about 153, 154
cross-origin requests, handling 154, 155
request credentials, managing 156
response caching, controlling 156, 157
response caching
polyfilling 62
response object, Fetch API
about 164
properties 165
successful response, verifying 165
RFC 5681
reference 276

routes
  matching, with caching strategies 233, 234, 235

S

Safari service worker support 97
scope 140
Secure Socket Layer (SSL)
  enabling 68
  history 67, 68
secure TLS connections
  properties 71
security properties, HTTPS
  confidentiality 72, 73, 74
  identity 72
  integrity 74
server auto-redirect, configuring of HTTP to HTTPS
  about 88
  canonical HTTPS link, defining 89
  domain protocol combinations, adding in webmaster tools 89
  domain protocol combinations, verifying in webmaster tools 89
  Google Analytics, updating to default to HTTPS 89
  robots.txt file, updating 91
  RSS feed, updating to HTTPS 91
  sitemap, updating to HTTPS 90
Server Name Indication (SNI)
  reference 68
service worker browser support
  about 96, 98
  Microsoft Edge service worker support 96
  Safari service worker support 97
service worker cache
  working 178, 179, 180
service worker clients
  about 140, 141
  reference 140
service worker fetch 110, 111
service worker scope 144, 145, 146
service worker shell
  creating 113
service workers
  about 94, 95, 96
  advanced pre-caching 293

  building 293
  cache-first network 293
  caching 114, 115
  creating, with Workbox 312
  events 148, 180, 181
  life cycle 113, 114
  offline copy of pages 293
  offline page 293
  old browsers, polyfilling 99
  registering 138, 139
  registration object 141, 143
  setting up 316, 317
  templating 201, 202, 203
  updating 143, 147, 148
  uploading 144
  user's subscription, managing 120, 121
single-page applications (SPAs) 252
site
  auditing, for HTTP link references 86
  content, auditing 87
  data, auditing 87
social media links
  updating 87
Sonar CLI
  using 307, 308
Sonar, components
  about 310
  configurations 310
  connectors 310
  formatters 311
  parsers 311
  rules 311
Sonar
  node module, used for automating site audits 311
  reference 260, 307
  used, for auditing web pages 307
SSL certificate
  domain-validated SSL certificate (DV certificate) 81, 82
  Extended Validation SSL certificates (EV certificates) 82, 83
  installing 84
  obtaining 84
  organization-validated SSL certificate (OV

certificate) 82
types 80

T

test devices 253
Time to Interactive (TTI) 273
Transport Layer Security (TLS)
  reference 77
  working 69, 70
Travis tool 306
Twitter Lite 7

U

uglify
  scripts, minifying 280, 283
UnCSS module
  reference 277

V

valid web manifest file
  generating 290, 291, 292, 293

W

Weather Channel
  reference 12
Web Manifest Validator
  reference 49
web manifest
  Apple Safari support 47, 48
  file, referencing 41
  files, validating 48
  launch style, controlling 45, 46
  properties 42, 43, 44
  specification 41
web pages
  auditing, with Lighthouse 296, 297, 298
  auditing, with Sonar 307
web performance optimization (WPO)
  about 248
  significance 248, 249
WebAPK 53
WebPageTest
  reference 260
  used, for benchmarking performance 260, 261, 262, 263
websites
  migrating, to HTTPS 85, 86
  reasons, for building in new way 10, 11
WordPress
  reference 84
Workbox
  background sync functionality, adding 327, 328
  cache invalidation 326, 327
  caching strategies 325, 326
  complex service workers, making 312
  dynamic routes with 323, 324, 325
  Google Analytics, using 328, 329
  installing 313, 314, 315
  pre-caching with 317, 318, 319, 320, 321, 322, 323
  reference 312
  structure 315, 316

Made in the USA
Monee, IL
17 June 2020

33788374R00195